ARCHITECTURE IN COLONIAL AMERICA

MARIAN C. DONNELLY

Leland M. Roth, Editor

UNIVERSITY OF
OREGON

PRESS
EUGENE

Published by:
University of Oregon Press
5283 University of Oregon
Eugene OR 97403-5283

Printed in the United States of America

ISBN: 0-87114-304-6

h g f e d c b a

⊰ Contents ⊱

NOTE

My wife, Marian Card Donnelly, intended to bring this manuscript, which was written in the 1980s, up to date for publication. Unfortunately, she passed away before she could engage this project. It seemed to me that leaving this comprehensive work unpublished would be a loss to architectural historians and other interested readers. Marian was interested in colonial architecture over the course of her life, and I'm sure she would be pleased to know that Professor Leland Roth, one of her colleagues at the University of Oregon, has edited and updated her manuscript for publication.

A number of people brought this volume to completion. Marian's original typescript was put into machine readable form by several of my assistants. Leland M. Roth expanded the abbreviated personal notations left by Marian, supplied the corrections outlined by readers of the manuscript, compiled the illustration captions, and worked closely with Amanda Clark who finished the notes and bibliography sketched out by Marian and who also carried out early copy editing. The illustrations were digitally prepared for publication by Marina Bergt.

I am most grateful to Professor Abbott Lowell Cummings for much help and advice, and in particular for keeping a complete copy of the manuscript at a time when I could not locate it all.

Russell Donnelly
May 2003

⊰ Introduction ⊱

THE MOST RECENT COMPREHENSIVE ACCOUNT of architecture in colonial America is Hugh Morrison's *Early American Architecture*, published in 1952. Since then this material has been treated in condensed form in several general histories of American architecture that bring the record nearly to the present. In some of these histories there are references to monographs and journal articles reporting studies of various sites and buildings undertaken since 1952.

The present book is intended to give an outline history of colonial architecture in what is now the United States from the Age of Exploration to the Revolutionary period. It is not intended to be comprehensive or definitive, if indeed such a work would be possible or even desirable. The buildings remaining from the colonial period are far too numerous to be encompassed in a single volume. Some of the examples chosen here are buildings already well known and carefully studied. Others have been chosen which have received less attention or for which recent intensive studies have not yet reached the general literature. For the latter the intention is to include references to such studies and indicate how they have brought forth new information and understanding and have on occasion corrected former errors. It will be evident that there is much unevenness in the available studies of early American buildings, and another purpose is to point out some of the gaps in our present knowledge and to encourage investigations of lesser known works.

In addition to the more conventional reports of structural and documentary findings, a number of American architectural historians are including more social and political factors in their detailed studies of building history. How effective this can be for the buildings of a particular group or region may be seen, for example, in some of the writings of Kevin M. Sweeney and Dell Upton, who have shown how many ideas about early American architecture remain to be explored.

The illustrations have been chosen partly to show some of the colonial buildings as they have survived and may be seen today. Much is also to be learned from drawings and prints from earlier times, before later structures have altered the appearance of the areas around the original buildings, before the buildings themselves have been altered, or, as has sometimes happened, been lost altogether. Another significant source of insight into these buildings is the substantial body of contemporary comments by travelers, diarists, and early historians, to say nothing of the official documents that have survived.

No better indication of the intrinsic value of colonial American architecture could be cited than the increasing quantity of responsible investigation in recent years. Historically these buildings have often been viewed as merely quaint at best or as provincial in its more derogatory sense at worst. Yet for two centuries these buildings sheltered a major venture, the transplanting of significant segments of western European populations across thousands of miles of water to an unknown land. A new continent was firmly settled by people whose culture was technologically, at least, advanced far beyond that of the native inhabitants. Colonial builders brought their traditions with them, necessarily creating new forms in unfamiliar circumstances, a remarkable process of artistic transformation. When viewed for their own merits, the finest colonial buildings reflect the vitality of the architectural traditions from which they came and the courage and ingenuity of their builders.

Marian C. Donnelly
1988

1-1. View of St. Augustine, 1588. (*From* Expiditio Francisci Draki Equitis Angli in Indias Occidentalis, *Leiden, 1588; courtesy of New York Public Library*).

⊰ *Chapter 1* ⊱

The Age of Exploration

"THE EARTH IS ROUND, circumscribed by antipodes, of a most insignificant smallness, and a swift wanderer among the stars."[1] When Johannes Kepler wrote these lines in 1609, the roundness of the earth had been successfully demonstrated for nearly a century, but its smallness had not been obvious to the European adventurers who claimed new lands in the Western Hemisphere. Spanish and English colonists were settling themselves at Santa Fe and Jamestown, inaugurating a remarkable period in the history of architecture. The Greeks and Romans had colonized, but not into such vast territories nor over such great distances. So energetic and, in spite of many setbacks, so successful was this undertaking that as early as 1654 Edward Johnson could make the observation that "Thus hath the Lord been pleased to turn one of the most hideous, boundless, and unknown Wildernesses in the world in an instant, as 'twere (in comparison of other work) to a well-ordered Commonwealth."[2] By the time of the American Revolution and the change of the English lands from a colonial to a new national status, part of the territory that is now the United States was settled. Growing knowledge of resources and climate, the immigration of builders with their tools and technical skills, and the instinctive urge to provide amenity had brought a high degree of sophistication to colonial building.

Even as early as the voyages of Columbus attempts were already being made to settle the new lands.[3] Confusion over the true relation of the western Atlantic islands which he encountered to the long-sought shores of Japan and China was not helped by the conflicting claims arising from Pope Alexander VI's Line of Demarcation of 1494. John Cabot's voyages to Newfoundland in 1497 and 1498, licensed by Henry VII, laid the basis for English claims in the New World, but here the venture yielded little but knowledge of the fisheries which the English were not to exploit until much later.[4]

The discoveries of Vasco da Gama in 1499 and 1501 and of Vasco Nuñez de Balboa in 1513 indicated that the problem of a western sea-route to China was very different from that undertaken by Columbus. The great voyage of Ferdinand Magellan (who died during it) and Sebastiano del Cano from 1519 to 1521 made clear that circumnavigation of the world was possible and set off a decade of rivalries between Spain and Portugal. While the Portuguese developed their trade routes but did not attempt extensive colonization, the Spanish added missionary enterprises to their search for gold and penetrated far into the interior of the newly discovered North American continent.

By the exploration of Hernando de Soto from Florida north to the Appalachians and west to the Mississippi in 1539-1542, and those of Francisco Coronado across the Rio Grande and west of the Mississippi in 1541, patterns of Spanish colonization were already regular. The Royal Ordinances for the Laying Out of New Cities, Towns or Villages proclaimed by Philip II in 1573 codified many established practices and give valuable insight into the history of Spanish planning.[5] These instructions stipulated a plaza with quarters for merchants, a town hall, hospital, other public buildings, and the church nearby if it was for a harbor town, at some distance and on a hill if for an inland town. These provisions were made in case the church was needed for refuge from attack. Individual properties were to be set out on a grid plan. In their probable dependence on the writings of Vitruvius and Alberti for literary sources and also on regular plans in Spain from as early as Roman times, these instructions indicate the orderly manner in which the Spanish proposed to settle.[6]

Indeed by 1502 the city of Santo Domingo on the island of Española "was laid out with ruler and compass, with all the streets being carefully measured."[7] As for settlements in what was later to become the United States, the founding of St. Augustine in 1570 was accompanied again by a grid plan, as recorded by Drake's expedition of 1586 [1-1].

There was, however, undoubtedly an extent to which Philip II's Ordinances represented wishful thinking. By the time they were issued, the fisheries of Newfoundland were being worked by Spanish Biscayan seamen, especially the Basques. Studies at Red Bay on the east coast of Labrador have revealed traces of cabins built partly into an outcrop of rock, with lower walls of stone and roofs of imported red Basque tiles.[8] Basque whalers were living here in the 1550s, and so far nothing more is suggested than a haphazard collection of dwellings and sheds for the processing of the catch.

IN CONTRAST TO THE MORE AMBITIOUS southerly voyages of the Spanish, the earliest French explorations across the Atlantic went north. Following the voyages of Giovanni da Verrazano in 1524, Francis I sent Jacques Cartier in 1534 to search for a northwest passage to Asia. Cartier reached the Lachine Rapids and the site of present Montreal, and he published his findings in his *Voyages* in French in 1545. From the account of his third voyage in 1540 comes the observation, "on both sides of the said River there are very good and faire grounds, full of as faire and mightie trees as any be in the world." As translated by Richard Hakluyt and published in 1589, this signaled decades of reports of geography and natural resources that were to entice further adventures and investment in North America.[9]

The English search for a northwest passage to Asia was accompanied by an equally serious search for sites for "plantations" which might supply raw materials for England. Impetus was slowed during the middle years of the sixteenth century because of internal disorders, partly following upon Henry VIII's break with Rome in 1534 and that monarch's disinterest in missions. Activity began to revive with the founding of the Muscovy Company in 1555 and, after the accession of Elizabeth I in 1558, the founding of the East India Company in 1559. Even before the completion of Sir Francis Drake's circumnavigation from 1577 to 1580, the queen's concern for development in North

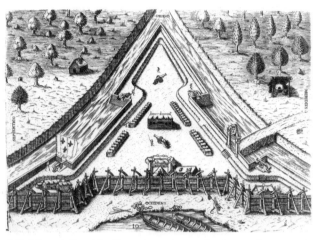

1-2. View of Fort Caroline, after a drawing by Jacques le Moyne de Morgues, 1564; published by Theodore de Bry, Brevis narratio eorum quae in Florida Americae…, *Frankfurt, 1591, Part II, Plate X. (Courtesy of New York Public Library).*

America led her to grant a patent to Sir Humphrey Gilbert "for the inhabiting and planting of our people in America," June 11, 1578. His charge was to "search, find out and view such remote heathen and barbarous lands, countries and territories not actually possessed of any Christian prince or people… to goe and travell thither, to inhabite or remaine there, to build and fortifie."[10] Although Gilbert's resulting expedition was a failure, the patent made clear that the English had no interest in respecting claims over land or sea that the Spanish or Portuguese might make on papal authority.

The fishing banks of Newfoundland were now being regularly visited by English ships. A letter to Richard Hakluyt from Anthony Parkhurst gave a "Report of the True State and Commodities of Newfoundland," also in 1578. In addition to describing the fishing he said, "The timber is most Firre yet plenty of Pineapple trees: fewe of these kinds meet to mast a ship of threescore and ten: but neere Cape Briton, and to the Southward, big and sufficient for any ship. There be also Okes & thornes, there is in all the countrey plentie of Birch and Alder, which be the meetest wood for cole, and also willow, which will serve for many other purposes."[11] Four years later Hakluyt published his monumental *Divers Voyages*, a collection of all the narratives he could find of voyages to the North American coast

claimed for England.[12] Until well into the next century, such accounts poured into England and other European countries, giving prospective adventurers much valuable information on the nature of the lands, peoples, and resources that they could expect to encounter. To the modern reader they give additional perception of the reactions of the explorers, their expectations, and their successes and failures.

Having thus become well informed about the resources of the New World, in 1583 Hakluyt presented his *Discourse of Western Planting* to Elizabeth 1, urging state support for plantations. He recognized the long-term advantage of acquisition in temperate lands, both for territory and for outlets for the woolen trade. He believed that colonization could only be successful with considerable numerical strength, and the failures up to that time could not have been lost upon him.

Although the *Discourse* itself was not printed until 1877, the ideas contained in it were also in the minds of other adventurers.[13] Sir Humphrey Gilbert voyaged to Newfoundland again in 1583, also unsuccessfully, and was drowned on the way home. Both Edward Hay and Sir George Peckham reported on that voyage, the latter addressing his message to "the noblemen and gentlemen, who doe chiefly seek a temperate climate, wholesome ayre, fertile soile, and a strong place by nature whereupon they may fortifie, and there either plant themselves, or such other persons as they shall think good to send to bee lords of that countrey."[14] He added that "there may be very easily made Pitch Tarre, Rosen, Sope ashes in great plenty, yea, as it is thought, inough to serve the whole realme in every one of these kinds."

Hakluyt had in fact written his *Discourse* at the request of Sir Walter Ralegh, who had already sent two captains, Philip Amadas and Arthur Barlow, to explore the more southerly coasts. They returned with an enthusiastic account, including a description of Roanoke Island as "a most pleasant and fertile ground, replenished with goodly cedars."[15] Since Ralegh was then in high favor with the queen, on March 25, 1584, he obtained letters patent for the discovery and plantation of new lands and countries, "To inhabite or remaine, to build and fortifie.[16] Despite Hakluyt's eloquence, the queen knew that full official funding of these attempts could only worsen the developing conflict with Spain, and she contented herself with supplying one of her own ships and a quantity of gunpowder.

Under Sir Richard Grenville, with Ralegh remaining in England, colonists settled at Roanoke in 1585, only to be taken away a year later by Sir Francis Drake. War with Spain was then imminent, the site proved less feasible than the reports had indicated, and there had been no effective efforts to start growing crops. A second attempt in 1587 resulted in the mysterious disappearance of this famous "lost colony" by 1589.[17] The great benefits historically were the drawings of John White, cartographer and illustrator to the expedition. These were published as engravings by Theodore de Bry in Frankfort in 1590, together with the official geographer Thomas Harriot's *Briefe and True Report of the New Found Land of Virginia*.[18] With these territories now named in honor of the queen the intentions of the English were unmistakable, but it was to be another twenty years before they could be realized successfully. For the next few years England was preoccupied with the war with Spain, which ended in 1604.

I N THE MEANTIME the French had not made much progress toward settlement in North America. Huguenots under René de Laudonnière built Fort Caroline at the mouth of the St. John River in Florida in 1564.[19] Thanks to his description of building the fort and the drawings and narratives by Jacques Le Moyne de Morgues a reasonably clear idea of this fort is available [1-2].[20] Le Moyne's account seems to have been based on that of Laudonnière, and his illustrations bear this out. The fort was triangular, with bastions consisting of sod walls on the land side and a plank wall on the river side. Cannon were mounted on a raised platform and positioned to cover the walls on the earth side. This was in the now well-established manner of European forts which had been developing since the introduction of cannon in the fourteenth century. A substantial literature on military architecture and the arts of siege and defense was already available, the earliest French book on the subject having been recently published.[21]

Although the natives could hardly be expected to attack with cannon, Laudonnière was also prepared for the Spanish and English, or so he thought. He found that in hurricane territory it was a mistake to have built one building too high, "for within a short while . . . the wind beat it down." He also built his own lodging within the fort, "round about which were galleries all covered," as became characteristic of French dwellings in these southern regions and also in the Mississippi valley. A precaution against fire was taken by placing the bake oven beneath a palm-branch shelter, across the ditch and at some

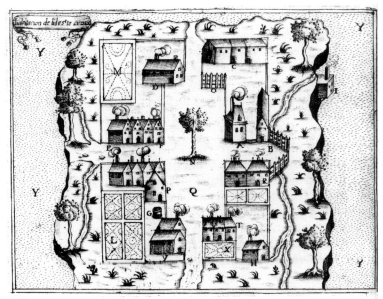

A Logis du sieur de Mons.
B Maison publique où l'on passoit le temps durant la pluie.
C Le magasin.
D Logement des suisses.
E La forge.
F Logement des charpentiers
G Le puis.
H Le four où l'on faisoit le pain.

I La cuisine.
L Iardinages.
M Autres Iardins.
N La place où au milieu y a vn arbre.
O Palissade.
P Logis des sieurs d'Oruille, Champlain & Chandore.
Q Logis du sieur Boulay, & autres artisans.

R Logis ou logeoiët les sieurs de Genestou, Sourin & autres artisans.
T Logis des sieurs de Beaumont, la Motte Bourioli & Fougeray.
V Logement de nostre curé.
X Autres iardinages.
Y La riuiere qui entoure l'isle.

1-3. Map of Ste. Croix, Maine, 1604, in Samuel de Champlain, Les Voyages du sieur de Champlain Xaintongeois, capitaine ordinaire pour le Roy, en la marine *(Paris, 1613), 38.*

A Logemens des artisans.
B Plate forme où estoit le canon.
C Le magasin.
D Logemét du sieur de Pont-graué & Champlain.
E La forge.

F Palissade de pieux,
G Le four.
H La cuisine.
O Petite maisonnette où l'on retiroit les vtansiles de nos barquesisque de puis le sieur de Poittincourt fit

rebastir, & y logea le sieur Boulay quand le sieur du Pont s'en reuint en France.
P La porte de l'abitation.
Q Le cemetiere.
R La riuiere.

1-4. View of fort, Port Royal, Nova Scotia, 1605. (From Champlain, Voyages..., *99).*

1-5. *Restored buildings, Port Royal, Nova Scotia, 1938-1940. (Photo: M. C. Donnelly).*

little distance from the fort. All to no avail, however, as the effort ended in massacre by the Spanish in September 1565.

It was not until 1604 that another serious attempt was made, this time under another Huguenot, Sieur de Monts, who received fur trading rights in Canada from Henry IV. The first site chosen for a trading post was the Isle Ste. Croix, but this was abandoned a year later in favor of Port Royal, near present Annapolis, Nova Scotia. Although Port Royal was totally destroyed by the English in 1613, the remarkable accounts and drawings published in the same year by Samuel de Champlain, geographer to the expedition, provide considerable information on how the French intended to begin settlement on the Isle Ste. Croix.[22]

Defense against Indian and other attackers being a prime consideration, an island site was chosen first [1-3]. The description by Marc Lescarbot, a member of the expedition, corresponds fairly well to Champlain's drawing.[23] The buildings are probably shown with some exaggeration, considering the speed with which they were built. The drawing shows an arrangement in four groups, each palisaded, and forming a central rectangular plaza with a tree in the middle. Lescarbot speaks of "Mons. de Monts's lodging, made with very faire and artificial carpentry work, with the banner of France upon the same... the storehouse, wherein consisted the safety and life of everyone, likewise made faire with carpentry work and covered with reeds."[23] These are shown as "A" and "C" on the drawing, and Lescarbot also mentions the public house where all might gather when it was raining, shown at "B." A bake house is at "H" and the main cooking place outside the enclosure at "I", as had been done with the bake oven at Fort Caroline. The well, however, so essential in case of siege, was inside one of the palisades at "G". Lescarbot went on to mention the gardens, "whereunto everyone exercised himself willingly." The rigors of the climate were also noted, in that the "houses need no opening, nor windows on the northwest side, being a wind very dangerous but rather on the east-side, or the

south."[24] Excavations carried out by the National Park Service in 1950 and again with the assistance of Temple University in 1968 revealed some stone foundations, enough to establish the site, but not enough to make definite its plan, which is thought to have differed from the arrangement shown on Champlain's drawing.[25]

After the move to Port Royal the plan was different. Here, with land approaches, the post was built like a French manor, all the buildings with common walls grouped around a courtyard [1-4]. A ditch on the land side and two palisaded gun platforms on the side toward the water provided the major defenses, while very small outside windows as indicated on Champlain's drawing would also be a deterrent to attack. Post life centered in the courtyard. To the right as one entered were the guard room, trading room, and storehouse. On the north side were the governor's house and three smaller dwelling houses, then came a third wing, with chapel, artisans' quarters, and a community room. On the entrance side were placed the bakery and kitchen, the blacksmith's shop, and an office/dwelling. Larger windows admitted more light through the walls on the courtyard side, and perhaps the working areas on the south side were placed there for the best use of daylight. Garden plots are indicated outside the habitation on Champlain's drawing, and again the patterns drawn upon them suggest some sense of formal planning. Champlain speaks of making a garden for pleasure, surrounded by ditches of fresh water stocked with trout, and he also constructed a summer house, "as a resort for enjoying the fresh air."[26] The reconstruction of 1940 is to some extent conjectural and can furnish only a general idea of the original structures [1-5].[27]

SHORTLY AFTER THE BUILDING of the habitation at Port Royal the Plymouth Company sent a "plantation" from Plymouth to Sagadahoc on the Kennebec River, with George Popham and Raleigh Gilbert as captains of the two ships. It lasted but a year as St. George's Fort, and Gilbert went down with his ship on the

1-7. *Excavated foundations, Pemaquid, Maine. (Photo: M. C. Donnelly).*

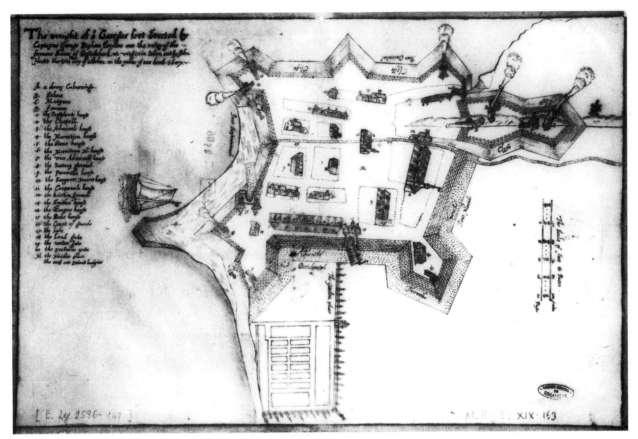

1-6. *Map of St. George's Fort, Sagadahoc, Maine, 1607. (Archivo General de Simancas).*

return voyage. A description of the enterprise, "Relation of a Voyage to Sagadahoc," probably written by the navigator James Davies, describes the building of the fort, begun August 20, 1607, and finished with trenches, fence, and cannon by October.[28] He speaks of fifty houses, a church, and a storehouse. A contemporary drawing by John Hunt, a member of the expedition, shows the fort to have been as English in character as Port Royal was French [1-6].

The drawing probably shows what was intended as well as what was completed. The area indicated by an accompanying scale was about 450 feet from north to south and 300 feet wide. It was fortified with earthworks, bastioned, and had a stream running through it from north to south. Two gates are indicated, a land gate on the west and a water gate on the north, the latter having a drawbridge over the trench, an arched opening and flanking turrets above. The water gate is likewise shown with battlements and turrets. Considering the circumstances and the speed with which the fort was constructed, however, it may be asked whether the gates as drawn are a true rendering of what was built or simply a conventional representation.

The houses and other buildings are shown as built with widely spaced vertical posts, gable roofs, and end or central chim-

neys. A key on the drawing identifies the different types of ordnance and the several buildings. The guard house was placed in the center and apparently built over the stream. On the south was the chapel, with tower and spire, and the admiral's house was in the southwest corner. The vice-admiral's house was across the central open space on the north side and the sargent major's house on the east. Munitions houses, storehouses, kitchen, bakehouse, and smithy were among the other buildings. More than any other English site up to that time, Fort St. George resembled an English village with an irregular market place, the guard house where the market hall would normally be, and the church on one side. On the west side, across the trench, a garden was laid out, about 150 feet long, fenced on two sides and divided into neat rectangular plots. Unfortunately attempts to confirm these features in the drawing have not been successful.[29]

The "Relation" concludes with a melancholy note on the abandonment of the site: "this was the end of that northern colony upon the river Sackadehoc."[30] In the meantime another site on the Maine coast was becoming known and by the 1620s would become settled.[31] At Pemaquid, about ten miles south of Damariscotta, sporadic fishing ventures in the second decade of the seventeenth century led to the founding of a modest town, which had no surrounding defenses. A number of French and Indian raids led to the building of a fort in 1664, which was also attacked, rebuilt, and destroyed by the French in 1696. Later attempts to revive the settlement were not successful, and by the mid-eighteenth century the site was abandoned. Its very remoteness, however, was a protection. Excavations in recent years have shown Pemaquid, like Jamestown, to be a storehouse of foundations and artifacts that reveal much about true conditions and ambitions of these Maine coastal settlers [1-7].

While the Pemaquid settlement apparently did not take form as early as was once thought, by the first decade of the seventeenth century enough had been learned about opportunities and dangers that the English were able to begin permanent settlement in the southern part of their North American claim.

Notes to Chapter 1

1. Johannes Kepler, *Astronomia Nova*, quoted in J. H. Parry, *Age of Reconnaissance* (Berkeley: University of California Press, 1981), 4.

2. Edward Johnson, *Wonder-Working Providence of Sions Saviour in New England* (Andover, Mass.: W. F. Draper, 1867), 209-210.

3. A site on the island of Española was proposed by Samuel Eliot Morison for the first landing of Columbus (Samuel Eliot Morison, *Admiral of the Ocean Sea: A Life of Christopher Columbus* (Boston: Brown and Co., 1942), 1:392-394, 2:96, and 113). A study of the probable route of Columbus puts his landing on Samana Cay in the Bahamas (see Joseph Judge, "Where Columbus Found the New World," in *National Geographic* 170, no. 5 (November 1986): 566-572, 578-599).

4. A good general account of the early voyages to America is to be found in Parry, "Notes for Further Reading," in *Age of Reconnaissance*, 348-351, which includes a discussion of the vast literature on this subject. Two other useful histories of the early voyages are in Samuel Eliot Morison, *The European Discovery of America* (New York: Oxford University Press, 1971-74), notable for its observations and illustrations from the seaman's point of view, and William Patterson Cumming, R. A. Skelton, and David B. Quinn, *The Discovery of North America* (New York: American Heritage Press, 1972), which is extensively illustrated with contemporary maps and views. Many of the early narratives have been published in new English translation in David B. Quinn, Alison M. Quinn, and Susan Hillier, eds., *New American World: A Documentary History of North America to 1612* (New York: Arno Press, 1979). A number of essays on political and social issues during this period are presented in Fredi Chiappelli, Michael J. B. Allen, and Robert Louis Benson, eds., *First Images of America: The Impact of the New World on the Old* (Berkeley: University of California Press, 1976).

5. The original document is in the Archivo General de Indias in Seville. It was published in Spanish by Zelia Nuttall, "Royal Ordinances Concerning the Laying Out of New Towns," in *The Hispanic American Historical Review* 4, no. 4 (1921): 743-753, and in translation in the same journal, 5 (1922): 249-254. A more recent translation, with commentary, is in Dora P. Crouch, Daniel J. Garr, and Axel I. Mundigo, *Spanish City Planning in North America* (Cambridge, Mass.: MIT Press, 1982), 1-65.

6. A comparison of the Ordinances of 1573 with the writings of Vitruvius was made by Dan Stanislawski, *Early Spanish Town Planning in the New World* (New York: American Geographical Society, 1947). Additional discussion of sources of inspiration for orderly planning of the new Spanish towns is in John William Reps, *The Making of Urban America: A History of City Planning in the United States* (Princeton: Princeton University Press, 1965), 27-28, and more recently in Crouch, Garr, and Mundigo, *Spanish City Planning*, 32-47.

7. Gonzalo Oviedo y Valdés, *Natural History of the West Indies* (Chapel Hill: University of North Carolina Press, 1959), 11.

8. James A. Tuck and Robert Grenier, *Red Bay, Labrador: World Whaling Capitol A.D. 1550-1600* (St. John's, Newfoundland: Atlantic Archaeology, 1989), 38-42. James A. Tuck, "A 16th-Century Basque Whaling Station in Labrador," *Scientific American* 245 (November 1981): 183.

9. Jacques Cartier, "Third Voyage of Discovery," in *The Principal navigations, voyages, traffiques & discoveries of the English Nation, made by sea or overland to the remote and farthest distant quarters of the earth at any time within the compass of these 1600 years*, comp. Richard Hakluyt, (London: J. M. Dent and Sons, LTD, 1927-28), 8:267.

10. Hakluyt, comp., *Principal navigations*, 8:17-23.

11. Ibid., 11.

12. Richard Hakluyt, *Divers voyages touching the discoverie of America* (Ann Arbor, Mich.: University Microfilms, 1966).

13. A more recent edition is Richard Hakluyt, "Discourse on the Western Planting," in *The Original Writings & Correspondence of the Two Richard Hakluyts*, ed. E. G. R. Taylor, Richard Hakluyt, and Richard Hakluyt (London: Printed for the Hakluyt Society, 1935), 2:211-326.

14. Sir George Peckham, "A true reporte of the late discoveries ... ," in Hakluyt, comp., *Principal navigations*, 8:113-117.

15. Philip Amadas and Arthur Barlow, "First Voyage," in Hakluyt, comp., *Principal navigations*, 8:309.

16. "The letters patents granted by the Queens Majestie to Sir Walter Ralegh," in Hakluyt, comp., *Principal navigations*, 8:290.

17. The history of the colony is set forth in David N. Durant, *Ralegh's Lost Colony* (New York: Atheneum, 1981). Durant is not convinced that the earthworks excavated by the National Park Service from 1947-1953 are those of the main fort built in 1685 (see pages 52-55 and 169-170). For those excavations see J. C. Harrington, *Search for the Cittie of Ralegh: Archeological Excavations at Fort Raleigh National Historic Site, North Carolina* (Washington D.C.: National Park Service, U.S. Dept. of the Interior, 1962).

18. Thomas Hariot, *A Brief and True Report of the New Found Land of Virginia* (New York: History Book Club, 1951 [1588]). John White's drawings preserved in the British Museum are reproduced in P. H. Hulton and David B. Quinn, eds., *The American Drawings of John White, 1577-1590: With Drawings of European and Oriental Subjects* (London: Chapel Hill, Trustees of the British Museum; University of North Carolina Press, 1964). For the documents see David B. Quinn, Alison M. Quinn, and Susan Hillier, eds., *English Plans for North America: The Roanoke Voyages, the New England Ventures* (New York: Arno Press, 1979). A discussion of the probable accuracy of the early drawings and prints of American discoveries is given in William C. Sturtevant, "First Visual Images," in *First Images of America*, Chiappelli, Allen, and Benson, 1:417-454.

19. Woodbury Lowery, *The Spanish Settlements within the Present Limits of the United States: Florida, 1562-1574* (New York: G. P. Putnam's Sons, 1905), 49-58.

20. R. G. de Laudonnière, "The Second Voyage into Florida," in *Principal navigations*, comp. Hakluyt, 9:16-18; Jacques Le Moyne de Morgues, "Narrative," in *The New World: The First Pictures of America*, ed. Stefan Lorant (New York: Duell, Sloan, and Pearce, 1965), 40, 53, and 55.

21. Horst de la Croix, *Military Considerations in City Planning: Fortifications* (New York: G. Braziller, 1972), 39-55. For studies of the literature see Horst de la Croix, and John R. Hale, *Renaissance Fortification: Art or Engineering?* (London: Thames and Hudson, 1977). The earliest French treatise seems to be Francois de la Treille, Giovanni Battista de' Zanchi, and Robert Corneweyle, *La manière de fortifier villes* (The maner of Fortification of Cities, Townes, Castles and Other Places) (Farnborough: Gregg, 1972) which is in turn a translation of Giovanni Battista de' Zanchi, *Del modo di fortificar le città* (in Venetia, 1560).

22. Samuel de Champlain, *Voyages of Samuel de Champlain, 1604-1618*, ed. William Lawson Grant (New York: C. Scribner's Sons, 1907), 21-118.

23. Marc Lescarbot, "Nova Francia: A Description of Acadia, 1606," in *A Collection of Voyages and Travels*, comp. Thomas Osborne (London: T. Osborne, 1745), 2:807.

24. Ibid., 812.

25. These excavations have not been fully published but are described in a paper by Gretchen F. Faulkner, "A History of Archaeological Investigation on St. Croix" (University of Maine, 1982). This paper was very kindly called to my attention by Dr. Robert L. Bradley of the Maine Historic Preservation Commission. See also Wendell S. Hadlock, *A Report of the Archeological Work Performed 1961-62 on United States Government Property: the Islesford Historical Museum Grounds, Islesford, Little Cranberry Island, Maine* (n.p., 1962).

26. Grant, ed., *Voyages of Samuel de Champlain*, 79-80.

27. The research for the reconstruction of the Port Royal Habitation, which was undertaken close to the original site, is described in Kenneth D. Harris, "Restoration of the Habitation of Port Royal, Lower Granville, Nova Scotia," *Royal Architecture Institute of Canada* 17 (July 1940): 111-116.

28. Benjamin Franklin de Costa, "A Relation of a Voyage to Sagadahoc," in *Early English and French Voyages, Chiefly from Hakluyt, 1534-1608*, ed. Henry S. Burrage (n.p.), 411-418.

29. The map was found in the Spanish archives, having apparently been sent to Philip II by the Spanish ambassador in London.

30. Burrage, ed., *Early English and French Voyages*, 419.

31. Helen B. Camp, *Archaeological Excavations at Pemaquid, Maine, 1965-1974* (Augusta: Maine State Museum, 1976).

2-1. Willem van de Velde, "Horsemen on the Beach," c. 1660, oil on canvas. (© 1986 Indianapolis Museum of Art).

Chapter 2

Early European Settlements on the North American Coast

N APRIL 10, 1606, JAMES I granted the first Charter of the Virginia Company of London: "…Our licence to make habitacion, plantacion and to deduce a colonie of sondrie of our people into that parte of America commonly called Virginia."[1] Two sub-colonies were identified, with overlapping territories. The First Colony, under the London Company, was to settle from 34°N to 41°N, or about from North Carolina to New York. The Second Colony, under the Plymouth Company, was to settle from 38°N to 45°N. or about from Virginia to Nova Scotia. The Crown also appointed a Council for Virginia.

2-2. *"Shipbuilding in the New World." Views of Native American houses are shown in the background. (From Theodore de Bry, Brevis narratio …, Part 4, courtesy of New York Public Library).*

In the same year there appeared anonymous "Instructions" for the intended voyage to Virginia. "It were necessary that all your carpenters and other such like workmen about building do first build your storehouse and those other rooms of publick and necessary use before any house be set up for any private person; and though the workman may belong to any private persons yet let them all work together for the company and then for private men. And seeing that order is at the same price with confusion, it shall be advisable done to set your houses even and by a line, that your streets may have a good breadth and be carried square about your market, and every street's end opening into it; from thence, with a few field pieces, you may command every street throughout, which market place you may also fortify if you think it needful."[2]

There is a clear analogy here to the plans for the slightly later Ulster Plantation and Londonderry in Ireland.[3] The ordering of market place, streets, and houses is also reminiscent of the "Ordinances" of Philip II thirty years earlier and probably had a similar source in planning theory. (Although these "Instructions" were evidently prepared by the time of the Sagadahoc expedition in 1607, the colonists of Fort St. George do not seem to have

followed so precise a scheme.) Giving the public buildings priority in construction recognized the most pressing needs, and it is interesting to note the reference to indentured workmen.

A remarkable number of narratives has survived from those who were sent with the first plantation to Jamestown in Virginia under the London Company in 1607. With the leadership of Captain Christopher Newport the expedition arrived May 13. John Smith later reported: "Now falleth every man to worke, the Councell contrive the Fort, the rest cut down trees to make place to pitch their tents; some provide clapboard to relade the ships; some make garden, some nets, etc."[4] Seven councilors had been appointed, most of whom were experienced seamen and adventurers who would have been well versed in the arts of quick fortification that had been practiced during the earlier years of exploration. The result was described by George Percy as being "triangle wise: having three Bulwarkes, one at every corner, like a half Moone, and foure or five pieces of artillerie mounted in them; thus we had made ourselves sufficiently strong for these Savages."[5] As for dwellings, John Smith writing in 1608 stated that the fort had been palisaded but that "we had no houses to cover us, our Tents were rotten and our cabbins worse than nought." [6]

"Tents" and "cabbins" have been likened to "subvernacular" buildings, especially the charcoal burners' shelters in the north of England.[7] These are also known in Sweden, along with the Lapp huts which they resemble.[8] Another kind of temporary shelter perhaps more familiar to the colonists was the seaside shelter for fisherfolk, used until recently on the west coast of the Jutland peninsula in Denmark and illustrated in a number of seventeenth-century Dutch beach landscapes [2-1].[9] These are all low A-shaped structures, not full houses, but merely roofs of thatch or board set directly upon the ground. For a single fisherman on

2-3. *View of buildings in reconstructed fort, Jamestown, Virginia, shown as built c. 1610. (Photo: M. C. Donnelly).*

a north European shore or for a single colonist in Virginia or Massachusetts Bay this kind of structure would provide a quickly built refuge from the elements and a place to keep personal possessions. At its highest point, however, there would still be minimal headroom, and such housing would be miserable indeed for a man and wife and family of one or more children.

However elementary the individual shelters at Jamestown were at the beginning, in the first month the fort had been finished and according to Percy "we had also sowne most of our Corne on two Mountains. It sprang a man's height from the ground."[10] Arrival in early summer had helped, since shelter for all activities had to be built from scratch. William Strachey indicated that to at least some extent Indian building materials were adopted by the colonists: "A delicate wrought kind of mat the Indians make with which our people do dress their chambers....The houses have wide and large country chimneys ...and they have found the way to cover their houses now (as the Indians) with barks of trees, as durable and as good proof against

storms and winter weather defending likewise the piercing sunbeams of summer and keeping weather would be like stoves, whilst they were, as at first pargeted and plastered with bitumen or tough clay."[11] In a drawing by John White two Indian buildings are shown and there are further descriptions in other contemporary writings [2-2].[12] Traditions were strong among the English colonists, however, and housing methods that were more familiar to them were soon developed. The comment about pargeting and plastering reflects the differences in climate between England and Virginia. A solution to housing that did not make a tight seal in hot, humid weather on the one hand nor was subject to destruction by violent rainstorms on the other was needed.

In John Smith's later *Advertisements* of 1631 he speaks of the church built in the Jamestown fort as "a homely thing, like a barne, set upon Cratchets, covered with rafts, sedge and earth; so was also the walls. The best of our houses were of the like curiosity."[13] "Cratchets" were forked poles, which when set upright as posts could carry horizontal poles to support the roof [2-3]. This was a common structural feature not only in England but elsewhere in north Europe. For the "best" of their houses, the Jamestown colonists were striving for a familiar form that could be easily constructed.

Smith's description of the first place of worship at Jamestown, also written in 1631, is equally revealing: "We did hang an awning (which is an old sail) to three or four trees to shadow us from the Sunne, our walles were rales of wood, our seats unhewed trees till we cut plankes, our Pulpit a bar of wood nailed to two neighboring trees. In foule weather we shifted into an old rotten tent…. This was our Church."[14] In contrast to what was to occur later in Massachusetts Bay, from the beginning in Jamestown it was considered appropriate to provide a place specifically for the worship in the Church of England, no matter how rudimentary that place might be.

In January 1608 a fire caused extensive damage to the fort and its buildings, which by April were rebuilt. From this building campaign we have dimensions and some detailed description from William Strachey: "The south side next the river…contains 140 yards, the west and east sides a hundred only. At every angle or corner, where the lines meet, a bulwark or watchtower is raised and in each bulwark a piece of ordnance or two well mounted. To every side, a proportional distance from the palisade, is a settled street of houses that runs along, so as each line of the angle hath his street. In the midst is a market-place, a store-house, and a corps-de-garde, as likewise a pretty chapel… a palisade of planks and strong posts, four foot deep in the ground, of young oaks, walnuts, etc…. The principal gate from the towne, through the palisade, opens to the river, as at each bulwark there is a gate likewise…."[15]

This description of the fort at Jamestown shows that it had certain features in common with that at Sagadahoc, that is, a central market place with storehouses, guardhouse, and chapel. Strachey suggests that within the Jamestown fort the placement of houses was more regular and he makes no mention of a trench such as the one at Sagadahoc. For the "pretty chapel" we are also indebted to him: "It is in length three-score foot, in breadth twentyfour, and shall have a chancel in it of cedar and a communion table of the black walnut, and all the pews of cedar, with fair broad windows to shut and open, as the weather shall occasion, of the same wood, a pulpit of the same, with a font hewn hollow, like a canoe, with two bells at the west end…. His Lordship hath his seat in the choir in a green velvet chair."[16]

Built for Anglican worship, with the Rev. Robert Hunt the first vicar at Jamestown, the chapel in the fort of 1608 was

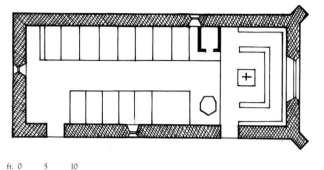

2-4. Chapel, Langley, Shropshire, England, c. 1601, plan. (After G. W. O. Addleshaw and Frederick Etchells, The Architectural Setting of Anglican Worship: An Inquiry into the Arrangement for Public Worship in the Church of England from the Reformation to the Present Day, London, 1948, plan 29.)

long and narrow, the "chancel" probably marked off by a communion rail, or even a screen, rather than being separate. This was the new "room" or "auditory" church then developing in England, as at the chapel of ease at Langley, Shropshire, c. 1601.[17] [2-4.] Nor was it necessary for the English churches to be built of stone, though only a limited number of the wooden ones survive, such as the church at Mattingly, Hampshire [2-5].[18] Like the chapel at Sagadahoc, the church in the fort at Jamestown reflected current English building practices.

By June 1610 the combined hardships of a poor location as to marshes and water, difficulties with the Indians, inadequate supplies, and disease had taken a severe toll on the small population at Jamestown. The decision by Sir Thomas Gates to abandon the settlement was turned around by word of approaching new supplies and settlers, but the episode of departure down the river has been viewed by some as shaking Jamestown's claim to be the earliest permanent English settlement in North America. Such a view seems difficult to maintain, however, since a small number of persons did remain and the site was reoccupied in a matter of hours.

TEN YEARS LATER came another critical moment in English settlement in America, this time in New England, and this time colonization for the purpose of gaining religious freedom. On December 21, 1620, a company of Separatists from the Church of England came ashore at Plymouth, Massachusetts, having been blown off their course for Virginia. Under the leadership of John Robinson they had left England for Leiden in 1619, seeking an atmosphere more suited to their preferences in worship. Disaffection with the Dutch Reformation set in, however, and they secured a patent for settlement in Virginia under the London Company, with which they severed relations in 1627.[19]

For all that their intentions for landing had been thwarted, they might have taken heart from the "Description" that John Smith had written in 1614: "Oke is the chiefe wood, of which there is great difference in regard of the soyle where it groweth, firre, pyne, walnut, chestnut, birch, ash, elme, cypresse, cedar, mulberries, plumtree, hazell, saxefrage, and many other sorts."[20] He further concluded: "And of all the foure parts of the world that I have yet seene not inhabited, could have but meanes to transport a Colonie, I would rather live here than anywhere."[21]

The hardships of the first winter at Plymouth as described by Governor William Bradford were survived by enough colonists that he was able to write that in the following summer "they

2-5. Church, Mattingly, Hampshire, begun fifteenth century. (Photo: M. C. Donnelly).

built a fort with good timber, both strong and comely, which was of good defense, made with a flat roof and battlements, on which their ordnance were mounted."[22] John Smith's observation in 1631 showed that the Pilgrims had overcome some of their hardships and were well established in the area of which he had spoken so enthusiastically: "Their Towne containes two and thirty houses... impaled about halfe a mile, within which a high Mount, a Fort, with a Watch-tower, well built of stone, loame, and wood, their Ordnance well mounted."[23] The town that grew here retained its Separatist character for many years, eventually being absorbed by the Massachusetts Bay Company in 1691. None of these first buildings have survived, and in spite of the drama of its founding, the Plymouth colony was to play a somewhat secondary role in the development of colonial building in New England.

The major impetus for this development came from the other religion-based colonial enterprise, the Massachusetts Bay Company, as well as its off-shoot, the Connecticut Colony. The full story of their first building efforts is gradually being unfolded. What is critical in the present account is the arrival in Salem, Massachusetts, of settlers under Roger Conant in 1626 and John Endicott in 1628, the latter armed with the Charter of the Governor and Company of the Massachusetts Bay in New England.[24] The site had been chosen as more sheltered than one previously used on Cape Ann. On August 6, 1629, the church was formally organized in Salem, though there was as yet no building provided specifically for worship.

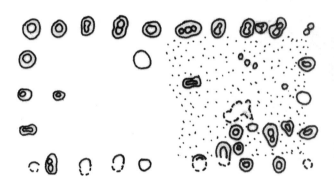

m. 0 1 2 3

2-6. Saxon hut, Holbeach St. John's, Lincolnshire, England, third century. (After Trudy West, The Timber-frame House in England, New York, 1971, Fig. 2).

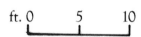

ft. 0 5 10

2-7. Anglo-Saxon house, Chalton, Hampshire, sixth century. (After P. V. Addyman, "Anglo Saxon Houses at Chalton, Hampshire," Medieval Archaeology 16 [1972], Fig. 2).

shelters, although they apparently did not use the word.[25] The precise nature of these various houses is still a matter of conjecture. Setting aside the matter of the dugouts for the moment, the others are all named as being in use around 1630. Few traces remain in New England, but archaeological investigations in Virginia and Maryland have substantially increased knowledge of some of the earliest English structures in the southern colonies.[26]

In both areas the terms "puncheon" or "palisade" are mentioned in documents from the earliest years of settlement. In Virginia in 1623 the majority of houses were described as "punches sett into the Ground. and couered with Boarde."[27] Within the decade Roger Clap found but one "house" among the "wigwams" at Charlestown in Massachusetts Bay, and that one "palisadoed and thatched."[28] The writers of these and similar passages may or may not have made the present distinction between "puncheon" construction, with posts set directly into the ground five to ten feet apart, and "palisades," with posts about six or seven inches apart, sometimes in trenches.

The scarcity of remains makes it difficult to determine much about what such buildings were like, although findings at Kingsmill and the Maine in James City County, Virginia, suggest "puncheon" buildings up to twenty-seven feet long.[29] Efforts to find English prototypes yield little apart from archaeological remains from the Middle Ages. Discoveries at Holbeach St. John's, Lincolnshire, included holes from a third- or fourth-century Saxon hut about fifteen feet long that might have been a "puncheon" hut.[30] [2-6.] Here the posts were set as much as seven feet apart. A quotation from Froissart's Chronicle states that with six or eight posts or stakes a house could be built.[31] The walls of such a house could be completed with wattle and daub, that is, an infill of thin upright poles, interwoven with thinner twigs, roots, or vines, and plastered with clay mixed with straw, moss, or other materials.[32] Another kind of covering was

THE WRITINGS OF THE COLONISTS in Massachusetts Bay and later histories giving traditional accounts of the first shelters at Salem and other places are difficult to interpret. John Smith's dismal mention of "tents" and "cabbins" has already been quoted. "Huts," "cottages," "wigwams," and "Pallizadoed houses" were mentioned by colonial writers who also described dugout

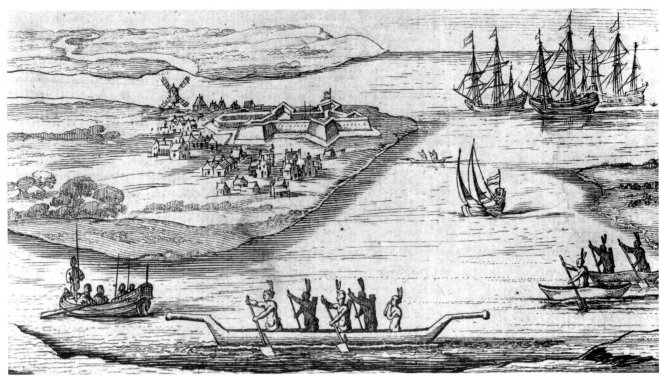

2-8. New Amsterdam, New Netherland. Hartgers view of 1628 (published 1651). (Courtesy of New York Historical Society).

horizontal boarding, as described in the "Notes" of 1623 and other documents.[33]

The "palisade" type of house is even more elusive, as none appear to survive, and the few contemporary references are not always clear as to whether the term refers to the house or the fence around it.[34] English parallels from the Middle Ages had walls of upright timbers set closely together, as at St. Andrew's Church, Greensted, Essex, a much-diminished but still extant example.[35] More significant for the colonial dwelling type may be Anglo-Saxon "stake-hole" buildings, the stakes fairly closely spaced, probably serving as framework for wattle and daub, and sometimes set with some regularity in trenches.[36] [2-7.] The most critical element for which direct archaeological evidence would be desirable is of course the roof. Precisely how the "puncheon" and "palisade" shelters were roofed is still a matter for conjecture, in spite of the occasional mention of the roofing material, as in Roger Clap's *Memoirs*.

One further matter might be considered in reading colonial statements about "palisaded" houses. There is a curious discrepancy between the use of this term by the builders or their observers and its absence from English writings on archaeology and vernacular architecture. Except for the English settlers and some of the American historians who have written about them, the term normally refers to fences, whether civil or military. The *Builder's Dictionary* of the early eighteenth century defines "pallisade" or "pallisado" as "a Sort of slight open Pale or Fence, set to beautify the Place, Walk; etc."[37] Considering the importance of defense in the English colonies and the extent to which mili-

tary men were among the first settlers, it could well have been easy for them to make the analogy between the fort and fence palisades and similarly placed timbers in their houses. The more frequent use of the term in colonial writings seems to be in reference to fences. For example, William Simmonds, writing of the fire at Jamestown fort in 1608, said it "was so fierce as it burnt their pallizadoes (though ten to twelve yards distant)" and that then the company engaged in "the rebuilding our towne, the repairing our pallisadoes."[38]

At this point, then, the question of the partially excavated shelter or "dugout" becomes appropriate. Edward Johnson scribed one practice of the settlers in Massachusetts Bay, saying, "They burrow themselves in the Earth for their first shelter under some Hill side, casting the Earth aloft upon Timber; they make a smoky fire against the Earth at its highest side" and he called these dwellings "Wigwames," evidently using this term in a generally derogatory sense rather than in any precise reference to Indian dwellings.[39] He also referred to the building of "huts for women and children," as if like the fishers' shelters such "dugouts" would hardly accommodate families.[40]

Tradition has it that the Dorchester Company had taken the frame, at least, of a house with them to Cape Ann in 1624 and that it was moved to Salem to house the Governor, Roger Conant, in 1626.[41] Francis Higginson, writing about two and one-half years later, spoke of "half a score houses, and a faire house newly built for the Governor."[42] By 1629 some of the most elementary shelters were giving way to more conventional and permanent houses. The success of the colony at Salem in surviving and having other communities grow out of it into a fully developed colonial region was the northern counterpart of the English success in establishing a southern foothold at Jamestown.

Between these English colonies lay the territories claimed by the Dutch and the Swedes. Robert Juet, reporting on the third voyage of Henry Hudson in 1609-1610, said that "The Countrey is full of great and tall Oakes… and Walnut Trees, and chestnut trees, yew trees and trees of sweet wood in great abundance, and great store of slate for houses, and other good stores."[43] By 1614 trading posts were set up on Manhattan Island, and in 1621 the Dutch West India Company was granted ownership of the territory claimed by the Dutch, powers of government, and exclusive trading rights.[44] The arrival of families by 1624 ushered in a settlement venture that was more explicitly commercial in intention than the cases in Virginia and Massachusetts Bay.[45] From the instructions with which the Dutch engineer Cryn Fredericksz was to lay out the fortifications and the principal buildings it could be said that New Amsterdam was begun, at least, as America's first "company town."

As these instructions have survived and been interpreted they were probably not influenced by the advice that Inigo Jones had sent to the Dutch East India Company in 1620.[46] Jones was thinking in terms of fort alone, and the dimensions for the moat that he recommended, for example, thirty feet wide and ten feet deep, are not those of the later document. Of considerable interest, however, is his last sentence: "My carvings and ornaments in the stone and to the gate and the arche are made clear to scale and to the mason." One is reminded of the York Water Gate in London, built in 1626 and heavily ornamented in the Tuscan Order, attributed by some to Sir Balthasar Gerbier and by others to Jones. Was this gate built on a model originally intended for New Amsterdam?

In a document dated April 22, 1625, Cryn Fredericksz was given instructions for more than the military defenses of New Amsterdam.[47] He was to start with a ditch, wider and shallower than Jones's moat, to be twenty-four feet wide, four feet deep, and to enclose the fort and an initial ten individual houses and gardens. The area to be enclosed was 200 feet wide and 1600 feet back from the water. Farm parcels and vineyards were to be developed outside the ditch. The town proper was to be inside the fort, protected by a much larger moat, fifty-four feet wide and eight feet deep. Twenty-five houses along a principal street, a market place in the middle 165 feet long and 100 feet wide, with church, school, and hospital upon it, and further houses were to complete the scheme. House lots were to be twenty-five feet wide and to vary in depth from thirty to fifty feet. The commercial nature of these instructions is nowhere so apparent as in the stipulation that the houses of the main street should be of uniform size (twenty-five feet square), all adjoining, and with doors to permit the access of the Commissary throughout the second level. This was to be reserved at first "for all the provisions of the Company" and later as grain-lofts, with the individual owners allowed to use the lofts above for their own goods. These houses would therefore have combined the residential and warehouse functions that survive in early merchants' houses of north European port towns. The fortress itself was to have five bastions. For all this Cryn Fredericksz was given five plans in addition to the written instructions.[48]

However commendable the idea of such a well-regulated planning and building program seemed to the Commissioners of the Dutch West India Company, in practice the individual more often overcame the general. The famous Hartgers View, published in 1651 but representing New Amsterdam about 1626-1628, may tell why.[49] [2-8.] It shows the fort empty, with houses scattered about and a windmill looming against the far shore, all lacking the precise order of the original instructions. In 1626 Nicolaes van Wassenaer, an Amsterdam physician who compiled a history of New Netherland, gave a report of this rather haphazard progress: "The colony is now established on the Manhaytes, where a fort has been staked out by Master Kryn Frederyckes, an engineer. It is planned to be of large dimensions …. The counting-house there is kept in a stone building, thatched with reed; the other houses are of the bark of trees. Each has his own house…. there are thirty ordinary houses on the east side of the river…. Francis Molemaecker is busy building a horse-mill, overwhich shall be constructed a spacious room sufficient to accommodate a large congregation, and then a tower is to be erected where the bells brought from Porto Rico will be hung…. The house of the Hollanders now stands outside the fort, but when that is completed, they will all repair within, so as to garrison it and be secure from sudden attack."[50]

From this account it appears that stone was hoped to give good protection for the counting house, though havoc would surely be wreaked by the fall of a burning thatch roof. The mill built for a horse walking in a circle to turn the wheel would not have the elaborate superstructure of a windmill and could therefore, as here, include an upper room large enough for a place of worship.

The outcome of these first years of building at New Amsterdam was so disorderly that an ordinance was issued by Director Peter Stuyvesant and the Council to clean up the worst abuses and order building of houses on unimproved lots.[51] The slow start toward reasonable living conditions was reported by the first minister to New Netherland, the Rev. Jonas Johannis Michaëlius, who wrote to his friend the Rev. Adrianus Smoutius in Amsterdam on August 8, 1628, that the colonists were "beginning to build new houses in place of the hovels and cots in which heretofore they nestled rather than dwelt."[52]

Here again is the question of "dugout," and a passage from a report by the Secretary of New Netherland, Cornelis van Tienhoven, March 4, 1650, described such shelters: "Those in New Netherland and especially in New England, who have no means to build up farmhouses at first according to their wishes, dig a square pit in the ground, cellar fashion, six or seven feet deep, as long and as broad as they think proper, case the earth inside all round the wall with timber, which they then line with the bark of trees or something to prevent the caving-in of the earth; Floor this cellar with plank, and wainscot it over for a ceiling; raise a roof of spars clear up, and cover the spars with bark or green sod so that they can live dry and warm in these houses with their families for two, three or four years."[53]

As in the case of the puncheon and palisade houses, excavations of medieval English buildings are illuminating. Many Anglo-Saxon "sunken huts" have been discovered which partly answer this description.[54] While evidence for living partly below ground level seems clear, more than one system can be proposed for reconstructing sunken huts so described. At West Stow, Suffolk, two different possibilities are shown in the reconstruction of buildings with sunken floors over examples of the same dimensions.[55] [2-9 and 2-10.] This is an Anglo-Saxon site, and part of the purpose

2-9. Hut, West Stow, Suffolk, 1972 reconstruction of sixth-century building. (Photo: M.C. Donnelly).

2-10. Hut, West Stow, Suffolk, 1972 reconstruction of sixth-century building. (Photo: M.C. Donnelly).

In New Amsterdam van Tienhoven's report of 1650 reveals that the use of dugouts had persisted for more than twenty years but that incoming settlers were expected to replace them with "good farmhouses and barns" and to start promptly the development of crops and livestock.[59]

FINALLY, one more European country engaged in the colonial adventure. An appeal from the Dutch West India Company to Gustavus II Adolphus of Sweden, after the failure of its attempt to colonize in Delaware in 1631, led to the formation of a joint Dutch-Swedish expedition under the former Dutch governor of New Netherland, Peter Minuit. By the time he was able to establish a settlement at the present Wilmington, Delaware, in 1638, the king had been killed in 1632, and the outpost was named Fort Christina in honor of the young queen.[60] Captain David de Vries noted in 1643 that the fort "was not

of this demonstration is to suggest that this kind of early English dwelling was not merely a hovel or pit. Closer in date to the seventeenth-century American "dugouts" are the cottages at Athelney, Somerset, much like the structures described by van Tienhoven.[56] [2-11.] This brings the use of such buildings down to much more recent times in England, and in the American colonies they were apparently also used as first shelters long after the initial period of settlement.[57] A colonial observer's approach to the matter was expressed by Richard Eburne in 1624: "Men must be contented at first with low and plain buildings. England hath been inhabited two or three thousand years at least, and yet what poor, what homely houses be there many till this very day."[58] He said that when better housing could be built the first shelters could be turned over to cattle and storage.

entirely finished; it was made after the English plan, with three angles close by the river."[61] Here in the colony called "New Sweden" a town was laid out by the military engineer Per Martensson Lindström in 1654. His plan shows the fort with four bastions rather than the three mentioned by de Vries.[62] [2-12.] Although this town, called Christinahamn, was projected in response to the queen's desire to expand her country's interests in America, it was to come to naught for Sweden.

In the same year Queen Christina abdicated the throne, moved to Rome, and embraced Roman Catholicism. Her successor, Charles X Gustavus, was fully occupied with a war with Poland, and New Sweden was far away. Little has survived of what was under construction for housing at that time. From documentary accounts it appears that the Swedish settlers built with logs laid horizontally, thereby bringing this technique to North America, where it was to have a long history of use. Jasper Danckaerts reported staying in a house "made according to the Swedish mode ."[63] An earlier reference of 1645 speaks of a house on Tinnicum Island near Essington, Pennsylvania, as being "constructed by laying very heavy hemlock logs the one on the other."[64]

Few, if any, such houses have survived from the original settlement period, although local traditions claim seventeenth-century dates for some log structures.[65] The so-called Swedish plan was used in this region, consisting of a major room with a corner fireplace and one or two smaller rooms, which might also have corner fireplaces. By 1655 Governor Rising of New Sweden sent a report showing that progress was being made only with difficulty: "The people are building houses as they are able and six or eight lots are now occupied. I expect that when more people come there will be more buildings, in the form of a city.... Fort Christina was built up last autumn with good ramparts of turf, on two sides where it had mostly fallen down. In the spring it was surrounded by palisades. Skilled workmen would be very useful to us, especially the following which are now needed: saltpeter-makers and powder-makers, ship-carpenters and house carpenters, those who understand how to cut all kinds of timber (yet we expect to obtain these best from New England)."[66]

This last remark suggests that the Swedish settlers had come to regard the framed house as preferable to the log cabin for a permanent dwelling. Their own traditions in wood being different from those of England, help from the English carpenters would indeed be desirable. Rising's letter asking for help arrived in Sweden too late, however, for the Dutch under Peter Stuyvesant not only recaptured their Fort Casimir, near present Newcastle, but took Fort Christina as well. The Swedish settlers now came under Dutch rule, which was in turn overthrown by the English in 1664.

As Rising's comment implies, by mid-century the houses and other buildings of European settlers in North America were more frequently permanent in nature and their European character firmly established. From these first successes the colonists could move to enlarging their holdings and setting forth in structural terms their increasing prosperity and confidence.

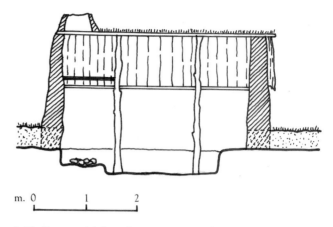

2-11. Cottage, Athelney, Somerset, nineteenth century. Section. (After H. Laver, "Ancient Types of Huts at Athelney," Proceedings of the Somerset Archaeological Society 55 [1909]:171).

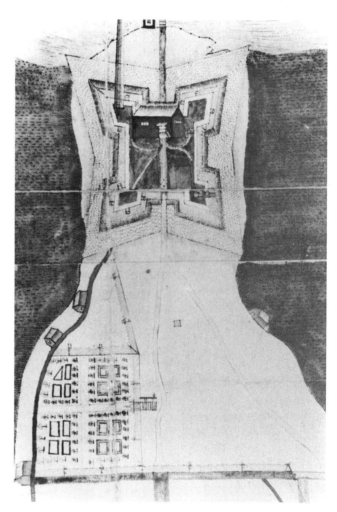

2-12. Per Lindström, Christinahamn (Wilmington, Delaware): 1654, plan. (Courtesy Stockholm, Hiksarkivet).

Notes to Chapter 2

1. Benjamin Perley Poore, comp., *The Federal and State Constitutions, Colonial Charters, and Other Organic Laws of the United States* (Washington D.C.: Government Printing Office, 1878), 2:1888.

2. From "Instructions by way of advice," in *Travels and Works of Captain John Smith: President of Virginia and Admiral of New England, 1580-1631*, ed. Edward Arber (Edinburgh: John Grant, 1910), 1:xxxvii.

3. John William Reps, *The Making of Urban America: A History of City Planning in the United States* (Princeton: Princeton University Press, 1965), 12-15. A detailed history of the towns in Ireland is in Sir Thomas Phillips, *Londonderry and the London Companies, 1609-1629: Being a Survey and Other Documents Submitted to King Charles I* (Belfast: H.M.S.O., 1928); for plan of Londonderry see Plate 3.

4. John Smith, "Description of Virginia," in *Narratives of Early Virginia, 1606-1625*, ed. Lyon Gardiner Tyler (New York: C. Scribner's Sons, 1907), 123; James O'Mara, "Town Founding in Seventeenth-Century North America: Jamestown in Virginia," *Journal of the Society of Architectural Historians (JSAH)* 8, no. 1 (1982): 1-11.

5. George Percy, "Observations gathered out of a Discourse of the Plantation of the Southerne Colonie in Virginia by the English, 1606," in *Travels and Works of Captain John Smith*, ed. Arber, 1.

6. John Smith, "A True Relation," in *Travels and Works of Captain John Smith*, ed. Arber, 1:9.

7. Fiske Kimball, *Domestic Architecture of the American Colonies and of the Early Republic* (New York: Dover Publications, 1966 [1922]), 4-5.

8. Sigurd Emanuel Erixon, *Svensk byggnadskultur studier och skildringar belysande den svenska byggnadskulturens historia* (Stockholm: Aktiebolaget Bokvert, 1947), 21-86.

9. Other examples are illustrated in Wolfgang Stechow, *Dutch Landscape Painting of the Seventeenth Century* (London: Phaidon, 1966), Plates 197, 207, 211, and 214.

10. Arber, ed., *Travels and Works of Captain John Smith*, 1:9.

11. William Strachey, "A true repertory of the wracke, and redemption of Sir Thomas Gates... his coming to Virginia, and the estate of that Colonie then, and after, vnder the gouernment of the Lord [de La] Warre, Iuly 15, 1610," in *A Voyage to Virginia in 1609; Two Narratives: Strachey's "True repertory" and Jourdain's "Discovery of the Bermuda,"* ed. Louis B. Wright (Charlottesville: University Press of Virginia, 1964), 81-82.

12. P. H. Hulton and David B. Quinn, eds., *The American Drawings of John White, 1577-1590, with Drawings of European and Oriental Subjects* (London: Chapel Hill, Trustees of the British Museum; University of North Carolina Press, 1964), plates 31 and 34A. The "six sorts" of buildings that could be put up by settlers in "New Albion," now New Jersey, are described in Beauchamp Plantagenet, *A Description of the province of New Albion...with a brief of the charge of victual, and necessaries, to transport and buy stock fro each planter, or labourer, there to get his master fifty pounds per annum, or more, in twelve trades, and at ten pounds per annum, or more, in twelve trades, and at tem pounds charges onely a man* (London: Printed by James Moxon, 1650). This includes as Type I a house that answers the written and pictorial descriptions of the Indian buildings. "Beauchamp Plantagenet" may have been Sir Edmund Plowden, and his treatise is excerpted in "American Notes," *JSAH* 15, no. 3 (October 1956): 2. Numerous references to colonial writings are made by G. Carroll Lindsay, "Plantagenet's Wigwam," *JSAH* 15 (November 1958): 31-35.

13. John Smith, "Advertisements," in *Travels and Works of Captain John Smith*, ed. Arber, 2:957. Figure 8 was based on an earlier engraving by J. Sadeler, with the background changed to show buildings from America (William Patterson Cumming, R. A. Skelton, and David B. Quinn, *The Discovery of North America* (New York: American Heritage Press, 1972), 13 and Figure 1).

14. Arber, ed., *Travels and Works of Captain John Smith*, 2:957.

15. Strachey, "True Reportory," 79 and 81.

16. Ibid, 80. By "His Lordship," Strachey means to refer to Lord De La Warr, the new Governor of the colony.

17. G. W. O. Addleshaw and Frederick Etchells, *The Architectural Setting of Anglican Worship: An Inquiry into the Arrangement for Public Worship in the Church of England from the Reformation to the Present Day* (London: Faber and Faber, 1948), 111, plan 29.

18. Frederick Herbert Crossley, *Timber Building in England: From Early Times to the End of the Seventeenth Century* (London: Batsford, 1951), 26-37.

19. Charles McLean Andrews, *The Colonial Period of American History* (New Haven: Yale University Press, 1934), 1:249-299.

20. Arber, ed., *Travels and Works of Captain John Smith*, 1:207.

21. Ibid., 1:193-194.

22. William Bradford, *Of Plymouth Plantation, 1620-1647*, ed. Samuel E. Morison (New York: Knopf, 1952), 111.

23. Arber, ed., *Travels and Works of Captain John Smith*, 2:943.

24. Poore, comp., *The Federal and State Constitutions*, 1:932-942.

25. See Kimball, *Domestic Architecture*, 3-91 for numerous references to seventeenth-century writings and also English construction techniques. For the Massachusetts Bay examples, see Abbott L. Cummings, *The Framed Houses of Massachusetts Bay, 1625-1725* (Cambridge, Mass.: Belknap Press, 1979), 18-21.

26. Cary Carson et al., "Impermanent Architecture in the Southern American Colonies," *Winterthur Portfolio* 16, nos. 2 and 3 (Summer/Autumn 1981): 196. For commentary on the early American use of earth-fast techniques in comparison with those in other geographical areas see Gordon Young, "Colonial Building Techniques," *Vernacular Architecture* 17 (1986): 6.

27. "Notes for an Answer," in *The Records of the Virginia Company of London*, ed. Susan Myra Kingsbury (Washington D.C.: Government Printing Office, 1906-1935), 4:259.

28. "Memoirs of Capt. Roger Clap," in Alexander Young, *Chronicles of the First Planters of the Colony of Massachusetts Bay, 1623-1636* (Boston: C. C. Little and J. Brown, 1846), 351.

29. Carson et al., "Impermanent Architecture." 148, 179, 192 and Figure 6.

30. Trudy West, *The Timber-frame House in England* (New York: Architectural Book Publishing Co., 1971), 16-21 and Figure 2.

31. Sir John Froissart, *The Chronicles of England, France, Spain, Etc.*, trans. Thomas Johnes (New York: J. M. Dent; E. P. Dutton, 1940 [1906]), 2:55.

32. A discussion of the many approaches to this technique is in Charles Frederick Innocent, *The Development of English Building Construction* (Newton Abbot, David and Charles, 1971 [1916]), 129-147.

33. Kingsbury, ed., *Records of the Virginia Company*, 4:259; and, Carson et al., "Impermanent Architecture," 149.

34. Cummings, *Framed Houses*, 21.

35. Innocent, *English Building Construction*, 110.

36. Philip Rahtz, "Buildings and Rural Settlements," in *The Archaeology of Anglo-Saxon England*, ed. David M. Wilson (London: Methuen, 1976), 84. See also P. V. Addyman, D. Leigh, and M. J. Hughes, "Anglo-Saxon Houses at Chalton, Hampshire," *Medieval Archaeology* 16 (1972): 13-21, esp. Figures 14 and 15.

37. *The Builder's Dictionary: or, Gentleman and architect's companion; being a complete unabridged reprint of the earlier works published by A. Bettesworth and C. Hitch* (Washington D.C.: Association for Preservation Technology, 1981 [1734]), 2:n.p.

38. Tyler, ed., *Narratives of Early Virginia*, 135 and 137.

39. Edward Johnson, *Johnson's Wonder-Working Providence, 1628-1651* (New York: C. Scribner's Sons, 1910), 83; and Cummings, *Framed Houses*, 19-21.

40. Johnson, *Wonder-Working Providence*, 38.

41. Frances James Rose-Troup, *John White, the Patriarch of Dorchester (Dorset) and the Founder of Massachusetts, 1575-1648, with an Account of the Early Settlements in Massachusetts, 1620-1630* (New York: G. P. Putnam's Sons, 1930), 105. No authority for such a tradition is given.

42. Francis Higginson, *New-Englands Plantation* (Amsterdam: Theatrum Orbis Terrarum; New York: Da Capo Press, 1970 [1630]), 51.

43. Robert Juet, "Third Voyage of Master Henry Hudson," in *Narratives of New Netherland, 1609-1664*, ed. Franklin J. Jameson (New York: Charles Scribner's Sons, 1909), 18-24.

44. Thomas J. Condon, *New York Beginnings: The Commercial Origins of New Netherland* (New York: New York University Press, 1968), 20-32.

45. Ibid., 71-75.

46. Jones's letter is in the private collection of Colin Johnston Robb, Loughgall, Ireland, and is reprinted in *Architectural Record* 98, no. 2 (August 1945): 146. The essay on Jones's letter is brief, and the letter itself appears to be brief as well. How Jones came to be engaged by the Dutch East India Company is not explained, nor is the exact date of the letter given. Jones reminds the company directors that to build "in stone and lime will be more lasting."

47. "Special Instructions for Cryn Fredericksz Regarding the laying out of the fort," in *Documents Relating to New Netherland, 1624-1626, in the Henry E. Huntington Library*, trans. and ed. Arnold van Laer (San Marino, Calif.: The Henry E. Huntington Library and Art Gallery, 1924), 131-169.

48. These plans, now lost, were given conjectural form by Frederik C. Wieder, *De Stichting von New York in Juli 1625. Reconstructies en nieuwe gegevens ontleend aan de van Rappard documenten* ('s-Gravenhage: M. Nijhoff, 1925). Three are reproduced in Reps, *The Making of Urban America*, 149, Figure 89.

49. Questions that have been raised about the date and authorship of the Hartgers View are discussed in Isaac Newton Phelps Stokes, *The Iconography of Manhattan Island, 1498-1909* (New York: Arno Press, 1967 [1915]), 1:133-135.

50. Nicolaes van Wassenaer, *Historisch verhael alder ghedenck-weerdichste geschiedenisse(n) die hier en daer in Europa, als in Duijtsch-lant, Vranckrijck, Enghelant... en Neder-lant, van den beginne des jaers 1621, tot den herfst toe, voorgevallen syn* (T'Amstelredam: Bij Ian Evertss, 1622-1635), 83-84.

51. Reps, John William. *The Making of Urban America.* (Princeton: Princeton University Press, 1965) 148-150.

52. Albert Eekhof, *Johas Michaëlius, founder of the church in New Netherland, his life and work, together with the facsimile, transcription and English of an extensive unknown autographical Latin letter* (Leyden: A. W. Sijthoff, 1926), 110.

53. Cornelis van Tienhoven, "Information Relative to Taking Up Land in New Netherland," in *The Documentary History of the State of New York: Arranged Under Direction of the Hon. Christopher Morgan, Secretary of State*, ed. E. B. O'Callaghan (Albany: Weed, Parsons & Co., Public Printers, 1849-1851), 1:368.

54. Addyman, "Anglo-Saxon Houses," 275-281 and Figures 2 and 4.

55. Stanley E. West, *West Stow, the Anglo-Saxon Village* (Ipswich: Suffolk County Planning Dept., 1985). See also Rahtz, "Buildings and Rural Settlements," 70-81.

56. Ibid., 79 and Figure 2.13.

57. Kimball, *Domestic Architecture*, 6.

58. Richard Eburne, *A Plain Pathway to Plantations (1624)* (Ithica, N.Y.: Cornell University Press, 1962), 47.

59. E. B. O'Callaghan, ed., *Documentary History of the State of New York*, 1:368.

60. The standard history of New Sweden is Amandus Johnson, *The Swedish Settlements on the Delaware, 1638-1664* (Baltimore: Genealogical Publishing Co., 1969 [1911]).

61. David Pietersz de Vries, *Korte historiael ende journaels aenteyckeninge van verscheyden voyagiens in di vier deelen des wereldtsronde, als Europa, Africa, Asia, ende Amerika gedaen* ('s-Gravenhage: M. Nijhoff, 1911 [1655]), 28-29.

62. Johnson, *Swedish Settlements*, 2:518-519.

63. Jasper Danckaerts, *Journal of a Voyage to New York* (Ann Arbor: University Microfilms, 1966 [1867]), 98.

64. Andries Hudde, "A brief, but true Report of the Proceedings of Johan Prints [Printz], Governor of the Swedish forces at the South-River of New-Netherland, also of the garrisons of the aforesaid Swedes, found on that River, the first of November 1645" [the date of Hudde's arrival there], 29. Published in Berthold Fernow, ed., *Documents Relating to the History of the Dutch and Swedish Settlements on the Delaware River* (Albany: The Argus Company, Printers, 1877), 12: 28-39. [Andries Hudde, in the service of the Dutch West India Company and appointed Commissary (Factor) on October 12, 1645, was dispatched from Manhattan to Fort Nassau on the east bank of what the Dutch called the South River of New Netherland (the Delaware). An aggressive proponent of Dutch trading and colonial interests, Hudde remained three years, eventually returning to Manhattan. On orders from Governor Peter Stuyvesant in Manhattan, Hudde submitted his "Brief and true Report," dated November 7, 1648, summarizing his activities with the Swedes and including brief descriptions of some of the Swedish settlements along the South River. Following orders from Manhattan, Hudde undertook building new Dutch forts and trading posts. For one of the buildings, boards, materials, and carpenters were sent from Manhattan, suggesting that a frame building was planned in contrast to the local Swedish log buildings that Hudde notes in his report. Fernow notes that Hudde's report was also published in the *Memoirs of the New York Historical Society*, vol.1, new series, page 429 (no date given). For Hudde's activities, see: Amandus Johnson, *The Swedish Settlements on the Delaware: Their History and Relation to the Indians, Dutch, and English, 1638-1664* (New York: D. Appleton & Co., 1911) 2 vols.; Stellan Dahlgren and Hans Norman, *The Rise And Fall Of New Sweden: Governor Johan Rising's Journal 1654-1655 in its Historical Context* (Uppsala: Almqvist & Wiksell International, 1988); and Carol E. Hoffecker et al., *New Sweden in America* (Newark: University of Delaware Press, 1995). Ed.]

65. The Morton Homestead and the Lower Swedish Cabin in Delaware County, Pennsylvania, for example, have been cited in discussions of the Swedish log houses. See Thomas Waterman, *The Dwellings of Colonial America* (Chapel Hill: University of North Carolina Press, 1950), 118-120; Harold Robert Shurtleff, *The Log Cabin Myth: A Study of the Early Dwellings of the English Colonists in North America* (Gloucester, Mass.: P. Smith, 1967 [1937]), 163-173; and C. A. Weslager, *The Log Cabin in America: From Pioneer Days to the Present* (New Brunswick, N.J.: Rutgers University Press, 1969), 148-180. As early as 1927 Henry C. Mercer expressed skepticism about these early survivals in "The Origin of Log Houses." p. 54. Firm dating of many of these structures awaits the results of modern archaeological and dendrochronological studies.

66. Johan Rising, "Report of Govenor Johan Rising," in *Narratives of Early Pennsylvania, West New Jersey and Delaware, 1630-1707*, ed. Albert Cook Myers (New York: C. Scribner's Sons, 1912), 164-165.

❧ Chapter 3 ❧

Early European Colonial Materials and Tools

I F THERE WAS TO BE ANY HOPE for securing and enlarging permanent European settlements on the North Atlantic coast, some kind of balance would have to be found between local and imported materials and tools and between the skills of the homeowner and those of the several craftsmen. The most important building materials needed were wood, brick, stone, glass, and iron, each having its specialized workers.

Some of the early explorers' lists of trees have already been cited, and they show a combination of astonishment at their variety and optimism for their use, undoubtedly with a certain amount of exaggeration.[1] Increasingly there were discussions of the suitability of these woods for specific purposes. John Smith wrote in 1612 of oaks "so tall and straight, that they will beare two foot and a half square of good timber for 20 yards long," and of cypress "neere 3 fadome [about eighteen feet] about at the root, very straight, and 50, 60 or 80 foot without a branch."[2] William Wood identified three kinds of oak in New England in 1634: "the red Oake, white, and black: as these are different in kinde, so are they chosen for such uses as they are most fit for, one kind being more fit for clappboard, others for sawne board, some fitter for shipping, others for houses....The Firre and Pine be trees that grow in many places, shooting up exceeding high, especially the Pine: they doe afford good masts, good board, Rozin and Turpentine."[3]

In the same year Thomas Morton spoke of only two kinds of oak, white and red, "excellent tymber for the building, both of howses and shipping: and they

3-1. The nailmaker. (From Jost Amman and Hans Sachs, The Book of Trades, Leipzig, 1568, 77).

are found to be a tymber, that is more tough then the oak of England."[4] And although John Josselyn of Kent was unsympathetic toward the Puritans, on his second voyage to Boston in 1663-1671 he took pains to write an extensive account of the trees he saw then.[5] Similar reports were written about the middle colonies, such as the list of trees drawn up in 1679, probably by Adriaen van der Donck, a traveller to New York.[6] William Penn also listed the major trees in Pennsylvania in 1683, calling particular attention to the swamp chestnut, "the most durable of all."[7]

The forests have changed since colonial times, and even then it was recognized that indiscriminate cutting of trees would prejudice the continuing supply. As early as November 7, 1632, the Massachusetts Bay General Court ordered that "For preservation of good timbr for more necessary uses, it is ordered, that noe man shall fell any wood for paleing but such as shalbe vewed & allowed by the nexte Assistant, or some whome they shall depute to doe the same; this order not to extend to ground that is or shall be assigned to ptculr psons."[8]

It has been estimated that only about 5 percent of the total area of New England remained covered with virgin forest to modern times. One such forest, at Colebrook, Connecticut, remaining in 1909 included "a mixture of immense hemlock, beech, yellow birch, sugar maple, fine black cherry, ash, chestnut and oak, with a few giant white pines."[9] There seems to have been a general preference for

21

oak or chestnut for framing, cedar for clapboard and roof shingles, and pine for partitions and door and window trim in New England, with locust also favored for framing in the South.[10]

As for the tools with which to work their wood, the colonists had a wide variety. In 1648 each settler was to have "a Spade, Axe and Shovell,"[11] while in 1684 it was observed of the Swedes in Pennsylvania that they "hardly use any toole but an Ax; They will cut down a Tree, and cut him off when down, sooner then two men can saw him, and rend him into planks or what they please; only with the Ax and Wooden wedges."[12]

English settlers, however, were generally advised to have a greater number of tools for building. A list of recommended equipment prepared by "Master Graves, Engineer," printed in 1630, includes "1 broad axe, 1 felling axe, 1 steel handsaw, 1 whipsaw, 1 hammer… 2 augers, 4 chisels, 2 piercers, stocked, 1 gimlet, 1 hatchet, 2 frowers, 1 handbill," and to keep them sharp, a grindstone.[13] Shortly thereafter William Wood, writing of "What Provision is To Be Made for a Journey at Sea, and what to Carry with Us for Our Use at Land," gave his recommendations: "All manner of tools for workmen… with axes, both broad and pitching axes. All manner of augers, piercing bits, whipsaws, two-handed saws, froes, both for the riving of pales and laths, rings for beetles heads, and iron wedges."[14] He also commented that although there were already blacksmiths working in New England it would probably

3-2. The scythe maker. (From Amman, Book of Trades, 78).

be more economical to bring such tools from England.

These and other tools to be used by carpenters and joiners are known to us from surviving examples as well as from early illustrations and dictionaries.[15] By the time of settlement in the American colonies they had evolved over thousands of years.

An endlessly fascinating source of information about tools is the vast body of early illustrations in various media. Even the blacksmiths were included in descriptions of trades, and as William Wood noted, they were the principal makers of tools which were not made by the builders themselves. From 1568 comes an illustration of a nail maker at work [3-1][16] and also a scythe maker [3-2].[17] While the latter shows the making of agricultural implements, carpenters' and joiners' tools were also made using the heavy furnaces and anvils of the blacksmiths. Possibly the cost of getting this equipment built and supplied with local iron put up the price of the earliest colonial tools in contrast to the cost of those made in established industries in England. The great bellows to keep the fire hot appears in a copperplate engraving of 1658 [3-3].[18]

The question of iron must be addressed, but first there is the matter of other early publications with illustrations of tools. The woodcuts of Amman and the engravings of Commenius were done for recording or didactic purposes, and they were not intended specifically to help the builder. By 1677, however, such a

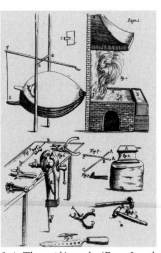

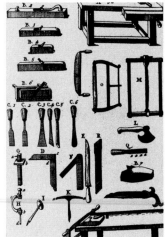

3-3. The blacksmith. Woodblock cut. (From Johann A. Commenius, Orbis Pictus, 85).

3-4. The smith's work. (From Joseph Moxon, Mechanick Exercises…, London, 1700, "Smith's Work," Plate 1).

3-5. The carpenter's tools. (From Moxon, Mechanick Exercises, "Carpenter's Work," Plate 8).

3-6. The joiner's tools. (From Moxon, Mechanick Exercises, "Joyner's Work," Plate 4).

guide did appear, in Joseph Moxon's *Mechanick Exercises: or the Doctrine of Handy-Works Applied to the Arts of Smithing, Joinery, Carpentry, Turning, Bricklaying.* Here the text and illustrations are directed to the user, with plates of the smith's forge and the tools of the carpenter and joiner [3-4, 3-5, and 3-6].[19] The earliest colonial builders did not have such printed guides, however, as until the latter part of the seventeenth century the apprentice was bound to keep the training from his master in confidence.

Two English dictionaries of the building trades were published in the early eighteenth century, *The City and countrey purchaser, and Builder's Dictionary…* by Richard Neve in 1703,[20] and the previously mentioned *Builder's Dictionary* of 1734,[21] neither illustrating the tools listed. Plates are included in two French eighteenth-century publications, the *Recueil de planches sur les sciences et les arts liberaux*, edited by Denis Diderot, and *L'Art du menuisier* by Audrè Roubo.[22]

A distinction was made between the work of the carpenter, "the Framing, Flooring, Roofing; the Foundation, Carcase, Doors, Windows, &c." and the joiner, who was skilled in "fitting and assembling various Parts or Members together."[23] The tools shown in the Amman illustrations of these workers in 1568 did not change radically during the American colonial period [3-7, 3-8, and 3-9].[24] In the Amman illustration the carpenter is shown working away from himself while he squares the timber, but in the Commenius illustration the more normal practice is shown. In contrast to these generalized illustrations, Moxon provides specific instructions for the use of these tools.

I N ADDITION TO hand tools for the preparation of wood there was of course the sawmill. Apparently invented in Germany, possibly as early as the fourteenth century, by the early seventeenth century sawmills were in use in Norway, Sweden, and Holland.[25] While England resisted the introduction of sawmills until the 1660s, fearing that they would add to an already acute unemployment problem, the colonies needed and built them. Long before permanent settlement began, Richard Hakluyt the Elder had said, in 1578: "…if neere such wood there be any river or brooke upon the which a sawing mill may be placed, it would doe a great service, and therefore consideration would be had of such a place."[26]

Fifty years later sawmills were starting up all along the Atlantic coast. The instruction to Willem Verhulst in January 1625 stated that he should "likewise see that a note be made of all falls or affluent streams whereby sawmills or other Mills might be operated and select some of the best that are the most suitable and nearest to the dwellings and the timber that is to be sawn in them, remembering as a general principle, if it can be done without hindrance or inconvenience, that the mills and other places should be down-stream from the woods or dwellings." [27]

Not all the sawmills that were subsequently built in New Netherland were driven by water power. In his letter of August 11, 1628, the Rev. Jonas Michaëlius said that the

3-7. *The carpenter. (From Amman, Book of Trades, 95).*

3-8. *The carpenter. (From Commenius, Orbis Pictus, 79).*

3-9. *The joiner. (From Amman, Book of Trades, 96).*

colonists were "making a windmill to saw lumber and we also have a gristmill."[28]

The Virginia colonists sought help from Germany, as reported in 1623: "Men skilful for sawe Mills were procured from Germany and sent to Virginia at the Companies great charge."[29] Here the hopes were not realized, as the "poor Dutchmen," as the writer called them, were harshly treated by the English settlers, had little food, fell ill, and those surviving fled to England. Another report, written about the same time, said that with setting up ironworks and sawmills and

3-10. A sawmill. (From Edward Williams, Explication of the saw-mill).

3-11. The brickmaker. (From Amman, Book of Trades, 94).

THE NEXT MOST important material, brick, had to be manufactured, but its use was thoroughly familiar and almost as old as human history. The fundamental material is clay, formed by the breaking down of stone to a finely textured earth, some of the best having been produced by the action of glaciers. A certain amount of sand is needed to keep the clay from shrinking and cracking when baked. Then lime is needed for mortar. These materials were also re-ported by early geographers such as Thomas Hariot, who ob-

planting mulberry and other specialized crops, all to come to productivity in two years' time, the colonists could not simultaneously build their own houses and raise food.[30] Reports going back to England in these years were by no means rosy.

Effective use of sawmills does not seem to have come about in Virginia until after 1650, to judge by the recommendations of Edward Williams in his tract of that year.[31] In another tract published in the same year, Williams described how such a mill should be built and included an illustration [3-10].[32] The Dutch in New Netherland were at least able to get sawmills up and running between 1630 and 1640, although evidently not very efficiently.[33] Apart from the personal hardships of the mill builders brought to Virginia, some of the difficulties in getting sawmills established may have come from lack of water power or scarcity of trees in certain locations. A suggestion of the latter is made in two comments in the *Journal* of Jasper Danckaerts, a Dutchman traveling in New Jersey and New York in the spring of 1680: "But although we found the stream suitable for mills, we did not discover proper wood sufficient for the purpose.... At the [Kaaterskill] falls on this river stands a fine saw-mill which has enough wood to saw."[34]

Matters went much better in New England. More than fifty mills are recorded as built in New Hampshire and Maine alone between 1633 and 1680, and more than thirty in Massachusetts and Connecticut in the same period.[35] These mills were supplying timber not only to their own local communities but also to other towns and colonies and to England. All the tools mentioned thus far, whether hand-powered or powered by wind or water, were used for building with wood, an abundant and natural material readily available to the European colonists.

served good clay and oyster shell lime in Virginia in 1587.[36] Peter Amman's illustration shows the brickmaker pressing the clay into a mold, while the kiln for firing is shown in the background, and finally a part of a wall under construction [3-11]. Kilns were built with three vertical sections, a lower opened for draft and ash removal, a fire chamber, and the oven itself. Another method of burning brick was to build the bricks into clamps, or a series of rows of brick with channels for fires in between. Neve described both processes in some detail, and the remains of both are sometimes discovered archaeologically [3-12].[37]

Simply having suitable clay and lime was, however, not the whole story of obtaining bricks. Isaack de Rasières wrote from New Netherland in 1626 that "As far as the burning of lime is concerned, that can certainly be done, and making bricks, too for there is clay enough here that could be used for brick-making and plenty of oyster-shells that are suitable for making lime; only we lack workmen who understand the burning and brick-making."[38] This lack was remedied soon after in the Van Rensselaer colony, where yellow bricks, favored by the Dutch, were produced by about 1630. Brick-making had started at Jamestown in 1607 and at Salem in 1629.[39] Variations in color and shape for special purposes seemed endless in number, and these are described in Moxon's work and the builders' dictionaries of the early eighteenth century.[40]

The size of the normal rectangular building brick was sometimes set by statute. Thomas Wilsford described bricks in 1659 as "commonly made of a reddish earth, which should be digg'd before winter, and made not until the Spring season, whose moulds (according to statutes) ought to be within Side in length 9 inches, in breadth 4½, and in thickness 2 ¼ inches."[41] As will be shown later, in the earliest stages of settlement in the English colonies brick was used principally for chimneys and infilling, while the Dutch made more use of brick for entire buildings.

Successful exterior use of brick depended a great deal on good mortar, and the quotations from Thomas Hariot and Issack de Rasières are only two among many reports of lime available or not. Beginning his seven-page discussion of "common mortar," Neve said: "As for making of common Mortar, and for the proportions of Lime and Sand to be us'd about it, as many Men are of many Minds, I shall give you their several Sentiments about it."[42] Among them is the formula of a "wise, wealthy, and ancient Soapboiler, dwelling without Aldgate… two Load of waste Soap-Ashes, one load of Lime, one Load of Lome, and one Load of Woolwich Sand."[43]

Nearly one hundred years earlier, in 1631, Governor Winthrop built a stone house, which was partly destroyed in a great October storm, "it being not finished and laid with clay for want of lime."[44] The arrival of the governor's wife and son aboard the Lyon three days later was clouded by this disaster. Winthrop apparently appealed to his friend Edward Howes in England for help, since Howes wrote the following March, giving precisely the same formula.[45] This alone would attest to the strong building traditions with which the English colonists worked, whether handed down in practice or perpetuated in handbooks and recipe books.

Like the carpenter, the bricklayer had his special tools, and Moxon illustrated them as well.[46] [3-13.] Here are the brick trowels, brick axe, saw of tin, rubstone, square, bevel, "trannel" of iron, float stone, little ruler, banker, pier, grinding stone, pair of line pins of iron, plumb rule, level, large square, ten foot rod,

five foot rod, jointing rule, joints of iron, compasses, hammer, rammer, crow of iron, and pickaxe. This list is even more impressive than the recommendation for carpenters' tools by "Master Graves" in 1630.

Moxon had also included a foot rule among the carpenters' tools in the first edition of his book in 1683, apparently the earliest known instance of showing numbers on a rule [3-14].[47] Moxon shows the foot divided into inches and the inches into eighths.[48] This was before the days of even inter-city to say nothing of international standard measures, and one needs to determine which foot or inch was meant before attempting to interpret colonial written dimensions in modern terms. A short time before Moxon's publication a little book on another kind of measuring instrument appeared, John Browne's *Description and Use of an Ordinary Joynt-Rule*.[49] [3-15.] This was "for the ready finding the Lengths and Angles of Rafters and Hips, and Collar-Beams in any Square or Bevelling Roofs at any Pitch, and the Ready Drawing the Architrave, Freize, and Cornice in any Order."[50] Browne's instrument is a sector, and he refers to "Mr. Gunter in his Book of the Sector,"[51] by which he means a work by Edmund Gunter (1581-1626), an English mathematician who invented a number of measuring devices and who improved upon the sector invented by Thomas Hood.[52] Neve did not include a rule in his dictionary, but in the *Builder's Dictionary* of 1734 the carpenter's rule is defined as "an Instrument most commonly made of Box Wood, 24 inches long and one and a half broad; each Inch being subdivided into 8 equal parts. On the same Side with these Divisions, is usually Gunter's Line of Numbers," and Gunter's Line is also described at some length.[53]

3-12. Brick clamp. (From Ivor Noël Hume, Historical Archaeology, New York, 1969, Fig. 28).

3-13. The bricklayer's tools. (From Moxon, Mechanick Exercises, "Bricklayer's Work," Plate 1).

3-14. The joiner's tools. (From Moxon, Mechanick Exercises, "Joiner's Work," Plate 5).

3-15. Folding rule. (From John Browne, Description and Use of an Ordinary Joynt-Rule, London, 1675).

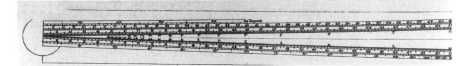

IN ADDITION TO the major building materials, wood and brick, the colonists also used stone for structural purposes and iron and glass as auxiliary materials. Stone was probably the most problematic of the three. It was expensive to quarry and dress, and Winthrop's miserable experience shows the hindrance brought on by lack of good mortar. Another factor was probably that so many colonists came from localities where stone was used for churches, fortresses, and other large public buildings but not as a rule for small single dwellings. Cellars and chimneys were sometimes built of stone in the early period, and the few stone buildings of which there are records will be noted later.

3-16. Reconstruction of the Saugus, Mass., ironworks, rebuilt as of c. 1642. (Photo: M. C. Donnelly).

As with brick, the manufacture of iron began far back in antiquity. By the end of the fifteenth century the medieval furnace for which forced draft was provided by hand or foot bellows had been improved by the addition of water-wheels to drive the bellows.[54] The iron ore and charcoal were poured alternately into the top of the massive furnace, the wheel driven by water operated the bellows, the molten iron was drawn off at the bottom into beds of sand to form the "sow" and "pigs," and the slag was carted away.

The basic requisites were, then, a source of iron, wood for charcoal, and water power. The latter two were fairly obvious, but from the early days of exploration deposits of iron were sought and noted despite the initial preoccupation with the search for gold. Jacques Cartier optimistically but mistakenly reported "a goodly Myne of the best yron in the World" at Cape Rouge in 1540, and Henry Parkhurst writing to the elder Hakluyt from Newfoundland in 1578 was alert to wood and water as necessary for the procuring of the ores he observed.[55] Along the eastern seaboard the first sources of iron ore to be exploited were the bog deposits, and later, as the hill regions inland were opened up for settlement, beds of ore were found that could be mined by the open pit method, while underground mining was in practice by the mid-eighteenth century.[56]

3-17. Glass Furnace. (From Georg Agricola, De Re Metallica, 1556, repub. New York, 1950, 591).

An interesting statement on the comparative qualities of European iron was made by Neve, who called English iron coarse, "hard and brittle," and said Swedish iron was "of all sorts the best we use in England. It is a fine tough sort of Iron, will best endure the Hammer, and is softest to file, and therefore most coveted by Workmen to work upon."[57] He did not like Spanish and German iron, and went on to say: "Generally the softest, and toughest Iron is the best. Therefore when you chuse Iron, chuse such as bows oftenest before it breaks, which is an argument of toughness, and see it breaks sound within, be of a grey Colour, like broken Lead, and free from such glittering specks as you may have seen in broken Antimony, and no Flaws of Divisions in it; for these are Arguments that tis sound, and was well wrought at the Mill."[58]

By great good fortune, archaeological remains and documentary evidence have made possible the restoration of the Hammersmith ironworks at Saugus, Massachusetts.[59] [3-16.] Here in addition to the blast furnace, of which parts of foundations remained, can be seen restorations of the forge, rolling mill, and slitting mill. A fragment of the original water wheel for the bellows is preserved in the restoration museum. The Ironmaster's House on the site belongs to the 1680s rather than to the time when the ironworks was founded in the 1640s.[60] In 1969 the property of the restoration came under the National Park Service to be administered as an historic site, thus providing an example of early colonial industry which is complemented by the restorations of the eighteenth-century ironworks at Cornwall and Hopewell in Pennsylvania.

Another important material desired for the finishing of houses and other buildings was glass. To import it was one possibility. In 1624 William Wood wrote that "Glasse ought not to be forgotten of any that desire to benefit themselves, or the Countrey: if it be well leaded, and carefully pack't up, I know of no commodity better for portage or sayle."[61] Glass was, however, something of a luxury, unlike iron. Vessels for food and drink came easily from the woodcarver and potter. Yet while only four or five glassworks went into operation in the colonies in the seventeenth century,[62] glass is known to have been widely used for windows, and much of it must have been imported.[63]

Neve devoted several pages to descriptions of various kinds of English and Continental glass and also the work of the glaziers, including the dimensions they used.[64] He described the method of packing "Tables" or the finished pieces of glass in cases tapering downward, the glass set on some straw, and straw placed between and above the cases. "These Cases are brought to London in the Coal-ships, they being set on End in the Coles more than half its depth, by which Means they are kept steady from falling and being broke by the Motion, and Rowling of the Ship."[65] Here he was referring to glass made in Newcastle and shipped to London but the method of packing for shipping to the American colonies must have been much the same.

When a glassworks was established it might consist of one or more furnaces for the preparation of the raw materials, melting the vitrified ingredients and annealing the blown pieces.[66] [3-17.] The glass might be cast, which then meant it had to be polished, or it might be blown by the "crown" or "cylinder" methods. The latter is described in some detail in the *Builder's Dictionary*, where this method is attributed first to the French.[67]

FROM THIS SHORT ACCOUNT of how the principal building materials were obtained in the American colonies, it should be evident that a certain number of skilled workers were essential to the success of permanent building programs in the newly settled lands. Although only a modest quantity of structures from the early colonial period has survived, there is enough that some ideas can be reached about the colonists' tastes, ambitions, and accomplishments, and to these the remainder of this study shall be devoted.

Notes to Chapter 3

1. See Notes 1:3, 5, and 6, and 2:7 and 12 above.

2. John Smith, "A Map of Virginia," in *Narratives of Early Virginia, 1606-1625*, ed. Lyon Gardiner Tyler (New York: C. Scribner's Sons, 1907), 90.

3. William Wood, *New England's Prospect*, ed. Alden T. Vaughan (Amherst: University of Massachusetts Press, 1977), 40.

4. Thomas Morton, *The New English Canaan* (London: 1634), in *Publications of the Prince Society* 14 (1883): 43.

5. John Josselyn, *An Account of Two Voyages to New-England, Made During the Years 1638, 1663* (Boston: Veazie, 1865), 50-57.

6. Adriaen van der Donck, attr., "The Representation of New Netherland Concerning its Location, Productiveness and Poor Condition," in *Narratives of New Netherland, 1609-1664*, ed. Franklin J. Jameson (New York: Charles Scribner's Sons, 1909), 295.

7. William Penn, "A Letter from William Penn proprietary and govenour of Pennsylvania in America, to the committee of the Free Society of Traders of that province, residing in London," in Albert Cook Myers, *Narratives of Early Pennsylvania, West New Jersey and Delaware, 1630-1707* (New York: C. Scribner's Sons, 1912), 227.

8. Nathaniel R. Shurtleff, ed., *Records of the Governor and Company of the Massachusetts Bay in New England 1628-1686*, 5 vols. (Boston: 1853-54), 1:101. See also Cummings, *Framed Houses*, 50-51.

9. Lucy E. Braun, *Deciduous Forests of Eastern North America* (New York: Hafner Pub. Co., 1964), 424-425.

10. Cummings, *Framed Houses*, 48-50; and Cary Carson et al., "Impermanent Architecture in the Southern American Colonies," *Winterthur Portfolio* 16, nos. 2 and 3 (Summer/Autumn 1981), 156-158.

11. Sir Edmund Plowden, attr., "A Description of the Province of New Albion," in *Tracts and other papers relating principally to the origin, settlement, and progress of the colonies in North America: from the discovery of the country to the year 1776*, ed. Peter Force (New York: P. Smith, 1947 [1836]), 2:31.

12. Thomas Paschall, "Letter to J.J. of Chippenham, January 31, 1684," in Myers, *Narratives*, 250-251.

13. "A Letter sent from New-England," in Alexander Young, *Chronicles of the First Planters of the Colony of Massachusetts Bay, 1623-1636* (Boston: C. C. Little and J. Brown, 1846), 267. This letter was appended to the third edition of Francis Higginson, *New-Englands Plantation* (London, 1630), in Young, *Chronicles*, 239-278; see note 2, p. 284.

14. Wood, *New England's Prospect*, 71.

15. Among the many notable collections of early American tools might be mentioned those in the Bucks County Historical Society, Doylestown, Pennsylvania, the Essex Institute, Salem, Massachusetts, the Smithsonian Institution, Washington, D.C., and the Henry Francis Dupont Winterthur Museum, Winterthur, Delaware. See also Carl Condit, *American Building: Materials and Techniques from the First Colonial Settlements to the Present* (Chicago: University of Chicago Press, 1982), 2-25; and Charles F. Hummel, *English Tools in America: the Evidence of the Dominys* (South Burlington, Vermont: Early American Industries Association, 1976).

16. Jost Amman and Hans Sachs, *The Book of Trades* (New York: Dover Publications, 1973 [1568]), 77. With woodcut illustrations by Jost Amman (1539-1591) and short didactic poems by Hans Sachs (1494-1576), this book was intended to explain the trades and also to exhort the artisans to virtuous lives. In the Dover edition the sense of the German verse is rendered as "The Nail Maker produces all sizes of nails and tacks for builders, coopers, shoemakers and other artisans."

17. Ibid., 78.

18. Johann Amos Commenius, *The Orbis Pictus of John Amos Commenius*, ed. C. W. Bardeau (Syracuse, N.Y.: C. W. Bardeau, 1887), 85. This book was the first illustrated primer "of all the Chief Things that are in the World, and of Mens Employment therein," according to the title page of the first English edition. (London, 1685). The plates of the 1887 edition are from the original edition of 1658. Of especial interest here is that Commenius had attained such fame as an educator that even before the English translation of his textbook he was invited to become President of Harvard College in 1654, although he declined (Ibid., ii).

19. Charles Franklin Montgomery, ed., *Joseph Moxon's Mechanick Exercises; or, The Doctrine of Handy-works Applied to the Arts of Smithing, Joinery, Carpentry, Turning, Bricklaying* (London: Praeger, 1970 [1703]). The "Exercises" were published in monthly installments beginning in 1677, and they were grouped to give instruction in smithing, joinery, house-carpentry, and turning, accompanied by eighteen plates. A section on bricklayer's work has eight plates, and it is thought to have been written by Moxon's son James. For an introduction to these "Exercises" by Benno M. Forman see pages IX-XXVII.

20. Richard Neve, *The City and countrey purchaser, and builder's dictionary, or, the compleat builder's guide* (London: Printed for J. Sprint, G. Conyers, and T. Ballard, 1703).

21. See Note 2.37.

22. Denis Diderot et al., *Receuil des planches pour la nouvelle èdition du Dictionnaire raisonnè... avec leur explication* (Geneva: Pallet, 1776-1777); and, Audrè Roubo, *L'art du menuisier*, 3 vols. (Paris: Leonce Laget, 1976).

23. *The Builder's Dictionary: or, Gentleman and architect's companion; being a complete unabridged reprint of the earlier works published by A. Bettesworth and C. Hitch* (Washington D.C.: Association for Preservation Technology, 1981 [1734]), 1:n.p.

24. The pioneering study of early American tools was in a series of articles entitled "Ancient Carpenters' Tools" published by Henry C. Mercer in *Old-Time New England* [*OTNE*] from April, 1925, through July, 1928. These were then collected and published first in 1929 and most recently as, Henry C. Mercer, *Ancient Carpenters' Tools: Together with Lumbermans', Joiners' and Cabinet Makers' Tools in Use in the Eighteenth Century* (Doylestown, Penn.: Horizon Press, 1975). Mercer's work has been followed by two other shorter American books: Eric Sloan, *A Museum of Early American Tools* (New York: Wilfred Funk, Inc., 1964), and Alex W. Bealer, *The Tools that Built America* (New York: Bonanza Books, 1980). For the English and Continental tools that the settlers used see also William Louis Goodman, *The History of Woodworking Tools* (London: G. Bell, 1964); Peter C. Welsh, *Woodworking Tools, 1600-1900* (Washington D.C.: Smithsonian Institution, 1966); and R. A. Salaman, *Dictionary of Woodworking Tools* (New York: Charles Scribner's Sons, 1980); the latter a massive collection, containing no less than sixty-nine listings for "Adze" alone, pages 23-30.

25. James Leander Bishop, *A History of American Manufactures from 1608 to 1860* (Philadelphia: Edward Young and Co., 1868), 1:93-94.

26. Richard Hakluyt the Elder, "Notes," in *The Principal navigations, voyages, traffiques & discoveries of the English Nation, made by sea or overland to the remote and farthest distant quarters of the earth at any time within the compass of these 1600 years,* comp. Richard Hakluyt (London: J. M. Dent and Sons, LTD, 1927-28), 7:248.

27. "Instructions for Willem Verhulst," in *Documents Relating to New Netherland, 1624-1626, in the Henry E. Huntington Library,* trans. and ed. Arnold van Laer (San Marino, Calif.: The Henry E. Huntington Library and Art Gallery, 1924), 44-47.

28. Albert Eekhof, *Jonas Michaëlius, founder of the church in New Netherland, his life and work, together with the facsimile, transcription and English of an extensive unknown autograph Latin letter* (Leyden: A. W. Sijthoff, 1926), 137.

29. "An Answer to a Declaration of the Present State of Virginia, May 1623," in *The Records of the Virginia Company of London,* ed. Susan Myra Kingsbury (Washington D.C.: Government Printing Office, 1906-1935), 4:143.

30. "Parts of Drafts of a Statement touching the Miserable Condition of Virginia, May or June 1623," in Kingsbury, ed., *Records,* 1:176.

31. Edward Williams, *Virginia: more especially the south part thereof, richly and truly valued viz. the fertile Carolana, and no lesse excellent isle of Roanoak, of latitude from 31. to 37. degr. Relating the meanes of raysing infinite profits to the adventurers and planters* (London: J. Stephenson, 1650).

32. Edward Williams, *Explication of the saw-mill* (London: 1650).

33. Bishop, *American Manufactures,* 1:105-106.

34. Jasper Danckaerts, *Journal of a Voyage to New York* (Ann Arbor, Mich.: University Microfilms, 1966 [1867]), 178 and 198.

35. Two excellent detailed studies of the New England sawmills and their builders are available whereas the mills of the other colonies have not yet been the objects of intensive research. See Richard M. Candee, "Merchant and Millwright," *OTNE* 60, no. 4 (Spring 1970): 131-149; and Benno Forman, "Mill Sawing in Seventeenth-Century Massachusetts," *OTNE* 60, no. 4 (Spring 1970): 110-130, 149. For the area of his investigation Candee offers some corrections to the data furnished in Bishop, *American Manufactures.*

36. Thomas Hariot, "A Brief and True Report of the New Found Land of Virginia," in Hakluyt, comp., *Principal navigations,* 8:373.

37. Neve, *City and countrey purchaser,* 48-51; and Ivor Noël Hume, *Historical Archaeology* (New York: Knopf, 1969), 172-175.

38. Isaack de Rasières, "Letter of September 23, 1626," in van Laer, trans. and ed., *Documents*, 235.

39. A general summary of brick-making in the colonies can be found in Bishop, *American Manufactures*, 1:216-231. See also Cummings, *Framed Houses*, 118-119, for records of brick made and used in Massachusetts Bay, and Henry C. Forman, *Jamestown and St. Mary's: Buried Cities of Romance* (Baltimore: Johns Hopkins Press, 1938), 81-89, for the early bricks of Virginia and Maryland. Further material on brick-making in Virginia is in J. C. Harrington, *Seventeenth Century Brickmaking and Tilemaking at Jamestown, Virginia* (Virginia Magazine of History and Biography, 1950); Herbert A. Claiborne, *Commentary on Virginia Brickwork Before 1800* (Boston: Walpole Society, 1957); and Calder Loth, "Notes on the Evolution of Virginia Brickwork from the Seventeenth Century to the Late Nineteenth Century," *Bulletin of the Association for Preservation Technology* 6, no. 2 (1974): 82-120. For the brick traditions with which the English builders were familiar see Alec Clifton-Taylor, *The Pattern of English Building* (London: B. T. Batsford, Ltd., 1962), 204-253.

40. *Moxon's Mechanick Exercises* describes and illustrates the tools for bricklaying, tiling and plastering, and he gives instructions for foundations, walls and mouldings, pages 237-287, and includes eight plates. Neve's entry on "Brick" in *City and countrey purchaser*, pages 37-56, includes clays, sizes, uses and a section on kilns and firing. He gave up on walls: "But finding of B. will be a very copious Letter, I shall refer it to Walls of Brick," and there follows another long discussion on pages 274-280. The anonymous *Builder's Dictionary* of 1734, unpaged, gives about the same coverage to "Brick," including directions for kilns and also tables of dimensions and costs, using twenty-eight pages in Volume I. Another five pages in Volume II under "Walling" are primarily concerned with the measurements for brick walls.

41. Thomas Wilsford, *Architectonice: The Art of Building, or An Introd. to All Young Surveyors in Common Structures* (London: Brook, 1659), 1.

42. Neve, *City and countrey purchaser*, 198.

43. Ibid., 203.

44. John Winthrop, *Winthrop's Journal, "History of New England," 1630-1649*, ed. James Hasmer (New York: C. Scribner's Sons, 1908), 1:69.

45. Letter from Edward Howes, March 26, 1632, in Adam Winthrop, *Winthrop Papers* (Boston: Massachusetts Historical Society, 1929-1947), 3:73.

46. Montgomery, ed., *Moxon's Mechanick Exercises*, 245-248. Some of these are also described and illustrated in Salaman, *Dictionary of Woodworking Tools*, 105, Figure 164.

47. Montgomery, ed., *Moxon's Mechanick Exercises*, "Joyner's Work," Plate 5, and Goodman, *Woodworking Tools*, 191.

48. Ibid., 193.

49. John Browne, *Description and Use of an Ordinary Joynt-Rule* (London: J. Brown and H. Sutton, 1675).

50. Ibid., title page.

51. Ibid., 2.

52. Edmund Gunter, *De sectore et radio* (The description and vse of the sector, the crosse-staffe and other instruments for such as are studious of mathematicall practise) (London: Printed by Willia[m] Jones, 1624).

53. *Builder's Dictionary*, 2:n.p. and 1:n.p.

54. F. Salzmann, *English Industries of the Middle Ages* (Boston and New York: Houghton Mifflin Company, 1913), 26-28.

55. Jacques Cartier, "Third Voyage of Discovery," in Hakluyt, comp., *Principal navigations*, 8:268; and Henry Parkhurst, "Report of the true state and commodities of Newfoundland," in Hakluyt, comp., *Principal navigations*, 8:15. A discussion of these early reports can be found in Edward Neal Hartley, *Ironworks on the Saugus; the Lynn and Braintree Ventures of the Company of Undertakers of the Ironworks in New England* (Norman: University of Oklahoma Press, 1957), 24-30.

56. A detailed state-by-state account of "Iron, Copper and Other Metallic Manufactures" is given in Bishop, *American Manufactures*, 1:465-631, references to the beginning of metal industry in each of the colonies being interspersed appropriately throughout. See also the more recent account by James A. Mulholland, *A History of Metals in Colonial America* (Tuscaloosa, Ala.: University of Alabama Press, 1981).

57. Neve, *City and countrey purchaser*, 179.

58. Ibid., 180.

59. As with many restorations, that of the Saugus ironworks is highly conjectural. See also Hartley, *Ironworks*, 165-184. These pages are devoted to the technology of the ironworks. Hartley's volume also includes a detailed history of early ironworks in the English colonies, taking into account the financial, management, and social factors involved.

60. Abbott L. Cummings, ed., *Architecture in Colonial Massachusetts* (Boston: Colonial Society of Massachusetts, 1979), 183-184.

61. Wood, *New England's Prospect*, 40.

62. George S. McKearin and Helen A. McKearin, *American Glass* (New York: Crown Publishers, 1941), 75-78, and Bishop, *American Manufactures*, 1:232-243.

63. Cummings, *Framed Houses*, 145-147.

64. Neve, *City and countrey purchaser*, 144-154.

65. Ibid., 157.

66. McKearin and McKearin, *American Glass*, 9-25; and Charles Joseph Singer et al., *A History of Technology* (Oxford: Clarendon Press, 1954-1978), 3:206-242.

67. *Builder's Dictionary*, 1:n.p.

4-10. *Fairbanks house, Dedham, Mass., begun c. 1637. (SPNEA).*

⊰ Chapter 4 ⊱

Housing in the Early Colonies

ONCE EUROPEAN COLONISTS had succeeded in establishing themselves on the east coast of North America, their approaches to more permanent housing were as varied as were their first temporary shelters. No orderly picture emerges of predictable developments in plans, materials, or technologies that can be applied to the colonial enterprise as a whole. In the 1630s the English in Virginia and Maryland and also in Massachusetts Bay, and the Dutch in New Netherland, were all creating their own solutions to their new situations, basing them on building types long familiar to them. By the third quarter of the century more recent fashions were often being adopted, and the next fifty years saw these becoming stronger and eventually dominant, side by side with the persistence of traditional styles and methods.

As the houses of these three groups are reviewed in turn, the fact that their builders were working simultaneously should be borne in mind. Further to be remembered is that the simplest and most complex dwellings do not necessarily represent opposite ends of a chronological scale but were constructed in different time patterns according to the needs of individual situations.

For the earliest decades only a few score houses survive, although from 1700 to 1725 there are hundreds of survivors; moreover, there is ample archaeological evidence and documentary information available about many of these houses, standing and long gone. Only a limited number of examples will be discussed here. Some of these houses have survived remarkably close to their original condition and are therefore informative about the colonial dwelling as originally intended. Some have been enlarged, perhaps more than once, and illustrate how the changing needs of their owners could be met by the ingenuity of the carpenters. Some that are no longer standing but are known through archaeological or documentary evidence are included in order to demonstrate the use of such materials.

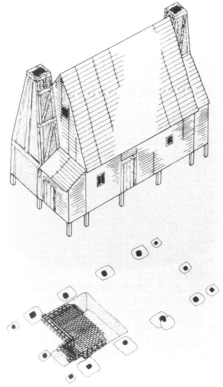

4-1. Utopia Leasehold, Kingsmill, James City Co., Va., 1660. Axonometric view with plan. (W. Kelso, Kingsmill Plantations, 1619-1800, Orlando, 1984, Fig. 41).

Concerning Virginia and Maryland, recurrent illustrations of the Adam Thoughgood House, Princess Anne Co., Va., and "Bacon's Castle," Surry Co., Va., leave the impression that such brick houses were the dominant form in the southern English colonies. Yet for many years serious investigators have recognized the widespread use of wood for southern houses, now lost to the casual observer by fire and demolition.[1] Henry C. Forman's pioneering efforts in the 1930s and 1940s to discover the true extent of colonial housing in Virginia and Maryland have been followed by the work of recent archaeologists in the same area. Far more information is now available, so that it is possible to surmise how climate, patterns of settlement, crop economy, and social factors affected the building of southern colonial homes, even though most are no longer standing above ground.

It should at once be understood, however, that the full story cannot yet be written. The major campaigns since Forman's time began with the excavations by the National Park Service at Jamestown in the 1950s.[2] Then, with St. Mary's City Commission taking the lead, the entire Chesapeake Bay area was searched for seventeenth-century sites by the Maryland Historical Trust and the Virginia Historic Landmarks Commission in the early 1970s. Excavations by the St. Mary's City Commission, the Virginia Research Center for Archaeology, Colonial Williamsburg, and the Department of Anthropology at the College of William and Mary have been undertaken at more than twenty-five sites in this region. While much remains to be done, the result so far has been the gathering of information about 150-odd buildings that the archaeologists describe as "impermanent" in character and "earthfast" in construction.[3]

These buildings, not all of which were houses, were those whose loss was mourned by Fiske Kimball sixty years ago. For the more "permanent" among them, parallels with English houses have long been readily available, as is the case with the early New England houses. For the "earthfast" buildings, however, such parallels depend largely on excavations in England since the 1950s, stemming from recent interest in vernacular architecture and medieval archaeology.

By "earthfast" is meant construction with timbers placed directly in the ground, whether set in holes, "hole-set," set on the surface, "ground-set," laid on the surface, "ground-laid," or placed in very shallow trenches, "trench-laid."[4] Three examples will be mentioned to indicate how some of these techniques could be used.

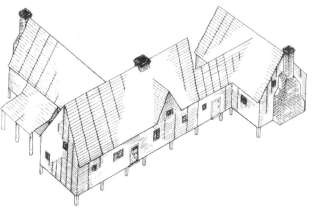

4-2. Pettus Manor, Kingsmill, James City Co., Va., c. 1660. Axonometric view. (Kelso, Kingsmill Plantations, Fig. 44).

At Kingsmill, James City Co., Va., the Utopia Leasehold by about 1660 had a dwelling twenty-eight feet by eighteen feet which was built with eight posts eleven inches square, set into square holes, so as to form a three-bay structure, probably of two rooms [4-1].[5] Outside the house at each end was a timber-framed and daubed fireplace. Under the west side was a bricked half cellar which was entered from the west wall. This

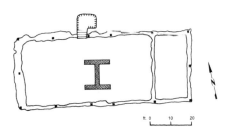

4-3. St. John's, St. Mary's City, Md., 1638. Plan. (From C. Carson et al., "Impermanent Architecture in the Southern American Colonies," Winterthur Portfolio 16 [1981], Fig. 2).

small dwelling was probably leased from the Pettus family, on whose land it stood, and where the Littletown (Pettus) Plantation was furnished with a much larger house [4-2].[6] This began c. 1640 as a fifty-by-eighteen-foot house, with twelve ten-inch hole-set posts forming five bays and probably a chimney at the back of the central bay.

The third house, built slightly earlier in 1638, was on the site known as St. John's in St. Mary's City, St. Mary Co., Md. [4-3].[7] It was about the same size as the Littletown (Pettus) dwelling, measuring fifty-two feet by twenty feet six inches. Here the house was framed, set on low cobblestone foundations, but with the floor joists trench-laid and independent of the sills. The chimney was set between the kitchen and parlor, the latter probably the room used for meetings of the assembly and provincial court, which were held in the house until 1645. At an early date, then, the earthfast and framed techniques might be combined.

Toward the end of the first period another house was built combining these techniques, but in this case a fully framed build-

ing raised on hole-set posts. Cedar Park, Anne Arundel Co., built in 1702, is a rare surviving example of a hole-set building [4-4].[8] It measures fifty feet by twenty feet eight inches, is one story high, and in five bays. The plan is of the hall and parlor type, with a central porch tower. The building has been enlarged and altered, but the original core can give some impression of the Littletown (Pettus) dwelling and St. John's, although it differs from them in having brick chimneys enclosed at each end rather than a central chimney as in the other two examples.

A mid-eighteenth-century encasing of Cedar Park in brick preserved its frame, which is an excellent example of Virginia colonial carpentry. The sills and posts are of cedar, the sleepers of locust, and the rest of oak and poplar. The interrupted sills

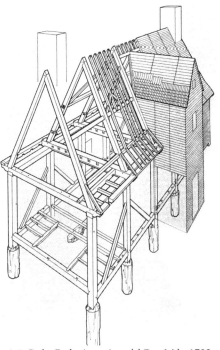

4-4. Cedar Park, Anne Arundel Co., Md., 1702. Framing diagram. (From Carson et al., Impermanent Architecture, Fig. 4).

were pegged to the posts and then the upright studs were mortised into them. The wall plates were put in place next, and then six tie-beams set above the posts and projected twelve inches beyond the plates. Joists were then mortised into the end girts. Erection of the six pairs of principal rafters was followed by the addition of common rafters, with additional members extending out to the false plates carried on the projecting tie-beams. The result was a sturdy frame and a house that turned out to be less "impermanent" than its original owner had perhaps intended.

We may well ask what the colonists themselves thought of these houses. The fortunes and misfortunes of the tobacco economy and eventual diversification of crops are thought to have been major factors in the persistence of earthfast buildings

4-5. *Pear Valley, Northampton Co., Va., late-seventeenth century. (Virginia Landmarks Commission).*

4-6. *Criss-Cross, New Kent Co., Va., late-seventeenth century. (Virginia Landmarks Commission).*

and their gradual replacement by more permanent structures in the eighteenth century. Called the "Virginia house" as distinct from the "great or English framed house,"[9] the planters "in them lived with continual repairs, and building new where the old had failed."[10] In 1647 it was observed that "the poverty of the countrey and want of necessaries here will not admit a possibilitie to erect other then such houses as wee frequently inhabitt."[11]

By contrast Ralph Hamor's description of Jamestown in 1614 indicates there, at least, more permanent framed houses at an early date: "The Towne...hath in it two faire rows of houses, all of framed Timber, two stories, and an upper Garret, or Corne loft high...there are also without this towne in the Island some very pleasant and beautifull howses."[12] Excavations begun in 1934 and renewed in 1954 revealed brick footings of about thirty framed houses, some of which were set in rows like town houses in England.

The matter of these row houses and town planning will be addressed later, but here the important point is the early building of framed houses in Virginia, which Hamor observed also at Henricopolis, Rocke Hall, and Bermuda City.[13] Whether these were framed in precisely the same manner as Cedar Park will probably never be known because of the disappearance of seventeenth-century timber houses in this region. Pear Valley, Northampton County,

4-7. *Adam Thoroughgood house, Princess Anne Co., Va., c. 1680. (Virginia Landmarks Commission).*

Virginia, is one of the few that remain, and even it has the chimney end of brick [4-5].[14] It is a one-room cottage, with a roof system different from that of Cedar Park. Scanty evidence indeed, but enough to raise the question as to whether there were preferences among Virginia and Maryland colonial carpenters related to their local English origins similar to those which have been discovered for Massachusetts Bay.[15]

Robert Johnson described "competent and decent houses, the first storie all of brick," at Henricopolis in 1611.[16] Although again an altered example, Criss-Cross, New Kent Co., Va., built c. 1690, has its lower main story of brick and then the gable ends are framed [4-6].[17] Whether Robert Johnson meant a full second story of timber or simple timber gables as at Criss-Cross is not clear. The use of brick for the lower story, however, serves to introduce the Virginia houses entirely built of the more durable material.

To return to the Adam Thoroughgood house, we find a good example of the modest one-and-a-half story house with end chimneys, gable roof, and two-room plan [4-7].[18] As it is now after restoration, the eighteenth-century dormers which appear in early photographs have been removed and the sash windows replaced with ones with leaded diamond panes and segmental arched tops. The arched tops were also

4-8. Smith's Fort plantation, Surry Co., Va.. (Photo: M. C. Donnelly).

replaced over the door. The date of the Thoroughgood house has not been fixed precisely, but it is thought to have been built c. 1680. The bricks are laid in Flemish bond on the west or entrance side and in English bond on the other three sides.

Somewhat later is Smith's Fort Plantation, in Surry County, Virginia.[19] It is also of brick, in Flemish bond with glazed headers, one-and-a-half stories high, with interior end chimneys. Here there is the more elaborate central-hall plan, which includes a passage from front to back, containing the stairway and providing cross ventilation [4-8]. Further elaboration of either the two-room or central-hall plan might be achieved by the addition of a front entrance porch, as at Malvern Hill, Henrico Co., Va., [20] and/or a rear stair porch, as at Bacon's Castle [4-9].[21]

Bacon's Castle is sometimes described as having a "cross plan" because the porches project from the central block to form a cross shape in outline. Houses with such porches might be better described as having two-room or central-hall plans with porches. In the latter case the central hall does not open out to the entrance or stair porch in such a way as to form a true cross axis, and the porch cuts off the cross ventilation. In summary, these several plan types formed the basis for the modest houses, "impermanent,"

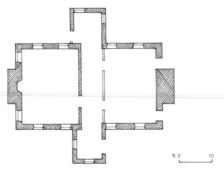

4-9. Arthur Allen house, "Bacon's Castle," Surry Co., Va. c. 1664. Plan. (After HABS).

framed, or brick, that sheltered the Virginia and Maryland settlers as they claimed and began to develop their lands.

IF WE TURN NORTH to New England, we find that while the general truth of the importation and adaptation of English building practices holds, the choice and application of these methods differ significantly from the southern colonial experience. Living closer together in towns rather than scattered on large plantations and having to cope with a much more severe climate, New England settlers more quickly moved to build well-framed houses than did their countrymen in Virginia.

By great good fortune more than seventy framed houses built before 1700 survive in Massachusetts alone, together with nearly fifty from the other New England states. Recent detailed analysis of the Massachusetts Bay houses has revealed the extent to which they perpetuate local English techniques, and it is to be hoped that similar modern studies will be made of houses in Rhode Island and Connecticut.[22]

While the nature of the Virginia houses made it seem logical to begin with the "impermanent" structures and proceed to the more permanent regardless of plan, the case of the New England houses is different. In both north and south, houses were built with one-room or two-room plans, regardless of material. But in Massachusetts, at least, the cellar and lean-to led to complexity in plans that does not seem to have been characteristic of the seventeenth-century southern houses.

Following English usage, the term "hall" is generally interpreted as the room having a fireplace in which the cooking was done. In a one-room house the bed might also be in this room or perhaps in a room above, commonly called a "chamber." In a two-room house with central chimney, as was customary in New England, the second room was called the "parlor" and contained the better furnishings, perhaps including the best bed. When the house was two stories high, the upper rooms were called the "hall chamber" and "parlor chamber." Identification of these rooms to show the size and nature of houses no longer standing is in many cases made possible by estate inventories which list possessions room by room.[23]

For storage of food the Massachusetts Bay settlers early began putting cellars beneath their houses, usually under the parlor in two-room houses, normally reached by a staircase going down from the hall. There was also the addition of lean-tos for downstairs bedrooms, kitchens, and dairies. The sloping roofs of the lean-tos give the "salt-box" appearance, whether they were additions to the original houses and thus come off at an angle from the main roof or whether, as late in the seventeenth century, they were part of the original framing with continuous roof lines. For the former the Fairbanks house at Dedham, Mass., c. 1637, is an early example [4-10].[24] The Thomas Painter house originally built in West Haven, Conn., c. 1685 (now moved to Litchfield), is an example of the latter [4-11].[25]

The fully-developed New England house, then, would be perhaps fifty feet by thirty feet, with central chimney, entered from the long side before the chimney, with a hall on one side and a parlor on the other. The lean-to would have a kitchen making use of the central chimney and also an extra room and a dairy. A cellar below would be reached by a stairway, and the chambers above would be reached by a stairway placed against the chimney.

Such a house was not necessarily so built in the first campaign, however, and it might be more appropriate to speak of a fully "equipped" house. Some of the better-known New England houses arrived at this point in stages, such as the Fairbanks house. The Whipple house in Ipswich, Mass., began as one-room c. 1655 and was enlarged to two rooms by 1683, with a partial lean-to added by 1721 [4-12].[26] In like manner the Scotch-Boardman house in Saugus, Mass., was first built about 1687, with hall and parlor on either side of a central chimney mass, but then soon enlarged about 1695 with a kitchen lean-to to the rear (with a bedroom to the left of the kitchen and a "milkroom" on the right).[27] Very similar is the Whitman house in Farmington, Conn., which also began as a two-room, two-story house about 1720, with its lean-to added after 1750 [4-13].[28] What makes the Whitman house so remarkable is that with its overhanging

4-10. Fairbanks house, Dedham, Mass., begun c. 1637. (SPNEA).

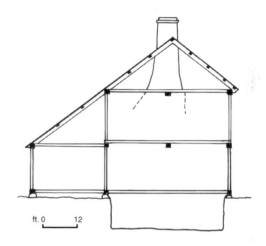
4-11. Thomas Painter house, West Haven, Conn., 1685. Section. (After Isham and Brown, Early Connecticut Houses, Fig. 65).

4-12. Whipple house, Ipswich, Mass., c. 1655 and c. 1683. (Photo: M. C. Donnelly).

upper story and descending pendants it would appear antiquated compared to contemporaneous eighteenth-century examples in Massachusetts, but in this area of Connecticut house design and construction followed very conservative patterns.

While archaeological remains such as those recently investigated in Virginia and Maryland furnish much information about the location, size, materials, heating, and furnishing of colonial houses, in the absence of numerous extant examples some frustration is bound to be encountered in determining the precise manner

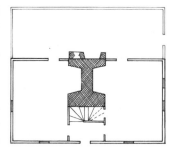

4-13. Whitman house, Farmington, Conn., c. 1720. Plan. (After Isham and Brown, Early Connecticut Houses, Fig.15).

of roofing these houses. The much greater number of seventeenth-century houses standing in New England makes the problem easier in this region, fortunately, since the shelter of a roof may be considered the primary reason for erecting a building in the first place. A diagram of the frame of the Fairbanks house illustrates the principal members of a simple gable roof and also the essential elements of an early Massachusetts Bay framed house [4-14].[29]

On a stone foundation rest the sills, which carry the upright members of the walls and into which may be framed the members of the ground-story floor. The upright framing members consist of the four corner posts, the chimney posts and intermediate posts, those at the gable ends called "prick posts," and those part-way along the sides called "story posts." The posts of the front and rear walls are set with their greater width running across the sills in order to provide the widest bearing for the beams they are to carry, and they are further widened at the top in the flared or "musket-stock" manner. Between the posts are set smaller vertical members, the studs, which help to support the roof and subdivide the main wall sections for application of the wall covering.

This vertical system is bound at the first story level by the principal horizontal members, the front and rear girts, mortised into the posts. End and chimney girts serve as binding beams to connect the front and rear sections of the frame. An alternative, and more economical, method is to insert smaller members between the posts, these "bearers" being grooved or trenched so that two-story studs can be pegged into them and so that they can also carry the second-story joists. Within

4-15. Parson Capen house, Topsfield, Mass., 1683. View of pendant. (Photo: M. C. Donnelly).

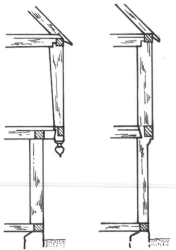

4-16. Framed and hewn overhangs. (After Isham and Brown, Early Connecticut Houses, Fig, 103).

the house the layer between the first and second stories has major subdivisions formed by the summer beams. When these run transversely between the front and rear story posts they perform a binding function; when laid from chimney girts to end girts they perform a bridging function to support the floor. The floor boards themselves are laid on smaller horizontal members, the joists, which are framed into the summer beams and are either framed into the girts or rest upon the bearers.

With the vertical and intermediate horizontal members thus provided, the success of the whole enterprise rests upon ensuring that the weight of the roof will not force out the walls. The New England builders solved this problem by connecting the posts along the front and rear with plates, which are then made secure by tie beams connecting the front and rear posts transversely, the three members of post, plate, and tie beam being locked together in a combination of mortise and tenon and dovetail joints. Principal rafters can then be mortised into the tie beams with common rafters between, on which the horizontal roof boarding can be fastened. The roof frame may be further stabilized by principal purlins, framed horizontally into the principal rafters, and by collars framed transversely into the principal rafters. The completed frame is then ready for wall and roof covering.

The New England climate rather promptly caused the colonists to choose clapboards rather than plaster for the outer covering of their walls. These boards, also called "weather boards," were about four feet long, riven from oak, cedar, or pine, and about five inches wide. They were tapered from a half-inch thickness to a "feather edge" so that they could be nailed to the studs with an overlap, leaving three or four inches exposed. Late in the period "beading" or molding the exposed edges gave additional embellishment to the pattern created by the clapboards. Horizontal boarding might be laid beneath clapboards, but it was rarely used as the final exterior finish. Further proof against the weather was secured by an infill, most often of brick and clay, in a few cases of wattle and daub or clay and chopped straw.

As for the roof, thatch and shingle were probably more widely used than slate and tile, in spite of many contemporary reports of fires. Thatch has not survived from the seventeenth century, at least in Massachusetts, but it would have been tied to laths or thin poles set between the rafters. Wheat straw, salt marsh hay, or reeds could be used, the latter "is said to last 40, 50, or 60 years."[30] This remark is accompanied by another: "Some are said to have pretended that they could thatch a Roof so that no Mouse could get in; but I know no Instance of any such Thing to have been done." Hence the family cat.

Shingles were generally of cedar or pine, thin boards four or five inches wide, half an inch thick, and from nine to eighteen inches long. The roof was covered with boards, laid horizontally if the frame was of principal and common rafters, vertically if it was of principal rafters and common purlins. Tiles could be of two kinds, one with holes for nails to fasten them to the roof boards, the other with knobs on the back by which they could be hung from laths. Slate was applied to roof boards with nails, and the *Builder's Dictionary* warns of another hazard, a slate "that soaks in Water, and therefore will not last long without rotting the Timber or Lath."[31]

Doors and windows in these framed houses varied in their size and placement. The main door was generally opposite the chimney as already noted, and fashioned from inch-thick vertical boards, held together on the inside with horizontal boards, all spiked together. Windows might be in single or double sets on the front of a one-room house and were placed more or less symmetrically on two-room houses. They were used on the end walls and sometimes in the gables, but at first apparently omitted in the rear wall. They could be framed into the main frame, as were the doors, or could be assembled whole and applied. Further, they could be simple casements, singly or in groups, or could be divided by transom bars. Glass was evidently the expectation of the builders, as attested by the early establishment of glassworks to supplement what was imported.

Little was done for exterior ornamentation as such. This has sometimes been interpreted as evidence for a "Puritan aesthetic." Were this the case, one would expect that there would have been no chamfering of door frames, no molding of window mullions, and certainly no use of roof pinnacles and elaborate overhang pendants [4-15]. Strength of English tradition on the one hand and the need for compact dwellings in a severe climate caused the New England settlers to construct box-like houses throughout the colonial period. The surviving refinements included in these houses, however, indicate that from the beginning the colonists were sensitive to appearance and desirous of making their houses as attractive as their means would allow.

This brings us to the vexed question of the overhang, or "jetty" as it was called then. Already familiar for centuries in

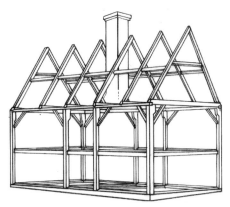

4-14. *House framing system as found in Massachusetts Bay. (After Isham,* Early American Houses, *Boston, 1928, Fig.18).*

England and on the Continent, the projection of one story outward from the one below on one or more sides of a house has been given a number of explanations. Considering that the need to provide more room in upper stories was less compelling in a comparatively spacious New England town than in a densely crowded medieval city and that framing such a projection could in fact cause more problems than it solved, another view would be that the overhang was an option to be adopted or not according to individual preference. The true overhang involves the projection of girts beyond the line of the posts by a foot or more, often with pendants carved from the downward-projecting ends of the second-story posts [4-16]. The "hewn" overhang, on the other hand, involves simply carving back the first-story posts so that the surface of the second story is slightly farther forward than that of the first. A simulation of distinction between first and second story was then achieved by simple means.

Without a chimney, however, the framed New England house would be of limited proof against the winter. Indeed, even from Paleolithic times the inclusion of a hearth was fundamental to a human dwelling in northern Europe. By the time of settlement in New England the hearth in the earth floor had developed to a brick chimney, founded on solid ground beneath the house, measuring about seven feet wide and ten feet deep and rising to carry the flues five or six feet above the ridge of the roof. Fireplaces opened into the parlor and hall, if serving a two-room house, the latter also having an oven. While wooden chimneys "catted" with clay are documented from the early days of settlement, their disadvantages were obvious and soon overcome, at least in part, by the more durable brick. The fireplace opening itself, revealing sometimes quite handsome brickwork, set off by the contrasting plain and massive oak lintel, was the focal point of domestic activity and has become a hallmark of the "colonial" dwelling [4-17].

Another major point of interest on the interior was of course the stair. Ordinarily opposite the entry and built against the chimney, the stair was at first enclosed and by the fourth quarter of the century was partly opened with a balustrade above the still closed string [4-18]. By this time newel posts and balusters could be shaped and turned in various patterns.

For the remainder of interior finish, once having been completed as far as the infilling, the walls might or might not have further interior covering. Nor, apparently, did the walls of all the rooms in a house necessarily get the same treatment. A frequent approach was to sheath the fireplace wall with vertical boarding and to lath and plaster the others. When other walls were sheathed, it could be with clapboard, with vertical overlapping boards, or with vertical boards joined at the edges. Whatever the

4-17. Abraham Browne house, Watertown, Mass., 1663. Interior of kitchen. (SPNEA).

choice, the walls formed a plain but often harmonious backdrop for the turned furniture, brilliantly-colored fabrics, and plates and vessels of wood, pottery, and pewter that were the household goods of the inhabitants.

While the framed house predominated in the New England colonies, brick and, to a lesser extent, stone were also used. Edward Johnson, writing his history of New England in 1652, spoke of "buildings beautiful and large, some of them fairly set forth with Brick."[32] He did not say "houses," and the earliest brick house we know from the New England colonies is the Peter Tufts house, Medford, Mass., built in 1675 [4-19].[33] Medford became a center for brickmaking, with several houses of brick there and also in nearby Haverhill, where brick was used for defen-

4-18. Parson Capen house. Detail of stair. (SPNEA).

sive "garrison" houses toward the end of the century.

The Tufts house seems imposing when compared to the Capen house, for example. Undoubtedly the colonists' familiarity with having lived in framed houses, especially in the East Anglian counties, disposed them to the same in New England, a disposition easily encouraged by the abundance of timber. Another factor was probably the scarcity of good lime for mortar in the early years. This scarcity limited the use of stone as well, as shown by John Winthrop's frustrating experience with the house built of stone in Medford in 1631.[31]

A partial use of stone for wall construction was popular late in the seventeenth century in Rhode Island, thanks to a locally reasonable supply of

4-19. Peter Tufts house, Medford, Mass., 1675. (SPNEA).

building stone and lime. (Another factor in the use of stone in this area was that the initial settlers came from regions in England where stone was a favored building material.) Exposing the stone chimney at the end of a one-room house and extending it to include a lean-to chimney produced a "stone-ender" such as the Eleazar Arnold house in Lincoln, R.I., 1687 [4-20]. Several other examples are known.[35]

4-20. Eleazar Arnold house, Lincoln, R.I., 1687. (Photo: M. C. Donnelly).

Much more ambitious is the Henry Whitfield house at Guilford, Conn., 1639-1640 [4-21].[36] Although much changed and heavily restored, its massive walls and steep roofs convey a sense of medieval building. With its end chimneys exposed and fashioned with offsets, the original two-room portion of the Whitfield house reminds one of the Adam Thoroughgood house in one-and-a-half stories, built about thirty years later. The stair tower off-center at the back and the kitchen wing on the south side of the back may or may not have been part of the original construction.

With the Whitfield house we have returned to the early part of the seventeenth century and a unique stone house. In approaching the brick houses of northeastern Massachusetts and the "stone-enders" of Rhode Island we were dealing with houses of more normal plans but built of less usual materials toward the end of the century. During these years colonial housing had also been developing in the Middle Colonies, and to this region we must now turn.

W E HAVE ALREADY noted the founding of New Amsterdam and considered the more elementary approaches to shelter there. By the time Charles II of England rather grandly presented the land from the

4-21. Henry Whitfield house, Guilford, Conn., 1639. (Photo: M. C. Donnelly).

Connecticut River to Delaware Bay to his brother, the Duke of York, and the Dutch surrendered to the English in 1664, New Amsterdam was becoming a notable town and several villages and manors had been established up the Hudson River as far as Albany. So little remains of Dutch building in the seventeenth century, however, that we are almost better informed by the documentary than by the structural evidence.

For the appearance of New Amsterdam just before the English seizure we have a view of "Novum Amsterodanum" issued in 1671 but probably from an earlier drawing [4-22].[37] As had been their custom in Holland, the Dutch built townhouses two or three stories high, with common walls and gable ends to the streets. Jasper Danckaerts evidently took the houses he saw in 1679 for granted, as he did not describe them.[38] A later visitor, the naturalist Peter Kalm from Sweden, remarked that most of the houses "are built of brick, and are generally strong and neat, and several stories high." Some had, in the old style, turned the gable end toward the street; but the new houses were altered in this respect.[39] The stepped gables were characteristic of contemporary Dutch townhouses, and the city must have been much like the village depicted in a drawing attributed to Cornelis Cort [4-23].

Kalm makes the further interesting observation that in Albany the houses were constructed in the rural manner except for the brick gable ends, so that "a stranger walking along the streets and not paying close attention might easily conclude that all houses here were of fired brick" [4-24].[40]

The Dutch farm dwelling built in connection with the barn was also used in New Netherland, although known only through contemporary descriptions. In 1643 Arendt Van Corlaer wrote back to Holland saying, "I had, moreover, contracted with Jan Cornelissen, carpenter, for a large farm-house; and he had promised to begin it in mid-April…. He must build for 700 guilders a house 120 feet long by 28 feet wide; 40 feet is deducted for a dwelling. There remain 80 feet for the farm-house. The dwelling part to be floored above and below; a cellar 20 feet long by 28 feet wide; a half-jutting chamber for the servants' sleeping room; a small room in the farm-house for the farm laborers; an enclosed stable for the studs, and further to make a horse and cow stable."[41]

Such buildings to shelter people and animals under the same roof had been in use in Germany and Holland since the Iron Age and were certainly one of the most ancient types of house to be transported to the New World.

The third material used by the Dutch in the Hudson Valley was stone. The house built c. 1662-69 by Pieter Bronck at West Coxsackie, N.Y., is a good example of a one-room, one-and-a-half story house, with the east gable end toward the street [4-25].[42] The chimney is in the original west wall, and the door on the north. Subsequent additions, including the adjacent Leendert Bronck house of 1738, reflect the growth of the family. The field-stone used in these houses was at first left quite rough, in later times more carefully dressed, and mortar was made from the coastal shell-lime or with Hudson Valley limestone.

In another direction from New Amsterdam, on Long Island, the seventeenth-century Dutch houses had a somewhat different aspect. Whether the Pieter Claesen Wyckoff house on Canarsie Lane in Brooklyn was actually built in the seventeenth century is uncertain.[43] [4-26.] Some portion may remain from that time, incorporated into an enlargement of 1737. Whatever the truth of the matter, the house was built of wood as was customary on Long Island. The shingles of the presumed older portion are of cypress, with fourteen of their forty-two inches exposed. The projection of the roof forward beyond the plate is more a Flemish than a Dutch device but was employed by the Dutch settlers in this region and also later in northern New Jersey.[44]

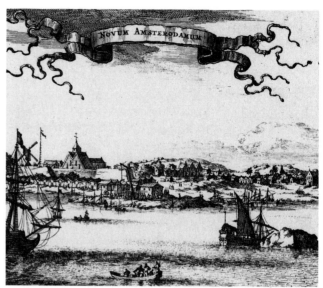

4-22. New Amsterdam, New Netherland. The Montanus View. (Courtesy of New York Public Library).

4-24. James Eights, "View of Albany," 1805. (Courtesy of Holland Society of New York).

4-23. Cornelis Cort, "A Dutch village." (New York Metropolitan Museum of Art, Rogers Fund, 1906, accession number 06.0142.6).

4-27. Lower Swedish Cabin, Darby Creek, Pa., seventeenth century. (Courtesy of Delaware County Historical Society).

4-26. Pieter Claesen Wyckoff house, Brooklyn, N.Y., seventeenth century. (Courtesy of Wyckoff House & Association, Inc.).

4-25. Pieter Bronck house, West Coxsackie, N.Y., c. 1662-1669. (Courtesy Holland Society of New York).

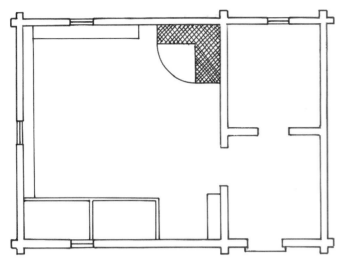

4-28. "Swedish" house plan. (After S. Erixon, Svensk byggnadskultur…, Stockholm, 1947, Fig. 452).

WE HAVE ALREADY NOTED the contribution made by Swedish settlers near the Delaware River.[45] Jasper Danckaerts did remark upon their houses: "…made according to the Swedish mode, and as they usually build their houses here, which are [like] block houses, being nothing else than entire trees, split through the middle, or squared out of the rough, and placed in the form of a square, upon each other, as high as they wish to have the house; the ends of these timbers are let into each other, about a foot from the ends, half of one into half of the other. The whole structure is thus made, without a nail or spike…. These houses are quite tight and warm; but the chimney is placed in a corner."[46] Peter Kalm's later report adds more information about the interiors: "The houses which the Swedes built when they first settled here were very poor. The whole house consisted of one little room, the door of which was so low that one was obliged to stoop in order to get in. As they brought no glass with them they were obliged to be content with little holes before which a moveable board was fastened. They found no moss, or at least none which would have been serviceable in stopping up holes or cracks in the walls. They were therefore forced to close them using clay both inside and out. The chimneys were masoned in a corner, either of gray stone (or in places where there were no stones) or mere clay, which they laid very thick in one corner of the house."[47]

In referring to the "Swedish" house it must be remembered that the mixed population of New Sweden included Finns and Germans as well as Swedes. In their home countries there were local preferences for round or hewn logs and a bewildering variety of cornering techniques.[48] Therefore when one of the few early surviving examples is illustrated it should be interpreted as representing these houses only in general terms [4-27]. The usual method of enlarging the one-room house was to add a small entrance room beside the main room, with another small chamber behind it, which might get some warmth from the chimney in the main room [4-28]. The great study of Swedish houses by Sigurd Erixon was based on buildings on their original sites.[49] Perhaps more accessible for travelers with little time are houses moved to the outdoor museums, such as the dwelling house of the sixteenth-century Mora farmstead from Dalarna, now in the Skansen Museum in Stockholm [4-29].

THE SWEDISH HOUSES bring to a close this general survey of the early more substantial dwellings erected by European colonists on the Atlantic seaboard during the seventeenth century. In concentrating upon the houses we have made only passing reference to the towns in which many of them were built. We have not considered the churches or other public buildings which served the communities, and to these equally important matters we shall now turn our attention.

4-29. Mora farmstead, Dalarna, Sweden, sixteenth century. Relocated to the Skansen Museum, Stockholm. (Photo: M. C. Donnelly).

Notes to Chapter 4

1. Fiske Kimball, *Domestic Architecture of the American Colonies and of the Early Republic* (New York: Dover Publications, 1966 [1922]), 9-10. Two books by Henry Chandler Forman describe his efforts: *Jamestown and St. Mary's: Buried Cities of Romance* (Baltimore: Johns Hopkins Press, 1938), and *The Architecture of the Old South: The Medieval Style, 1585-1850* (Cambridge, Mass.: Harvard University Press, 1948). The first major publication on the recent studies is in Cary Carson et al., "Impermanent Architecture in the Southern American Colonies," *Winterthur Portfolio* 16, nos. 2 and 3 (Summer/Autumn 1981). Additional valuable articles are by Dell Upton, "Ordinary Buildings: A Bibliography on American Vernacular Architecture," *American Studies International* 19, no. 2 (Winter 1981): 57-75 and Upton, "Traditional Timber Framing," in *Material Culture of the Wooden Age*, Brooke Hindle, ed. (Tarrytown, N.Y.: Sleepy Hollow Press, 1981), which includes a comparison between framing methods in the northern, southern, and middle colonies. See also Upton, "The Power of Things: Recent Studies on American Vernacular Architecture," *American Quarterly* 35, no. 3 (1983): 262-79.

2. John L. Cotter, *Archaeological Excavations at Jamestown Colonial National Historic Park and Jamestown National Historic Site, Virginia* (Washington D.C.: National Park Service, U.S. Dept. of the Interior, 1959).

3. Carson et al., "Impermanent Architecture," 135-139.

4. Ibid., 36.

5. Ibid., 180-181, 193, and Figure 9; William M. Kelso, *Kingsmill Plantations, 1619-1800: Archeology of Country Life in Colonial Virginia* (Orlando: Academic Press, 1984), 72-76.

6. Carson et al., "Impermanent Architecture," 180 and 193, and Figure 9; Kelso, *Kingsmill Plantations*, 76-80.

7. Carson et al., "Impermanent Architecture," 185-187, 190, and Figure 2. More detailed material on St. John's is given in Garry Wheeler Stone, "St. John's Archaeological Questions and Answers," *Maryland Historical Magazine* 69, no. 2 (Summer 1974): 146-168; in Robert W. Keeler, *The Homelot on the Seventeenth-Century Chesapeake Tidewater Frontier* (Ann Arbor, Mich.: University Microfilms International, 1980); and in Garry Wheeler Stone, "Society, Housing, and Architecture in Early Maryland: John Lewger's St. John's," (Ph.D. diss., University of Pennsylvania, 1952), n.p.

8. Carson et al., "Impermanent Architecture," 187-189 and Figure 4, 145. See also J. Reaney Kelly, "Cedar Park, Its People and Its History," *Maryland Historical Magazine* 58, no. 1 (March 1963): 30-53.

9. Richard B. Davis, ed., *William Fitzhugh and his Chesapeake World, 1676-1701: The Fitzhugh Letters and Other Documents* (Chapel Hill: University of North Carolina Press, 1963), 202-203.

10. H. R. McIlwaine, ed., *Journals of the House of Burgesses of Virginia, 1619-[1776]* (Richmond, Va.: [Colonial Press, E. Waddey Co.], 1905-1915), 1:33.

11. William Waller Hening, ed., *The Statutes at Large; Being a Collection of all the Laws of Virginia, from the First Session of the Legislature in the Year 1619* (Charlottesville: University Press of Virginia, 1969 [1819]), 1:340.

12. Ralph Hamor, *A True Discourse of the Present State of Virginia* (Richmond: Virginia State Library, 1957), 30-31, 33.

13. Ibid., and Peter C. Marzio, "Carpentry in the Southern Colonies during the Eighteenth Century with Emphasis on Maryland and Virginia," *Winterthur Portfolio* 7 (1972): 229-250.

14. Historical American Buildings Survey (HABS): *Virginia Catalog* (Charlottesville: University Press of Virginia, 1976), 238. Pear Valley does not have the extra extension of the rafters to the false plate that is shown in the drawing of Cedar Park.

15. Abbott L. Cummings, *The Framed Houses of Massachusetts Bay, 1625-1725* (Cambridge, Mass.: Belknap Press, 1979), 95-117.

16. Robert Johnson, "New Life of Virginia," in Peter Force, *Tracts and other papers relating principally to the origin, settlement, and progress of the colonies in North America: from the discovery of the country to the year 1776* (New York: P. Smith, 1947), 1:14.

17. Forman, *Architecture of the Old South*, 72-73; HABS: *Virginia*, 180; Harden de v. Pratt, "The Restoration of Christ's Cross, New Kent County, Virginia," *Virginia Magazine of History and Biography* 65, no. 3 (July 1957): 328-331.

18. Thomas Waterman and John Barrows, *Domestic Colonial Architecture of Tidewater Virginia* (New York: Charles Scribner's Sons, 1932), 3-7; HABS: *Virginia*, 262; Daniel Reiff, *Small Georgian Houses in England and Virginia: Origins and Development Through the 1750s* (Newark: University of Delaware Press, 1986), 202-203.

19. Forman, *Architecture of the Old South*, 50; Herbert A. Claiborne, *Comment on Virginia Brickwork Before 1800* (Boston: Walpole Society, 1957), 41; Mark R. Wenger, "The Central Passage in Virginia: Evolution of an Eighteenth-Century Living Space," *Perspectives in Vernacular Architecture* 2 (1986): 137-149.

20. Forman, *Architecture of the Old South*, 70-71; HABS: *Virginia*, 234; Reiff, *Small Georgian Houses*, 212-214.

21. Waterman and Barrows, *Domestic Colonial Architecture*, 19-27; *HABS: Virginia*, 59; Stephenson B. Andrews, ed., *Bacon's Castle* (Richmond, Va.: Association for the Preservation of Virginia Antiquities, 1984).

22. Abbott Lowell Cummings's monumental study of the framed houses of Massachusetts Bay has already been cited (note 2.25 above). It has been the most important source for the discussion here of New England domestic architecture in the seventeenth century. The extant houses to which he refers are catalogued and described in Abbott L. Cummings, ed., *Architecture in Colonial Massachusetts* (Boston: the Colonial Society of Massachusetts, 1979), 113-121.

23. Cummings, *Framed Houses*, 216-222.

24. Cummings, ed., *Architecture*, 135-137.

25. Norman Morrison Isham and Albert F. Brown, *Early Connecticut Houses: An Historical and Architectural Study* (Providence, R.I.: Preston and Rounds, 1900), 133-136.

26. Cummings, ed., *Architecture*, 157-159.

27. Cummings, *Framed Houses*, 24-25.

28. Isham and Brown, *Early Connecticut Houses*, 31-36.

29. Cummings, ed., *Architecture*, p. 174, and Cummings, *Framed Houses*, 52-94. See also Upton, "Traditional Timber Framing."

30. *The Builder's Dictionary: or, Gentleman and architect's companion; being a complete unabridged reprint of the earlier works published by A. Bettesworth and C. Hitch* (Washington D.C.: Association for Preservation Technology, 1981 [1734]), 2:n.p.

31. Ibid.

32. Edward Johnson, *Johnson's Wonder-Working Providence, 1628-1651* (New York: C. Scribner's Sons, 1910), 43.

33. Hugh Morrison, *Early American Architecture: From the First Colonial Settlement to the National Period* (New York: Oxford University Press, 1952), 72-73.

34. John Winthrop, *Winthrop's Journal, "History of New England," 1630-1649* (New York: C. Scribner's Sons, 1908), 1:69.

35. Norman Morrison Isham and Albert Frederic Brown, *Early Rhode Island Houses: An Historical and Architectural Study* (Providence, R.I.: Preston & Rounds, 1895), 41-44; Antoinette Forrester Downing, *Early Homes of Rhode Island* (Richmond, Va.: Garrett and Massie, Inc., 1937), 38-47; Russell H. Kettel, "Repair and Restoration of Eleazar Arnold's Splendid Mansion," *OTNE* 43, no. 2 (October 1952): 29-35; and Dell Upton, "Architectural Change in Colonial Rhode Island: The Mott House as a Case Study," *OTNE* 69, nos. 3 and 4 (Winter/Spring 1979): 19-20 and 26-28.

36. Isham and Brown, *Early Connecticut Houses*, 112-124; J. Frederick Kelly, "Restoration of the Henry Whitfield House, Guilford, Connecticut," *OTNE* 29, no. 3 (January 1939): 75-89.

37. Isaac Newton Phelps Stokes, *The Iconography of Manhattan Island, 1498-1909* (New York: R. H. Dodd, 1915-28), 1:142-143.

38. Jasper Danckaerts, *Journal of Jasper Danckaerts, 1679-1680* (New York: C. Scribner's Sons, 1913 [1867]), 46.

39. Adolph B. Benson, rev. and ed., *Peter Kalm's Travels in North America* (New York: Dover Publications, 1966), 1:132.

40. Ibid., 2:612.

41. E. B. O'Callaghan, *History of New Netherland or New York under the Dutch* (New York: D. Appleton, 1966 [1846]).

42. Helen Wilkinson Reynolds, *Dutch Houses in the Hudson Valley before 1776* (New York: Payson and Clarke, 1929), 66-68.

43. Rosalie Fellows Bailey, *Pre-Revolutionary Dutch Houses and Families in Northern New Jersey and Southern New York* (New York: Dover Publications, 1968), 88-91; *Historic American Building Survey (HABS): New York*, 8 vols. (New York: Garland Publishing, Inc., 1979), 1: 172.

44. The flared eave also appears in seventeenth- and early eighteenth-century French houses in Quebec.

45. See Chapter 2, pages 16-17.

46. Danckaerts, *Journal of Jasper Danckaerts*, 98.

47. Benson, rev. and ed., *Peter Kalm's Travels*, 1:272.

48. Sigurd Erixon, "The North-European Technique of Timber Construction," *Folkliv* 1 (1937): 13-60. See also Terry G. Jordan, *American Log Buildings: An Old World Heritage* (Chapel Hill: University of North Carolina Press, 1985), 41-85.

49. Sigurd Erixon, *Svensk byggnads kultur* (Stockholm: Aktiebolaget Bokvert, 1947).

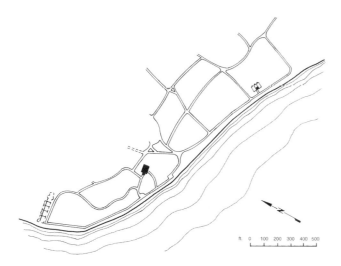

5-1. Jamestown, Va. Plan of the town. (After C. E. Hatch, Jamestown, Virginia: The Townsite and its Story, *Washington, D.C., 1957, 43*).

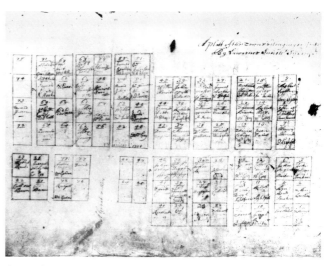

5-2. Yorktown, Va. Plan drawing, 1691. (Virginia State Library).

5-4. St. Mary's City, Md. State House, 1674. Reconstruction of 1934. (Photo: M. C. Donnelly).

Chapter 5

Early Colonial Public and Religious Buildings

BY THE END of the seventeenth century some of the early European settlements on the north Atlantic coast had grown into small cities, while the increase in population also furthered the founding of small towns. As approaches to housing differed between the southern, New England, and middle colonies, so did the development of communities.[1]

The effect of the tobacco economy on the growth of towns in the Tidewater colonies of Virginia and Maryland was apparent even in the colonial period. We have already noted the intentions of the London Company for an orderly approach to the initial settlement in 1606.[2] The palisaded towns such as Jamestown and Henrico probably were closest to that ideal. Otherwise these proposals came to little at first.[3] In 1724 the Reverend Hugh Jones could write: "Thus neither the interest nor inclinations of the Virginians induce them to cohabit in towns; so that they are not forward in contributing their assistance towards the making of particular places, every plantation affording the owner the provision of a little market; wherefore they most commonly build upon some convenient spot or neck of land in their own plantation."[4]

In both Virginia and Maryland between 1662 and 1706, however, the colonial legislatures were pressured by the authorities in London to pass several Acts to create new towns.[5] An earlier attempt to enlarge Jamestown in 1623 and make it the sole port of entry for cargo had resulted in a rather scraggly gridiron plan for the "New Towne" near the fort [5-1].[6] From the slender evidence available in contemporary drawings and descriptions it seems that the simple gridiron plan was considered the most suitable [5-2]. A Maryland Act of 1683 gave important instructions regarding public buildings: "...Open Space places to be left on which may be Erected Church or Chappell, & Marckett house, or other publick buildings."[7] Clearly the central

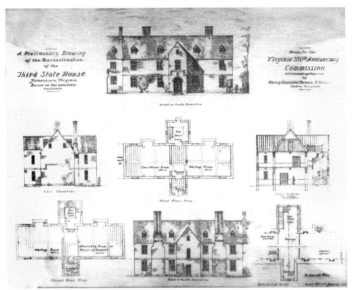

5-3. Third State House, Jamestown, Va., 1661-1665. Conjectural drawing. (Virginia State Library).

space reserved for these public buildings that was proposed for military reasons by the Spanish in 1573 and the English in 1606 was for everyday practical reasons still desirable. Because of the plantation-oriented way of life in Virginia and Maryland, however, such towns were few in the seventeenth century.

LOCAL GOVERNMENT in the southern colonies required a place of assembly, and the slow pace of town development was not conducive to energetic public building projects.[8] From 1641 to 1656 the Assembly of Virginia met in a house in Jamestown purchased from the former Governor, John Harvey [5-3].[9] When it burned in 1656, the Assembly moved to another house, which burned in 1660. This led to a contract for a new "state house," which was completed in 1665, only to be burned in Bacon's Rebellion in 1676.[10] The Assembly then met in taverns and Governor Berkeley's home, Green Spring, until the Fourth State House was completed in 1685.[11] While its exterior appearance must have been essentially domestic, with its two stories, central porch, and symmetrically placed chimneys, the interior was specifically planned for legislative use. If the surviving foundations and documents have been interpreted correctly, the court room, Secretary's office, and Clerk's office were on the ground floor, the stairs were in a porch projecting on the back, or north, side, and the Assembly Room with antechamber and offices were on the second floor.[12] Since it was built on the foundations of the Third State House, it must have been quite similar in appearance. The building was already in need of repair by 1693, and when it burned in 1698, the seat of government was moved to the Plantation, soon to be renamed Williamsburg.

As can be seen from the plan of Jamestown, no attempt was made to provide a central "open space" for a church and State House. For St. Mary's City in Maryland the original plan is

5-5. Bacon's Castle, Surry Co., Va.. Overall plan of plantation compound. (After H. C. Forman, The Architecture of the Old South, the Medieval Style, 1585-1850, Cambridge, Mass., 1948, Fig. 61).

unknown. The "Instructions" from Lord Baltimore in 1634 were for marking out the streets and for the settlers "to build their houses in an decent and uniform a manner as their abilities and the place will afford, and neere adjoyning one to another."[13] By 1678 the few houses that had been built were "at a considerable distance from each other," and the new State House apparently had not been made the focus of a regular plan.[14] The Assembly had met at St. John's in February 1638 and at other times thereafter.

Not until 1676 was a State House built, only to be abandoned when the capital of Maryland was moved to Annapolis in 1694. Smith's Town House, or tavern, in St. Mary's City had been purchased by the Government of Maryland in 1662, with the idea of using it as a State House, and in 1664 a new State House was proposed but never built. This was to have been forty feet square, two-and-a-half stories high, with a hip roof and turret.[15]

Ten years later a successful project was ordered, for a State House forty-five feet by thirty-six feet, with entrance porch on the front and stair tower at the rear.[16] As reconstructed for the Maryland Tercentenary Celebration in 1934, the building is near the original site rather than on the remaining foundations. Measurements of these foundations are slightly different from those specified in the Act for construction. The resulting structure has a basically house-like appearance, with its central porch, symmetrically placed windows in two stories, and end chimneys [5-4]. The interior, however, is reconstructed with the Assembly Room occupying the entire first floor, and the Council Chamber is set off on the second. The success of the original building was short-lived, since it needed repairs in less than a decade and was abandoned as a house of government with the removal of the capital to Annapolis in 1694. Converted to a church in 1720, it was finally demolished in 1829.

We can see, then, that for each Tidewater colony the place of legislative assembly was at first a house made available for the purpose and then a building domestic in its external appearance with the appropriate assembly rooms and offices arranged within. In each case the capital city was not much more than a village and lacked a fully developed formal plan. The Virginia county courthouse square began to appear late in the seventeenth century, with a few notable examples remaining from the eighteenth century. Otherwise there is little to be said of secular public building in the early southern colonies.

What did, in fact, occur was that many a plantation resembled a village, as a French visitor remarked in 1686, "you would believe you were entering a rather large village," only to learn that the buildings he saw were all part of his host's estate.[17] The self-sufficiency of an establishment like Bacon's Castle, for example, with its barn, tool shed, smoke house, etc., would last through the eighteenth century [5-5]. While grist mills, iron works, and other works might be included, all were primarily for the use of the individual plantation, in contrast to the primarily communal purpose of these works in New England towns.

There was, however, one public building that did have to be provided for communal use. Whether in Virginia under the Church of England, or in Maryland with its generous religious toleration for that day, places of worship were clearly required. With a few exceptions, churches were placed in comparative isolation, sometimes at crossroads where they could be reached from several plantations.

The story that began with John Smith's famous description of the first church at Jamestown entered upon a new chapter when more substantial churches could be built. In 1724 Hugh Jones described the pattern that developed: "The parishes being of great extent (some sixty miles long and upwards) many dead corpses cannot be conveyed to the church to be buried: So that it is customary to bury in gardens or orchards, where whole families lye interred together, in a spot generally handsomely enclosed, planted with evergreens, and the graves kept decently."[18] Jones goes on to report that funeral sermons, baptisms and marriages were performed in the houses of such estates, adding religious observances to the village-like character observed by the Frenchman.

The churches built in Virginia after the first settlement period continued the English parish church tradition, as shown by the description of the church in the fort at Jamestown. When Captain Samuel Argall arrived to be Governor at Jamestown in 1617 he found the church that had been built for the town in ruins and proceeded to build a church "wholly at the charge of the inhabitants of that cittie, of Timber, beinge fifty foote in length and twenty foote in breadth."[19] It has been thought that the footings of this building were discovered during the excavations of the present church in 1906.[20]

While it is known that brick was also used for building churches in seventeenth-century Virginia, how early this took place is another matter. For at least two, dates of construction in the 1630s have been firmly held on the one hand and seriously questioned on the other. The earliest date proposed is that for the Newport Parish Church, commonly called St. Luke's, at Smithfield in Isle of Wight County, Virginia [5-6].[21] It is now believed to date closer to 1680. The church is a simple rectangular building with a square entrance tower, such as would have been built in England. The brick is laid in Flemish bond. Salient buttresses divide the exterior side walls into four bays, with brick tracery dividing the windows in each bay. The east end has a large traceried window, and at both ends the gables are stepped in the Dutch manner, long since adopted in England. The tower may have originally been finished with crenelations, as it was at first only two stories high. Whereas the roof and part of the east gable fell in a storm in 1857, enough remained to allow reconstruction in the 1950s.[22] The interior is fitted up with rows of pews on either side of the central aisle, and the pulpit is on the south side just before the sanctuary, which is marked off by a low step and

communion rail. This is the pattern found in English churches of the time, such as the chapel at Great Houghton, Yorkshire, c. 1650 [5-7].[22]

Then the James City Parish Church at Jamestown has also been variously dated from 1639 to the 1680s (but now thought to date to about 1680 also) [5-8].[23] It too is a simple rectangular building with buttressed walls and a western tower. By 1907 it had long been abandoned and only the tower and foundations remained. Even more than at St. Luke's what is seen today is almost entirely restoration. Whether it had the stepped gables and traceried windows of St. Luke's can only be conjectured. The exterior restoration, under the direction of Edward M. Wheelright in 1907, depended partly on the St. Luke's, while the interior furnishings had to be based on English models.

For the date of the first brick church of Bruton Parish, in Williamsburg, Virginia, there is good evidence for completion in 1683.[24] It was sixty feet by twenty-four feet internally, with no

5-6. Newport Parish Church, St. Luke's, Smithfield, Isle of Wight Co., Va., c. 1680. (Photo: M. C. Donnelly).

5-7. Chapel, Great Houghton, Yorkshire, England, c. 1650. (National Monuments Record).

tower, and had five buttresses on each side. A drawing by a Swiss traveller, Franz Ludwig Michel, of 1702, lacks the buttresses excavated in 1939, perhaps because of difficulty in drawing [5-9]. Michel did attempt to show what was probably a stepped gable, and also the wall around the churchyard with a lych gate.[25] This was soon to be replaced by the present church in 1715.

If we turn to Maryland in the period of early settlement, we find even less evidence for church building. Lord Baltimore's report of March 26 included the comment that "There are not fifty houses in the space of Thirty Myles And for this Reason it is that they have beene hitherto only to divide this Provynce into Countys without beeing able to make any subdivision into Parishes or Precincts."[26] In this colony, which was distinctive for its early religious toleration, only the foundations remained of the Roman Catholic chapel built at St. Mary's City in 1634-1638, since the building was closed and taken down in 1704.[27] Excavations in 1938 showed it to have been a cruciform building, fifty-five feet long and fifty-seven feet wide, built of brick.[28] Not until

later in the century was there much substantial church building in the Maryland colony, and by that time Gothic traditions were all but spent.

THE MIDDLE COLONIES were settled more by trading companies than by plantation owners, but even here there was no rush to build civic and religious structures. Probably the most famous of the former was not built as a government building but as an inn, in 1641 [5-10]. David de Vries, writing his "Short Historical and Journal-Notes" of 1655, described it as "a fine inn, built of stone, in order to accommodate the English who daily passed with their vessels from New England to Virginia."[29] Elsewhere public meetings were being held in forts. The tavern at New Amsterdam was designated as the "Stadthuys" in 1654, and it was finally replaced by a City Hall proper in 1699.[30]

Religious commitments among the early settlers of the middle colonies were more varied than in Virginia and Maryland and resulted in the building of several kinds of churches. The

"Provisional Regulations" adopted by the Swedish West India Company in 1624 stipulated to prospective colonists that "They shall within their territory practice no other form of divine worship than that of the Reformed religion as at present practiced here in this country.[31] Gustavus II Adolf had in fact wished to see a colony from Sweden established in America to be a stronghold of Protestantism against the Spanish, but after his death the emphasis turned more to trade. When the colony of New Sweden had finally been established on the Delaware, Governor Johan Printz was able to report in 1647 that "I have caused a church to be built in New Gothenburg, decorating it according to our Swedish fashion, so far as our resources and means would allow."[32]

This remark tells us that at least once a Swedish village church was built in the New World. The New Gothenburg church was undoubtedly a wooden structure with single nave and chancel, much like the church at Granhult in Smoland, built c. 1300 [5.11].[33] Built of horizontal timbers, it is one of two medieval examples that have survived in Sweden, and such churches in wood continued to appear down into the eighteenth century. The decorations to which Printz referred were also of long tradi-

tions, consisting of floral and geometrical ornaments as well as paintings of Biblical scenes to form a "Biblia Pauperum."

The New Gothenburg church was also described by the Rev. Israel Acrelius (1714-1800) in the history of New Sweden that he published in 1759: "A handsome wooden church was also built at the same place, which Magister Campanius consecrated, on the last great prayer-day which was celebrated in New Sweden, on the 4th of September, 1646."[34] Writing of the period after the Dutch took over the colony in 1655, Acrelius quoted the account of settlement by Andrew Rudman, first Provost of Swedish churches in America: "The churches were so built that, after a suitable elevation, like any other house, a projection was made some courses higher, out of which they could shoot, so that if the heathen fell upon them, which could not be done without their coming up to the house, then the Swedes could shoot down upon them continually, and the heathen, who used only bows and arrows, could do them little or no injury."[35]

From the context of the account by Acrelius we may surmise that Rudman was referring to a church built at Tranhooke. The "any other house" was probably similar to the one at the

5-8. Brick Church, Jamestown, Va., seventeenth century. (Photo: M. C. Donnelly).

Mora Farmstead from Dalarna. [See 4-29.] In any event we have these two possibilities for early Swedish churches, a more conventional building or something rather like a fort, both of timber. Acrelius also tells of the provision for worship at Wicacoa, a site now within Philadelphia: "On the strand at Wicacoa stood a blockhouse, which some years after was changed to a church, so that service was held here and at Tenakong (New Gothenburg) alternately. A block-house answered the purpose very well, for the churches generally were of the same material."[36] Acrelius may have been referring to a structure such as the storage lofts of Sweden [5-12]. None of the wooden churches or other early places of worship have survived from New Sweden, and consequently we are dependent on documentary accounts for our conjectures about them.

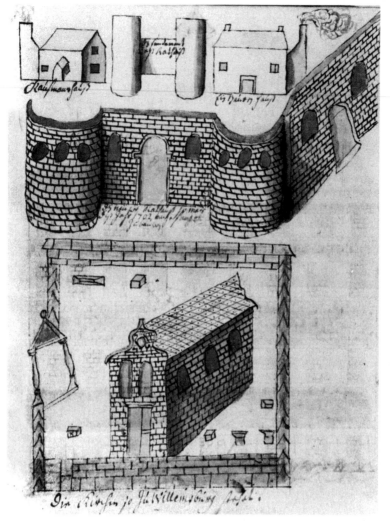

5-9. Brick Church, Williamsburg, Va., 1683. Drawing by Franz L. Michel, c. 1702. (Bern, Stadsbibliothek [Mss.hist.helv.X.152, f. 63ᵛ]).

it when they recovered their senses, they were nevertheless compelled to pay—nothing could avail to prevent it. The church was then, contrary to every one's wish, placed in the fort."[39]

To return to de Vries's *Notes*: "The church should be built in the fort, to guard against any surprise by the savages. Thus were the walls of the church speedily begun to be laid up with quarry-stone, and to be covered by the English carpenters with overlapping shingles cleft from oak, which, by exposure to the wind and rain, turn blue, and look as if they were slate."[40] The Montanus View of c. 1650 shows the church with its belfry and the M-shaped roof built by the English carpenters, the roof sloping nearly to the ground, giving the impression of a Friesland farmhouse. [See 4-22.]

While all this was going on, the colony up the river at Rens-

For the Dutch in New Netherland, building of churches also began slowly. By 1642 no church had yet been erected in New Amsterdam, and "it was a scandal to us when the English passed there and saw only a mean barn in which we preached."[37] The "mean barn" was perhaps the horse-mill built by Francis Molemaecker in 1626, "over which shall be constructed a spacious room sufficient to accommodate a large congregation."[38] Director General Willem Kieft, however, encouraged by promises of funds and help from some of the citizens, seized his chance and presided over New York's first fund-raising party.

"It happened about this time that the minister, Evardus Bogardus, gave his step-daughter in marriage; and on the occasion of the wedding the Director considered a good opportunity for his purpose. So after the fourth or fifth round of drinking he set about the business, and he himself showing a liberal example let the wedding guests subscribe what they were willing to give towards the church. All then with light heads subscribed largely, competing with one another; and although, some well repented

selaerwick was still without a church, the minister's house being "in which service is performed."[41] The patron, Kiliaen van Rensselaer, had sent a wooden model for a church to his agent at Rensselaerwick in 1641. Knowledge of this perhaps spurred Director Willem Kieft to get a church built for New Amsterdam. The type of church proposed seems to have been exclusive to the Dutch, at least at this early period. Van Rensselaer wrote to one of the colonists, Arendt van Corlaer, "please use diligence in erecting it. It ought not to be a very complated matter, the shape being mostly that of an eight-cornered mill."[42] In other letters he indicated that the upper story of the church be used for the storage of grain and that it should be covered with tiles in order to protect it from fire during Indian attacks.[43]

This church may not have been built, but other Dutch churches were built on octagonal or hexagonal plans.[44] The idea may have come from the great octagonal church built at Willemstad by Prince Maurice in 1596.[45] Among those built by the Dutch in New Netherland was the church at Bergen, N.J.,

5-10. The Tavern (later Stadthuys), New Amsterdam, New Netherland, c. 1650. (Courtesy of the New York Public Library, Eno Collection, 1679-80, #12).

5-11. Church, Granhult, Smoland, Sweden, c. 1300. (Stockholm, ATA).

5-12. Storehouse, Björvik, Östergötland, eighteenth century. Relocated to Stockholm, Skansen. (Photo: M. C. Donnelly).

built by William Day in 1680 [5-13].[46] It was stone, octagonal, "and when ringing the bell the sexton stood in the centre of the building. In the interior, pews were placed only around the wall and were occupied solely by the male attendants. The remainder of the floor was used by the females, each having a chair."[47] Further description of a typical interior comes for the church at Claverack, N.Y., built somewhat later: "Above their heads is a wooden ceiling with prodigious rafters. The walls are plastered and meant to be white; the wood-work is painted blue.... The pulpit stands at the north end...shaped like a wineglass, and surmounted by a sounding board."[48] These octagonal and hexagonal plans never became widespread. The only known example among the New England meeting houses was the one at Fairfield, Conn., of 1698, which Alexander Hamilton described in 1744 as "an octogonall church or meeting built of wood like that of Jamaica upon Long Island, upon the cupolo of which is a public clock."[48] Kiliaen van Rensselaer had stipulated that the church at Rensselaerwick be forty-eight feet wide, which could not result in a very large building, and by the middle of the eighteenth century these little Dutch churches were being replaced with larger and more conventional buildings.

As for the model sent by Kiliaen van Rensselaer, no such models seem to have survived from the colonial period in the American colonies. A late medieval example from Sweden, however, suggests the nature of such a model. This is the model of the church at Norra Ny in Värmland, demolished in the 1760s [5-14].[49] The making of such models might have been more frequent than we might think if we recall carved and painted figures of donors holding models of churches in medieval times.

THE SITUATION WAS DIFFERENT in New England. Here there were no patrons and no royal governors until the appointment of Sir Edmund Andros over the "Dominion of New England" in 1684. Until then the five colonies were administered under the Council for New England. Maine had had its first permanent settlement at Monhegan in 1622 and for the rest of the century was involved in conflicting claims for jurisdic-

5-13. Dutch Reformed Church, Bergen, N.J., 1680. (From C. H. Winfield, History of the County of Hudson, New Jersey, *New York, 1874, 381*).

5-14. Model of the church at Norra Ny, Värmland, Sweden, eighteenth century. (Stockholm, ATA).

tion, and from the earliest settlement at Portsmouth, or possibly Dover, about 1631, a similar course of events took place in New Hampshire.[50]

Dissent arising early among the Dissenters, a number of Puritans (having become dissatisfied with matters in Massachusetts Bay) moved to Connecticut in 1634-1635 under the leadership of Thomas Hooker, founding the towns of Wethersfield, Windsor, and Hartford. Shortly thereafter, another Puritan colony was founded at New Haven by John Davenport and Theophilus Eaton. A royal charter of 1662 intended the union of the two colonies, which was accomplished in 1665. Here there were again chronic boundary disputes with Massachusetts and also with Rhode Island, which was founded by yet another dissenter, Roger Williams, in 1636 and chartered in 1644.

After the initial settlements of these New England colonies, further expansion tended to cling to the ports and navigable rivers, with only a slow spread into the interior. Lack of suitable agricultural lands meant that no large staple crops could form the basis of the economy, as was the case in the southern colonies. Lumber and shipbuilding were the leading sources of trade with England, and a great deal of self-sufficiency was necessary for the survival of individual households. The fields and forests were held and worked both individually and in common, with life centering where the landholders had their dwellings.

In Massachusetts and Connecticut, government was based on religious principles, the "theocratic commonwealth," in the early years at least, having church membership a requirement for voting privileges. The meeting house accordingly dominated the town. An anonymous "Essay on the ordering of towns" written about 1635 said: "Suppose the Town square 6 miles every way, the houses orderly placed about the midst, especially the meetinghouse, the which we will suppose to be the center of the whole circumference."[51] By this time only nine or ten of the towns in Massachusetts had built or begun meeting houses, but the comment makes clear that already these buildings were the center of town life. This is confirmed by the early records of specific towns, such as those of March 1636 which instructed that the bounds of Cambridge, Charlestown, and Watertown "shall run 8 miles into the country from their meeting house."[52] On September 3, 1635, it had been ordered that "no dwelling house shall be built above half a mile from the meeting house in any new plantation."[53] As the number of properties increased in each town this became impractical, and the order was repealed on May 13, 1640. Some towns developed along the meandering lines of an English village, especially Boston, where in 1665 the Commissioners found the "streets crooked, with little decency and no uniformity."[54] Elsewhere the more regular grid was adopted, as at New Haven in 1636, illustrated on the famous Wadsworth map of 1748 [5-15]. This has been thought to have been based on the principles of Vitruvius, or on Biblical references and the proposals of Villalpandus.[55] Here the Congregational meeting house is shown in the central square.

As the town meeting became the focus of government in New England towns, the meeting house obviously occupied a central position in civic and religious affairs as well as a central geographical position. Although this building might not be erected until some years after a town was founded, the normal expectation for its position was such that it is central to discussion of the First Period public and religious buildings in New England.

T HE TERM "MEETING HOUSE" itself appears to have been introduced in New England. The last reference to building "churches" as places of worship for the Puritans seems to have been at a meeting in London on February 10, 1629/30.[56] Two years later John Winthrop wrote of the "new meeting house" at Dorchester, Mass., to date the earliest known use of the term in a New England document and also a reference to the earliest known "meeting house" built as such.[57] The intention had been to build "houses for God's worship" as distinct from houses for the ministers, and the "faire house newly built for the Governor" was the first place of worship in Salem.[58] From the first known meeting house at Dorchester to the year 1700, more than 200 were built in New England, of which only one enlarged and much altered example survives.

For our knowledge of these buildings we are indebted to the town records which in many cases have survived, giving the original detailed instructions to the carpenters and subsequent orders for additions and repairs. Three examples may be chosen to represent the various possible types: the first meeting house in Sudbury, Mass., of 1643, the second meeting house in Malden, Mass., of 1658, and the second meeting house in Weymouth, Mass., of 1682.

The Sudbury building was to be "thirty foote longe twenty foote wide eight foot be…ioynte three footte between studde two crosse Dorments in…house six clearstory windowes two with foure light a peece and foure with three lights a peece and to entertise between ye studde."[59] This information is sufficient for preparing a conjectural elevation of the building, especially since contemporary English carpenters' manuals explain terms unfamiliar in modern usage. The result was a modest rectangular building, thatched or shingled, probably with the entrance in the middle of one of the long sides and the larger windows

5-15. New Haven, Conn., Wadsworth Map, 1748. (Yale University Map Collection).

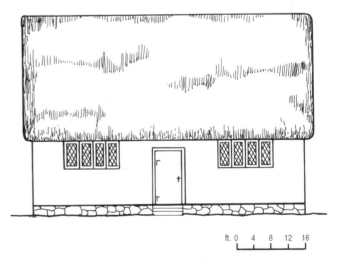

5-16. Meeting house I, Sudbury, Mass., 1643. Conjectural drawing. (After M. C. Donnelly).

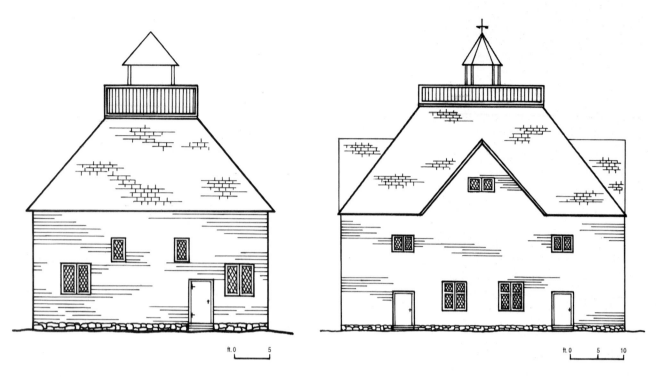

5-17. *Meeting house II, Malden, Mass., 1658. Conjectural drawing. (After M. C. Donnelly).*

5-18. *Meeting house II, Hingham, Mass., 1681. Conjectural drawing. (After M. C. Donnelly).*

5-19. *Town house, Boston, Mass., 1657. Conjectural drawing. (After M. C. Donnelly).*

flanking it [5-16]. Within the residents would be seated according to their "dignity," men on one side, women on the other. Numerous records of seating reveal what is known from later buildings, that the pulpit and communion table would be placed in the middle of the long wall opposite the main entrance. Benches or pews were arranged accordingly, the whole plan representing the Puritan response to what was considered unacceptable in the practices of the Church of England.

At Malden fifteen years later a second and less frequent type of meeting house was constructed. It was slightly larger than the Sudbury building, being thirty-three feet square, and with galleries was two stories high.[60] It was also provided with a turret on the roof [5-17]. Here the seats were set in rows facing the pulpit, which was in the center of the front, to the left of the door as one entered. In the conjectural drawing the small windows in the second level have been placed so that they would conveniently light the pulpit, as indicated in the records. Turrets were often built on the meeting houses, sometimes at the time of initial construction and sometimes added later. They served both

as watch towers and to house bells. The builder at Malden was v, who was to do some of the carpentry for Harvard College several years later, as we shall see.

The Malden meeting house was square, and the "four-square" myth dies hard. Of the more than two hundred built by 1700, twenty-one are known to have been precisely square. The sixty-three others for which either shapes or actual dimensions are known were planned as rectangles of varying proportions. No evolution of shape can be determined from the extant records. In 1632 the first meeting house at Cambridge, Mass., was square, and nearby in Dedham in 1638 the first meeting house was rectangular, thirty-six feet by twenty feet.[61] In 1700 the second meeting house in Clinton, Conn., was square, whereas the second meeting house in Middleboro, Mass., of the same year was "36 foot in length: 30 foot in breadth."[62] To argue that a short rectangle still meant a "four-square" meeting house plan in the minds of the builders is to ignore their clear awareness that a rectangle has "length" and 'breadth." When the New England authorities wanted a "square" meeting house, they said so.

5-20. Market hall, Midhurst, Sussex, late seventeenth century. (Photo: M. C. Donnelly).

The third example is the meeting house that in 1682 the Weymouth, Massachusetts, carpenter Jacob Nash was instructed to build "45 foot in length 40 foot bredth," with a "platform" on the roof.[63] With its four-gabled roof and galleries on three sides it resembled the somewhat larger second meeting house at Hingham, Mass., as it was originally built in 1681 [5-18].[64]

5-21. Old Harvard College, Cambridge, Mass., 1638-1642. Conjectural restoration drawing. (SPNEA).

A PROGRESSION FROM small to large during the seventeenth century is no more discernible than a progression from rectangular to square. More important is that by the end of the century with the Brattle Street Church in Boston, 1699, there began a reversion to the longitudinal plan with entrance tower at one end.[65] Here too the word "church" was now used to designate a Congregational place of worship. Significant changes had occurred in the New England colonies. The original fervor of the Puritan settlements had abated. In 1684 the Massachusetts Bay Charter was revoked and a royal governor appointed, putting an end to the exclusive rule of the Congregational Church and introducing the Church of England as well as other Christian sects. Growth in the size of towns put pressures on the first meeting houses, many of which were pulled down to make way for larger structures. In Boston particularly, even as early as 1657, more than one parish of the church had been formed, and it was necessary to build the first Town House for city-wide civic use [5-19].[66]

It will at once be seen how much like the meeting houses this building was in appearance. It was, in fact, the other way around. Needing a place for worship according to Puritan rather than established principles, and founding their towns on religious principles, the New England colonists adapted the town halls or market halls familiar to them in England [5-20].[67] The basic requirement for these buildings since medieval times was a room

for civic meetings and the court, with perhaps a clerk's office for securing records. If raised upon posts, as at Midhurst, the town hall provided shelter for the market folk. Modest in the English village, the town hall was related to the imposing examples built in Continental cities. From early times the market cross had been a place for preaching as well as for assembly, especially in Elizabethan England when there was need to keep preaching the Reformation. For the Puritans in New England, rejecting the altar-oriented liturgy of the Church of England, to use the familiar village hall for both religious and civic meetings was a natural convenience. This transformation of a traditional building, even to its site, to new use was perhaps the most notable innovation made by the colonial builders in the American colonies.

Little is known of one other important kind of building in the early colonies, the school. By 1700 two colleges had been chartered, Harvard and William and Mary, and there is some information available about the first buildings of the former. An Act passed by the General Court of Massachusetts on October 28, 1636, founded Harvard College, and by 1642 the "Old College" was ready for use [5-21].[68] The conjectural drawing of

5-22. William Burgis, View of Harvard College, Cambridge, Mass., engraved 1726. From left to right: Harvard Hall, 1674-77 (burned and demolished 1764); Stoughton Hall, 1698-99 (demolished 1781); and Massachusetts Hall, 1718-20. (Courtesy of the Massachusetts Historical Society).

1933 was based on college records and other descriptions, which tell a surprising amount about the building. It was built of wood, three stories high, and most probably in the E-shaped form illustrated here. The ground floor held the principal hall, the kitchen, buttery, etc., and two chambers with small cubicles or "studies" within. The library was on the second floor, along with more chambers and studies, while there were additional chambers and studies on the third floor. No single person is credited with the design in the records, but strong resemblances to Eton College in particular suggest that the Reverend John Wilson, on the Board of Overseers of the new college, may have furnished some initial ideas based on his years of study at Eton. For the present discussion we may note that the Provisions of Old College were consistent with those of the English colleges where the founders of Harvard had been educated.

Old College was far from satisfactory structurally, however, and by 1672 plans were begun for a New College, begun in 1674, completed in 1677, and known as "Harvard Hall" [5-22].[69] The designer is not known for this building, either, but again, it may have been one of the Overseers. The master builder was Samuel Andrew, "well skilled in the mathematics," and the timber work was done by Job Lane, who had built the Malden meeting house of 1658. Old Harvard Hall was a more conventional rectangle, ninety-seven feet by forty-two feet, two stories high with two additional stories in the gambrel-roofed attic. The view of 1726 shows gables on the long sides, a balustraded deck, chimney clusters, and belfry, and a fashionable touch in the mouldings over the windows. The Hall occupied the center of the first floor, with kitchen, buttery, and chambers on either side. On the second floor the library was over the Hall, with the chambers on either side, as well as in the two attic stories. Old College, then ruinous, was taken down, and Old Harvard Hall served until it burned in 1764.

WITH BOSTON NEEDING a Town House by 1657 and Harvard College needing a new building by 1674, the colonists in Massachusetts Bay and indeed in New England generally had firmly established themselves. The last years of the seventeenth century and the first of the eighteenth were to bring changes and new enterprises all along the Atlantic seaboard. Traditions remained strong, however, and we must now turn our attention to a period of mixed old and new.

Notes to Chapter 5

1. For a more extensive account of early colonial towns see Carl Bridenbaugh, *Cities in the Wilderness; the First Century of Urban Life in America, 1625-1742* (New York: The Ronald Press Company, 1938); and John William Reps, *Town Planning in Frontier America* (Princeton: Princeton University Press, 1965).

2. See note 2.2.

3. John William Reps, *Tidewater Towns: City Planning in Colonial Virginia and Maryland* (Williamsburg, Va.: Colonial Williamsburg Foundation; University Press of Virginia, 1972), 24-64.

4. Hugh Jones, *The Present State of Virginia* (London: 1724), ed. Richard L. Morton (Chapel Hill: University of North Carolina Press, 1956), 73-74.

5. Reps, *Town Planning*, 114-124.

6. Charles E. Hatch, Jr., *Jamestown, Virginia: The Townsite and its Story* (Washington, D.C.: U.S. Dept. of the Interior, National Park Service, 1957), 40-45.

7. William H. Browne, ed., *Archives of Maryland, Proceedings and Acts of the General Assembly of Maryland, October 1678 – November 1683* (Baltimore: Maryland Historical Society, 1889), 5:612.

8. Chapter 1, page 2; Chapter 2, page 9.

9. Charles E. Hatch, Jr., *America's Oldest Legislative Assembly* (Washington D.C.: n.p., 1956), 10.

10. Ibid., 27-29.

11. Ibid., 29-31.

12. Henry C. Forman, *Jamestown and St. Mary's: Buried Cities of Romance* (Baltimore: Johns Hopkins Press, 1938), 172-174.

13. "Instructions…directed by the Right Honorable Cecilius Lord Baltimore….," in Clayton Coleman Hall, ed., *Narratives of Early Maryland, 1633-1684* (New York: C. Scribner's Sons, 1910), 20-22.

14. Browne, ed., *Archives of Maryland*, 5:266.

15. Forman, *Jamestown and St. Mary's*, 274.

16. Ibid., 282-292.

17. Gilbert Chinard, ed., *Un Français en Virginie* (Paris: Librairie E. Droz, 1932), 92.

18. Jones, *Present State of Virginia*, 96-97.

19. From "A Briefe declaration of the plantation of Virginia during the first twelve years," quoted in George C. Mason, "The Colonial Churches of James City County, Virginia," *William and Mary Quarterly* 19, ser. 2, no. 4 (October 1939): 515.

20. Opinions have varied on this matter. Some historians have held that these footings are those of Argall's church, although they are twenty-one and a half feet wide instead of twenty, as in the documentary mention of Argall's church in 1624. See Forman, *Jamestown and St. Mary's*, 154 and 163; Mason, "Colonial Churches," 518-519; and James Scott Rawlings, *Virginia's Colonial Churches* (Richmond: Garrett & Massie, 1963), 20-22.

21. The date of 1682 was held by George C. Mason, *Colonial Churches of Tidewater Virginia* (Richmond: Whittet and Shepperson, 1945), 192-198. Discoveries made during the restorations of 1953-1959 led those participating in the investigations to accept 1632, with which Mason later concurred. See James Grote van Derpool, "The Restoration of St. Luke's, Smithfield, Virginia," *JSAH* 17, no. 1 (March 1958): 12-18. The church is described in Herbert A. Claiborne, *Commentary on Virginia Brickwork Before 1800* (Boston: Walpole Society, 1957), 24-25; Rawlings, *Virginia's Colonial Churches*, 31-38; and Harold W. Rose, *The Colonial Houses of Worship in America* (New York: Hastings House, 1963), 458-460. The most recent discussion, arguing for a date in the 1680s, is in Dell Upton, *Holy Things and Profane: Anglican Parish Churches in Colonial Virginia* (New York and Cambridge: Architectural History Foundation and MIT Press, 1986), 58-63.

22. Van Derpool, "Restoration of St. Luke's," 14-15.

23. Forman, *Jamestown and St. Mary's*, 154-163; Mason, *Colonial Churches*, 7-15; Claiborne, *Comments on Virginia Brickwork*, 18; Rawlings, *Virginia's Colonial Churches*, 18-27; Rose, *Colonial Houses of Worship*, 450-451; and Upton, *Holy Things and Profane*, 60-62.

24. Marcus Whiffen, *The Public Buildings of Williamsburg* (Williamsburg: Colonial Williamsburg, 1959), 75-78.

25. For the drawing see ibid., 211, notes 32 and 33.

26. Browne, ed., *Archives of Maryland*, 5:266.

27. Forman, *Jamestown and St. Mary's*, 202-203.

28. Ibid., 248-251.

29. Franklin J. Jameson, ed., *Narratives of New Netherland, 1609-1664* (New York: Charles Scribner's Sons, 1909), 212.

30. Isaac Newton Phelps Stokes, *The Iconography of Manhattan Island, 1498-1909* (New York: Arno Press, 1967 [1915]), 1:231-232.

31. Arnold van Laer, trans. and ed., *Documents Relating to New Netherland, 1624-1626, in the Henry E. Huntington Library* (San Marino, Calif.: The Henry E. Huntington Library and Art Gallery, 1924), 2.

32. Governor Johan Printz, "Report to the Right Honorable West India Company," in Albert Cook Myers, *Narratives of Early Pennsylvania, West New Jersey and Delaware, 1630-1707* (New York: C. Scribner's Sons, 1912), 122.

33. Marian Ullén, *Medeltida träkyrkor* (Stockholm: Riksantikvarieämbetet, 1983), 19-30.

34. Israel Acrelius, *A History of New Sweden*, William M. Reynolds, trans. and ed. (Philadelphia: The Historical Society of Pennsylvania, 1874), 43.

35. Ibid., 176-177.

36. Ibid., 176.

37. David Pietersz de Vries, *Korte historiael ende journaels aenteyckeninge van verscheyden voyagiens in di vier deelen des wereldtsronde, als Europa, Africa, Asia, ende Amerika gedaen* ('s-Gravenhage: M. Nijhoff, 1655 [reprinted 1911]), 212.

38. Nicolaes van Wassenaer, *Historisch verhael alder ghedenck-weerdichste geschiedenisse(n) die hier en daer in Europa, als in Duijtsch-lant, Vranckrijck, Enghelant... en Neder-lant, van den beginne des jaers 1621, tot den herfst toe, voorgevallen syn* (T'Amstelredam: Bij Ian Evertss, 1622-1635), 83-84.

39. Adriaen van der Donck, attr., "The Representation of New Netherland," in Jameson, *Narratives*, 326.

40. De Vries, *Korte historiael*, 213.

41. Father Isaac Jogues, "Novum Belgium," in Jameson, *Narratives*, 262.

42. Arnold van Laer, trans. and ed., *Van Riensselaer Bowier Manuscripts* (Albany: University of the State of New York, 1908), 561.

43. Ibid., 82, 414, and 551.

44. Thomas J. Wertenbaker, *The Founding of American Civilization: The Middle Colonies* (New York: C. Scribner's Sons, 1938), 77-81.

45. Frans Audré Jozef Vermeulen, *Handboek tot de geschiedenis der Nederlandsche bouwkunst* ('s-Gravenhage: M. Nijhoff, 1931), 2:363-364.

46. Benjamin C. Taylor, *Annals of the Classis of Bergen* (New York: Board of Publication of the Reformed Protestant Dutch Church, 1857), 112-113; and Charles H. Winfield, *History of the County of Hudson, New Jersey* (New York: Kennard and Hay, 1874), 380-381.

47. Taylor, *Annals*, 123.

48. Carl Bridenbaugh, ed., *Gentleman's Progress* (Chapel Hill: University of North Carolina, 1948), 167.

49. Erland Lagerlöf, *Medeltida träkyrkor II* (Stochholm: Riksantikvarieämbetet, 1985), 211.

50. For general histories of this period in New England see Charles M. Andrews, *The Colonial Period of American History*, 4 vols. (New Haven: Yale University Press, 1934-1938), 1:375-461; and a shorter summary in Peter T. Mallary, *New England Churches & Meeting Houses, 1680-1830* (New York: Vendome Press, 1985), 6-18. See also Thomas J. Wertenbaker, *The Puritan Oligarchy* (New York: C. Scribner's Sons, 1947), 159-338.

51. Adam Winthrop, *Winthrop Papers* (Boston: Massachusetts Historical Society, 1929-1947), 5:181-182. For further discussion of New England town planning see John D. Cushing, "Town Commons of New England, 1640-1840," *OTNE* 51, no. 3 (January-March 1961): 86-94; Joseph Wood, "Village and Community in Early Colonial New England," *Journal of Historical Geography* 8, no. 4 (October 1982): 333-346; and Joseph Wood, *The New England Village* (Baltimore: Johns Hopkins University Press, 1997).

52. Nathaniel B. Shurtleff, ed., *Records of the Governor and Company of the Massachusetts Bay in New England*, 5 vols. (Boston: 1853-1854), 1:166-167.

53. Ibid., 1:157.

54. Hugh Morrison, *Early American Architecture: From the First Colonial Settlement to the National Period* (New York: Dover Publications, 1987 [1952]), 50.

55. Anthony N. B. Garvan, *Architecture and Town Planning in Colonial Connecticut* (New Haven: Yale University Press, 1951), 44-49; and John Archer, "Puritan Town Planning in New Haven," *JSAH* 35, no. 2 (May 1975): 140-149.

56. Shurtleff, ed., *Records*, 1:68.

57. John Winthrop, *Winthrop's Journal*, "History of New England," 1630-1649 (New York: C. Scribner's Sons, 1908), 1:75.

58. Great Britain Public Records Office, *Calendar of State Papers, Colonial Series* (London: 1860-1969), 8:164.

59. Town Records, Sudbury, Mass., 1:43.

60. The contract is quoted in *The Bi-centennial Book of Malden* (Boston: 1850), 123.

61. *The Records of the Town of Cambridge* (Cambridge, Mass.: 1901), 85; and *Early Records of the Town of Dedham*, 3 vols. (Dedham: 1892-1899), 1:38.

62. *Two Hundredth Anniversary of the Clinton Congregational Church* (Clinton, Conn.: 1867), 7; and Town Records, Middleboro, Mass., 1:117.

63. Town Records, Weymouth, Mass., 1:162.

64. Marian C. Donnelly, *The New England Meeting Houses of the Seventeenth Century* (Middletown, Conn.: Wesleyan University Press, 1968), 72-77; and Mallary, *New England Churches*, 41-45.

65. *Records of the Church in Brattle Square* (Boston: 1902), 4 and 9. Brattle Street Church, 1699, is notable for two things, one its being the first Congregational religious structure to be labeled a church instead of a meetinghouse, and the other its being the first church in America to have been designed with a Christopher Wren-like tower and steeple, a feature that would become widely seen in the next century. The design of the tower is credited to Thomas Brattle, a mathematics instructor at Harvard College who had recently been to London, met Wren, and seen his churches under construction; see Rick Kennedy, "Thomas Brattle, mathematician-architect in the transition of the New England mind, 1690-1700," *Winterthur Portfolio* 24 (Winter 1989): 231-45. The Brattle Street church is illustrated in Marian C. Donnelly, *The New England Meeting Houses of the Seventeenth Century* (Middletown, Conn., 1968). [ed.]

66. Morrison, *Early American Architecture*, 88-89. The Agreement for building the Town House is published in *Re-dedication of the Old State House, Boston, July 11, 1882*, 3rd ed. (Boston: 1885), 129-130.

67. Donnelly, *New England Meeting Houses*, 94-108. For a good discussion of the role of the churches in governmental affairs in Virginia see Upton, *Holy Things and Profane*, 5-10.

68. Samuel Eliot Morison, "A Conjectural Restoration of the 'Old College' at Harvard," *OTNE* 23, no. 4 (April 1933): 131-138. The full story of the buildings at Harvard is given in Bainbridge Bunting, *Harvard: An Architectural History* (Cambridge, Mass.: Belknap Press of Harvard University Press, 1985). For the first college building see pages 5-13.

69. Samuel Eliot Morison, *Harvard College in the Seventeenth Century*, 2 vols. (Cambridge, Mass.: Harvard University Press, 1936), 2:423-430, and Bunting, *Harvard*, 16-21.

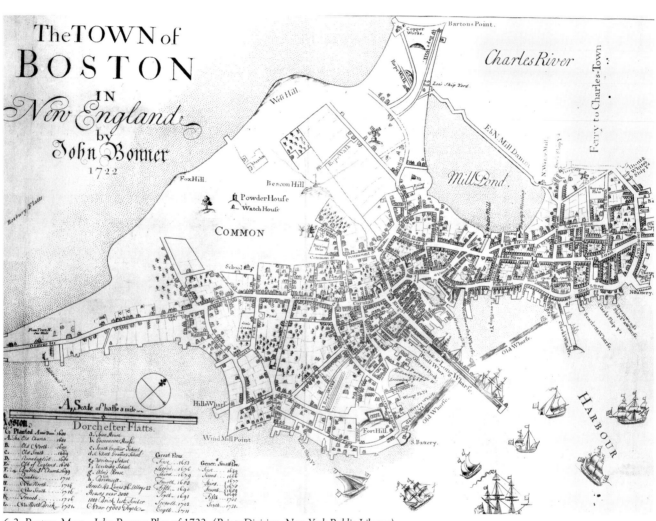

6-2. Boston, Mass., John Bonner Plan of 1722. (Prints Division, New York Public Library).

⊰ Chapter 6 ⊱

Survivals and Innovations

B

Y EXTENDING our consideration of early colonial buildings into the 1680s we have begun to deal with a period of about forty years during which well-established, familiar methods of planning and construction were continued but were increasingly accompanied by new fashions, which were to culminate in the Georgian style. As we examine some of the principal towns, houses, churches, and public buildings from about 1680 to about 1720, we will see that in less than a century from the earliest permanent European settlements in North America the centuries-old pattern of the persistence of tradition amid innovation was at work as soon as permanent footholds had been secured.

For the towns themselves, founding, growth, and change took a number of guises, most clearly related to political history. New Amsterdam, for example, fell with little struggle to the English in 1664 and was promptly renamed New York. By this time the town had grown well beyond the fort and was contained within the wall crossing the island from the Hudson to the East River [6-1]. Under English rule, expansions were only sporadically determined by regular planning projects.[1] In 1794 the English visitor Jedidiah Morse could still observe the character of the early part of the city: "The most convenient and agreeable part of the city is the Broadway. It begins at a point which is formed by the junction of the Hudson and East rivers, occupies the height of land between them, upon a true meridional line, rises gently to the northward, is near 70 feet wide, adorned, where the fort formerly stood, (which has lately been leveled) with an elegant brick edifice for the accommodation of the governor of the State, and a public walk from the extremity of the point, occupying the ground of the lower

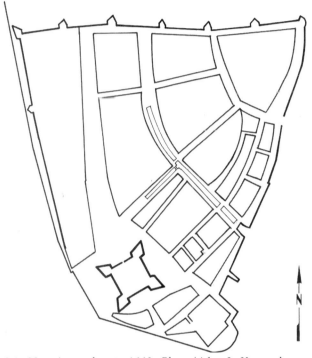

6-1. New Amsterdam in 1660. Plan. (After J. Kouwenhoven, The Columbia Historical Portrait of New York…, Garden City, N.Y., 1953, 41).

battery, which is now demolished [1791]."[2] The southern part or the modern city, then, keeps some of the original features, including the meridian line that was laid out for the benefit of navigation.

In like manner Boston, founded in 1630 and said to have "comly streets" in 1654,[3] was still irregular in plan by the time John Bonner drew his map in 1722 [6-2]. The town had not begun with a fort, but grew from the good harbor, the streets winding about the hilly portions and inlets of the peninsula on which it was located. The principal street from the dock led to the market place, beside which stood the Old Brick Meeting House and the Town House, much as they would have been placed in an English village.[4]

Their predecessors of 1669 and 1657 had been destroyed in the great fire that began October 2, 1711, and to the buildings shown on Bonner's plan we shall later devote some attention. The fire did not, however, result in basic alteration of the pattern of streets, much of which survived into the present century to confound the inhabitants of the Age of Automobiles.

Similarly, the centers of the smaller towns were little changed by the mid-eighteenth century. Alexander Hamilton, writing of New Castle, Delaware, in 1744, said, "The houses are chiefly brick, built after the Dutch modell, the town having been originally founded and inhabited by the Dutch when it belonged to the New York government. It consists chiefly of one great street which makes an elbow at right angles. A great many of the houses are old and crazy. There is in the town two publick buildings, viz., a court house [1676] and a church [1710]."[5] The town had begun at Fort Casimir in 1651 during the days when Governor Peter Stuyvesant at New Amsterdam was pressing Dutch claims against the Swedish settlements on the Delaware. Captured by the Swedes in 1654, it was recaptured in 1655 by Stuyvesant, who laid out streets and named the ensuing town New Amstel. In 1664 it was taken by the British and renamed New Castle.

Under British rule the town flourished, with a brief recapture by the Dutch in 1673. A century later another English traveler reported that "there are scarcely more than a hundred houses in it, and no public buildings that deserve to be taken notice of. The church, Presbyterian and Quaker meeting-houses, court-house and market-house, are almost equally bad, and undeserving of attention."[6] Harsh words, indeed, for a town that now prides itself on the survival of some of those very buildings and the "great street" with the town Green.[7]

In the last years of the seventeenth century there were still extensive lands to be occupied, and four cities were deliberately planned and founded with much more formal purpose than had been exerted in Boston and New York. Charleston, Philadelphia, Annapolis, and Williamsburg all reflect the grand designs of their founders, though in significantly different ways. Charleston began as the principal town of the Carolina Territory, bestowed on eight Lords Proprietors by Charles II in 1663, for which John Locke proposed a feudal system of government which came to nothing. The site for the town was chosen by 1672, however, and a portion of the proposed plan laid out by 1680. In that year Maurice

Mathews commended its regularity in comparison to "the indecent and incommodious irregularities which other English Collonies are fallen unto for want of ane early care in laying out the Townes."[8] His description of four large streets sixty feet wide with a two-acre square in the center for the courthouse is borne out by a plan of 1704 [6-3]. Only the half on the Cooper River side was yet built, and it was surrounded by defenses. Later expansion carried out the remaining part of the original plan, but later buildings on the courthouse square took away that central space.[9] The original plan was conservative, following the Vitruvian model that we have previously noted.

Meanwhile a most important development was taking place in the Middle Atlantic region. Not long after the Restoration William Penn's father lent Charles II £16,000, the indebtedness left owing to the estate when the Admiral died in 1670. Ten years later William Penn requested to be repaid in "a tract of land in America," the grant for which was signed March 4, 1681. Energetic plans for colonization followed, and in September Penn issued his "Instructions…for the Settling of the…Colony."[10] These instructions included choice of site for "navigation, healthy situation, and a good soil for provision," specific instructions for planning a town, and were sent with three commissioners and a contingent of settlers to what is now Philadelphia. When Penn followed a year later in October 1682, having landed first at New Castle, he found the section of land beside the Delaware partly

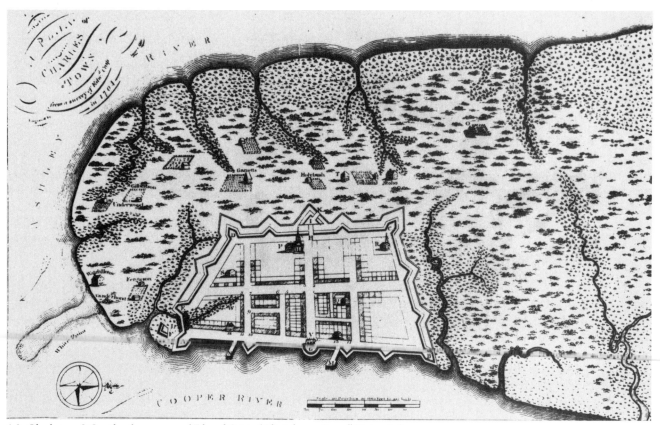

6-3. *Charleston, S.C., plan from survey of Edward Crisp. (Olin Library, Cornell University).*

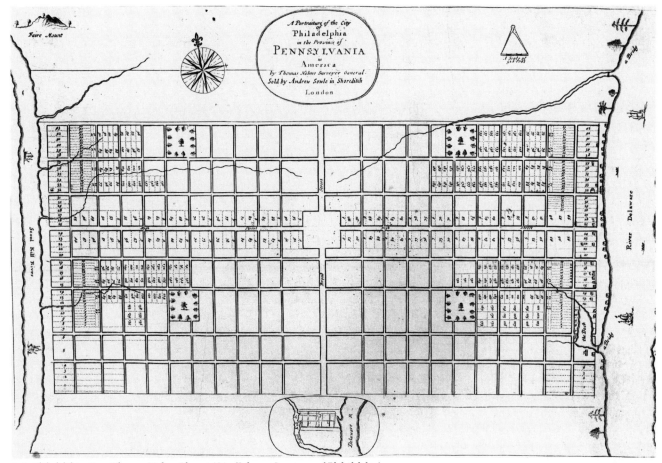

6-4. *Philadelphia, Pa., Thomas Holme Plan, 1683. (Library Company of Philadelphia).*

built and proceeded to have the rest laid out to the banks of the Schuylkill.[11] He had earlier sent Captain Thomas Holme as Surveyor General of Pennsylvania, who in 1683 published his famous description and plan of the new city [6-4].[12]

Holme wrote that the city "hath a Front to each River...the least hath room enough for House, Garden and small Orchard, to the great Content and Satisfaction of all here concerned....In the Center of the City is a Square of ten Acres; at each angle are to be Houses for Publick Affairs, as a Meeting-House, Assembly or State-House, Market-House, School-House, and several other Buildings for Publick Concerns." Later modifications included moving Broad Street to higher ground two blocks west and diminishing the four park squares. Furthermore, as early as 1698 additional streets were beginning to turn the "green country town" that Penn had proposed in his "Instructions" to a far more crowded city.[13]

With the memory of London's great fire in 1666, Penn had wanted ground for planting gardens or orchards on either side of each house, so that the town "will never be burnt, and always be wholesome."[14] To this extent Penn's idea differed from the Vitruvian plan as proposed for Charleston. It is unlikely that Penn

had any more theoretical source for his house-lot instructions, since what he described was the familiar English Cottage garden. Nor was this idea unprecedented in the English colonies. In 1660 Samuel Maverick said that in Newbury, Massachusetts, "The houses stand at a good distance each from the other, a field and a garden between each house, and so on both sides the street for four miles or thereabouts."[15] Penn's contribution was to incorporate such lot planning into a formal urban proposal.

Philadelphia was founded as a result of a financial settlement between Penn and the Crown. A different set of circumstances brought about the moving of the capital of the Maryland colony from St. Mary's City to the then Anne Arundel Town in 1693. Maryland had in fact become a royal province rather than a proprietary colony in 1691 as a result of disputes following the Revolution of 1688. Lord Baltimore, proprietor and governor, was a Catholic, and although measures of religious tolerance had been developed in the colony, his tenure could not survive the anti-Popish sentiments of the late 1680s.

Sir Francis Nicholson was appointed governor in 1691, and he brought about the new location of the capital on the grounds of better accessibility, and convenient excuse for removing the seat of government from strongly Catholic St. Mary's City.[16] An Act of October 11, 1694, designated Anne Arundel Town as the new capital, with the name changed to Annapolis to honor Princess Anne on May 18, 1695.[17]

What had been a modest village was now given a new layout with diagonal streets leading from a "Public Circle" and a "Church Circle," with "Bloomsbury Square" as a third large open space, planned but not carried out [6-5].[18] The author of this plan, known from the drawing of 1718, is uncertain, but Nicholson was probably the one most responsible. He was undoubtedly acquainted with the plans for the rebuilding of London after 1666, and he could have consulted Wren while in London in 1691, the English architect then holding the position of Royal Surveyor. As the first attempt to build a Baroque city in America this gallant effort did not result in a fully workable system of plazas and vistas. Not even the east-west axis of St. Anne's Church is in line with West Street, although this comment is offered with caution, since the present building dates from 1839. Whether the pattern formed by Main, Duke of Gloucester, and Green Streets was intended to honor the princess with an "A" is also a matter of conjecture.

We may suspect that the topography of Anne Arundel Town led the planner of Annapolis to this Baroque approach rather than to adopt the more traditional grid plan for new settlements. The land between the Delaware and the Schuylkill was comparatively flat, and the original intention to have Philadelphia develop evenly across it almost dictated a grid plan. At Anne Arundel Town, however, a hill rose sharply from the harbor, providing inviting sites for State House and church. Now that long straight streets were fashionable, it is not surprising that these were used rather than the meandering streets that wound among the hills of Boston in the 1630s.

With this possibility in mind we can follow Nicholson to his next governorship, that of Virginia in 1698. The Fourth State House at Jamestown burned in October 1698, shortly before his arrival, and he seized the opportunity to move the capital to Middle Plantation.[19] The "Act directing the building the Capitoll and the City of Williamsburg" was resolved by the House of Burgesses on June 7, 1699. The site was attractive because it was deemed to be "healthy, and agreeable to the constitutions of the inhabitants of this his majesty's colony," and because the College was already there. Support for the idea of a symbolic "A" in the plan of Annapolis comes from the assertion of at least two writers by 1724 that Nicholson's original plan for the city included "W" in honor of King William.[20] This was not carried out, however, the present arrangement of streets being planned under Governor Alexander Spotswood in 1712.[21]

If we look at the map drawn by a French army officer in 1782, we can see the nature of the site, which for the town itself consisted of 200 acres on a neck of land between the York and James Rivers [6-6]. With the College already built and the purpose of the new town unmistakable, it was logical to lay out a principal street from the College to a balancing site, for the

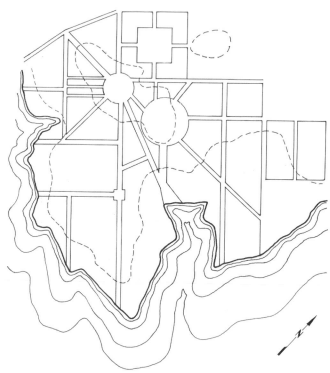

6-5. Annapolis, Md., plan of 1718. (After J. Reps, Town Planning in Frontier America).

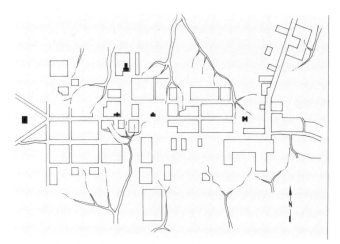

6-6. Williamsburg, Va., plan of 1782. (After M. Whiffen, The Public Buildings of Williamsburg..., Williamsburg, Va., 1956, Fig. 2).

Capitol, along the comparatively narrow strip between the tributaries of the two rivers. The major public services of the ordinary English town, the market place and the church, could be centrally located. Then the Governor's Palace could be set off like a manor house, with the avenue off the Palace Green leading to it at right angles from the principal, or Duke of Gloucester Street. An orderly town was thereby achieved, the key buildings within easy walking distance of each other. Vistas of College, Capitol, and Palace were provided. The church, built in 1683, was

6-7. *Nelson-Galt house, Williamsburg, Va., c. 1709. (Courtesy of Colonial Williamsburg).*

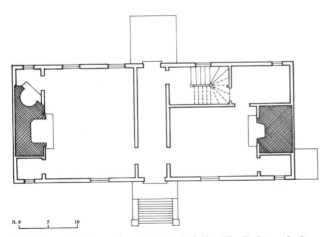

6-8. *Nelson-Galt house, plan. (After M. Whiffen,* The Eighteenth-Century Houses of Williamsburg, *Williamsburg, 1984, Fig. 41).*

already in place just northwest of the present building, and may well have helped to determine the village-like plan. It was located beside one of the larger areas that were not interrupted by the tributary streams. The plan of 1782 shows how these streams made it impossible to carry out a full grid plan in 1712.

Williamsburg, then, in the middle of this transitional period, was planned with several elements at work: the English village, the Vitruvian grid city, and the Baroque vista. Had it remained the state capital, a century and a half of growth would undoubtedly have altered its character. As it was, a second removal of the capital, this time to Richmond in 1780, caused the town to lapse into comparative obscurity until its revival as a museum village in the 1930s.[22]

SOME OF THE HOUSE TYPES developed in the colonies in the seventeenth century survived well into the eighteenth century. Because of its fall from prominence, Williamsburg retained a number of its eighteenth-century houses, two of which may be

6-9. *Bracken house, Williamsburg, Va., c. 1760-1770. (Courtesy of Colonial Williamsburg).*

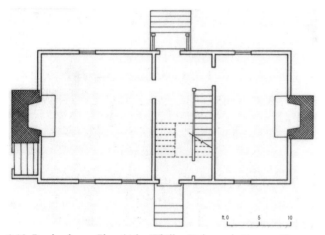

6-10. *Bracken house. Plan. (After Whiffen,* Eighteenth-Century Houses, *Fig. 6).*

chosen to illustrate the case in the Southern colonies.[23] Among the more recent restorations is that of the Nelson-Galt house in 1951-1953 [6-7 and 6-8].[24] As done elsewhere, the Act of 1699 specified location and dimensions of the house that were required for the holding of one's lot, and these were modified in 1705. Because it stands behind the building line on Francis Street, which was not affected by that part of the law in 1705, the house is believed to have been built shortly after the deed of the lot in 1707. It is eight feet longer than the stipulated twenty by forty, perhaps because of framing in the end chimneys. These were normally left open in such story-and-a-half houses. The central hall plan that was used for the Rolfe house appears here, although there is some reason to believe that the Nelson-Galt house may have been first built on a hall-and-parlor plan like that of the Adam Thoroughgood house. This is the important survival, the two-room, end-chimney house, in which the details of windows, panels, door frames, etc., were provided in the current mode.

By this time the pedimented doorway, sash windows[25] with panelled shutters, modillioned cornice, and dormer windows were common features. For the persistence of these plans and details over a considerable span of time it is instructive to compare the elevation and plan of the Nelson-Galt house with those of the Bracken house, built c. 1760-1770 [6-9 and 6-10].[26] Both even have the same proportion of the height of the walls equaling that of the roofs. For centuries, in the days before central heating and indoor plumbing, this kind of small English house had proved to be a convenient and workable shelter, comfortably adaptable to conditions in the Southern colonies.

Building traditions also continued strong in New England, a good surviving example being the Parson Barnard house at North Andover, Massachusetts, of c. 1715 [6-11].[27] Here is the central chimney more favored in the New England colonies, with a lean-to projecting to the rear. The original building of the Hyland house in Guilford, Connecticut, c. 1720, was also a hall-and-parlor house with a central chimney [6-12 and 6-13].[28] The Hyland house originally had a hewn overhang on all four sides, notable for finely carved detail.

THE ENGLISH COLONISTS, then, once settled, were content to build their homes for many years according to familiar methods, with modifications to suit their new locations. In the Middle Atlantic colonies by the second decade of the eighteenth century the population included English colonists but was also strong in Dutch, Swedish, and German settlers. In the wide area that the Dutch had once commanded, a lone survivor at New Castle, Delaware, built at the end of the seventeenth century, shows the small Dutch house still in use long after the takeover by the English [6-14].[29] The ground floor of the Old Dutch house has brick walls, with timber for the upper half-story. Within are two rooms below, with a central chimney and the stair closed off. The eave projects along the front, the ridge is parallel to the street. At the time of its construction, New Castle must have looked much like the little village sketched by Cornelis Cort. [See 4-23.]

Later, in 1738, Leendert Bronck built his new brick house next to the stone house built by his grandfather, Pieter Bronck, in West Coxsackie, New York, about 1663 [6-15].[30] The Leendert Bronck house is one-and-one-half stories high, with an attic above provided with granary doors. There is a room on either side of the central chimney, each opening directly onto the street. The brick is laid in English bond, with the "mousetooth" pattern along the gable ends. On the interior the lower-story ceiling beams are exposed, as are the curved braces. The characteristic cupboard bed in the south room is the type noted by Alexander Hamilton in 1744: "They have their beds generally in alcoves so that you may go thro all the rooms of a great house and see never a bed."[31]

For the houses of this period in Philadelphia the situation was different. Here the city was newly planned, primarily as a refuge for English Quakers. William Penn at one point held some

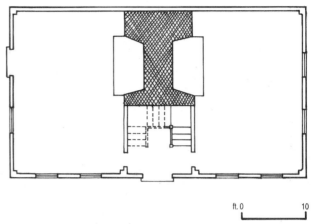

6-13. Hyland house. Plan. (After Isham and Brown, Early Connecticut Houses, 147).

6-11. Parson Barnard house, North Andover, Mass., c. 1715. (SPNEA).

6-12. Hyland house, Guilford, Conn., c. 1720. (Photo: M. C. Donnelly).

interests in East and West Jersey, but in any event there were already strong settlements of Dutch, Finns, and Swedes on both sides of the Delaware, virtually surrounding the site laid out by Thomas Holme. Penn arrived in 1682 and returned to London in 1684. In the same year was issued "Information and Directions to Such Persons as are inclined to America, more Especially Those related to the Province of Pennsylvania."[32] This proposed that a settler should build "a House of thirty foot long and eighteen broad, with a partition neer the middle, and an other to divide one end of the House into two small Rooms."

The Letitia Street house in Philadelphia, now re-erected in Fairmount Park, belongs to this early period [6-16 and 6-17].[33] Because of its corner chimneys it has been classed as having a "Swedish" plan similar to that described in Chapter Four.[34] It was, however, built as a town house such as those illustrated in Moxon's *Mechanick Exercises* [6-18 and 6-19].[35] The rear room or kitchen, added apparently after the main house, was not included in the re-building, though Waterman included it on his plan. A drawing of 1825 shows the house in its original location and with the entrance to one side rather than in the center.[36]

While the Letitia Street house has been moved, the Betsy Ross house of c. 1700 remains on its original site [6-20].[37] It is narrower, with the door on the right and only one window in the first level. Both houses have the now-common sash windows, generously proportioned shutters, and broad cornices characteristic of the Philadelphia area. The Betsy Ross house also has the "pent eave" across the front, a survival of a European practice designed to help shed rain away from the walls.[38]

Neither of these houses surviving from the early period of building in Philadelphia appears to have been built according to the Instructions, and how widely they were applied is difficult to determine. One question is still unanswered. As early as the first reprint of the Instructions in 1880 skepticism was expressed about an attribution to William Penn. Although they were surely published at his behest, he was not a carpenter or mason, and if he didn't write them, who did? The author was certainly knowledgeable about house carpentry and able to furnish practical directions. If a plan is drawn according to the Instructions and compared with the two plans illustrated by Moxon in his sections on "Carpentry" and "Bricklaying," the similarities are suggestive [6-21]. Moxon and Penn were both Fellows of the Royal Society of London, having been elected the one in 1678 and the other in 1681. They may or may not have been acquainted through this distinguished association. The truth of the matter may never be known, but it is difficult to escape the conclusion that a leading English writer on carpentry prepared instructions specifically for use by settlers in the New World.

To turn to the larger houses of this period, we can find several examples illustrating the changes that were taking place as well as the ideas that persisted. We have already given some thought to the plan and site of Bacon's Castle, and now we should look more closely at the house itself [6-22].[39] It was built 1664-1665 by the planter Arthur Allen and takes its name from

6-14. *Old Dutch house, New Castle, Del., late-seventeenth century.* (Photo: M. C. Donnelly).

6-16. *Letitia Street house, Philadelphia, Pa., c. 1715. Perspective drawing.* (Courtesy of Historical Society of Pennsylvania).

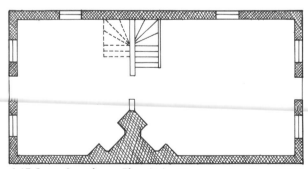

6-17. *Letitia Street house. Plan.* (After Waterman, Dwellings, 129.)

6-15. *Leendert Bronck house, West Coxsackie, N.Y., c. 1738. (Photo: M. C. Donnelly).*

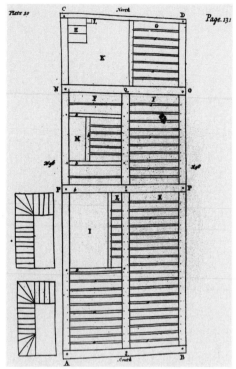

6-18. "The Draft of a Foundation." (From Moxon, Mechanick Exercises, "Carpenter's Work." Plate 10).

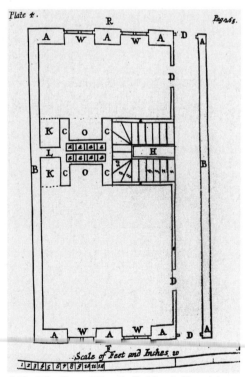

6-19. "The Ground Plat of a Building." (From Moxon, Mechanick Exercises, "Bricklayer's Work." Plate 4).

6-20. Betsy Ross house, Philadelphia, Pa., c. 1700. (Photo: M. C. Donnelly).

having been seized as a strong-hold by the rebellious Nathaniel Bacon in 1676. This is in itself an indication of the place it held as a large, two-story brick building in an area of predominantly framed houses. The building has undergone a number of changes, notably the loss of the pediment over the original porch door and alteration of the windows on the exterior. The interior paneling was also changed, and by 1970 the whole structure had deteriorated to the point where a major conservation program was necessary. More recently some indications of the original formal gardens have been discovered.

The most remarkable features of Bacon's Castle are the curvilinear gables, above which rise diagonally placed chimneys [6-23]. Much has been made of the "medieval" character of these gables, but they should probably be more properly regarded as "early Renaissance." Netherlandish Renaissance gables such as

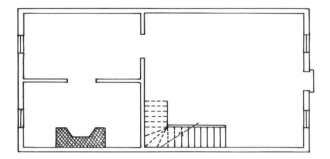

6-21. Conjectural plan of a Philadelphia town house, based on Moxon. (After M. C. Donnelly).

these had long since been adopted in England, and it is not at all surprising that Arthur Allen should have chosen them for his Virginia manor house [6-24].[40] It would be better to restrict the term "medieval" to those buildings which manifest unmistakably Romanesque or Gothic rather than clearly later stylistic features. Allen arrived in Virginia in 1649, more than twenty years after Inigo Jones had introduced the Palladian version of Renaissance style in England, but before the new taste had spread much beyond London. To one of Allen's means, a Netherlandish gable was still a fashionable embellishment.

The same choice was made by Peter Sergeant for his house in Boston, completed in 1679 [6-25].[41] The illustration shows the house as rebuilt with the roof altered in 1728, but in the course of demolition in 1922 it was discovered that here too there had originally been curved gables and perhaps even diagonally set

6-22. Arthur Allen house, "Bacon's Castle," Surry Co., Va., 1664-1665. (Photo: M. C. Donnelly).

6-23. *Arthur Allen house, "Bacon's Castle." Detail of chimney stack. (Photo: M. C. Donnelly).*

6-24. *House at Ludham, Norfolk, seventeenth century. A good provincial example of curvilinear Netherlandish gables. (Photo: M. C. Donnelly).*

6-25. *Peter Sergeant house, Boston, Mass., 1676-1679. Drawing shows house as modified in 1728. (From J. Winsor,* The Memorial History of Boston, *Boston, 1880-81, 2:89).*

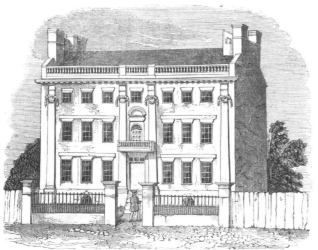

6-26. *Foster-Hutchinson house, Boston, Mass., c. 1688. (From American Magazine, 1836; courtesy of the University of Oregon Library).*

6-27. *Nicholas Stone, Lindsey house, London, England, 1640. (National Monuments Record).*

chimney shaftes.[42] At first it was two stories high and two rooms deep, like the Tufts house in Medford of 1675. The famous description in Hawthorne's *Twice Told Tales* of 1837 is mainly concerned with its state then as a boarding-house, but the staircase was little altered: "The great staircase, however, may be termed, without much hyperbole, a feature of grandeur and magnificence. It winds up through the midst of the house by flights of broad steps, each flight terminating in a square landing place, whence the ascent is continued toward the cupola. A carved balustrade, freshly painted in the lower stories, but growing dingier as we ascend, borders the staircase with its quaintly twisted and intertwined pillars, from top to bottom."[43]

From this description of the staircase we can see that the Tufts and Sergeant houses had, by the 1670s, the elements of the so-called "Georgian plan" or "double pile plan," that was to dominate house design in the English colonies for over a century. A typical house would be two stories high, with a central door leading into a staircase hall. The two sets of rooms on either side of the hall would be furnished with two sets of chimneys, either built at each end of the house or built dividing the front and rear rooms. As a convenient dwelling for its time, such a house only remained to be clad in what fashion might suggest for its exterior and interior finish.

A marked change from early Netherlandish Renaissance ornamental schemes appeared a decade later at the Foster-Hutchinson house in Boston, 1689-1692 [6-26].[44] If a seventeenth-century facade with giant Ionic pilasters seems startling, the century was, after all, drawing to a close. This motif had been used on Lindsey house in London, perhaps attributable to Nicholas Stone, c. 1640, and it was by no means exceptional [6-27].[45] The illustration was published in 1836, three years after the house was demolished. While it was still standing, in 1828, a Boston historian published an account written by a British officer who had witnessed a riotous attack upon the house in 1765:

> As for the house which from the structure and inside finishing seems to be from a design of Inigo Jones or his successors, it appears they were a long time resolved to level it to the ground. They worked three hours at the cupola before they could get it down, and they uncovered part of the roof; but I suppose, that the thickness of the walls, which were of very fine brick-work, adorned with Ionic pilasters worked into the wall, prevented their completing their purpose.[46]

The "Ionic pilasters worked into the wall" were probably original and not applied at the time of repairs after a fire in 1748. As for the reference to Inigo Jones, the officer reporting the riot could well have been one of those eighteenth-century gentlemen priding himself on knowledge of architecture and possessing one or more of the publications then emerging. Lindsey house in London is

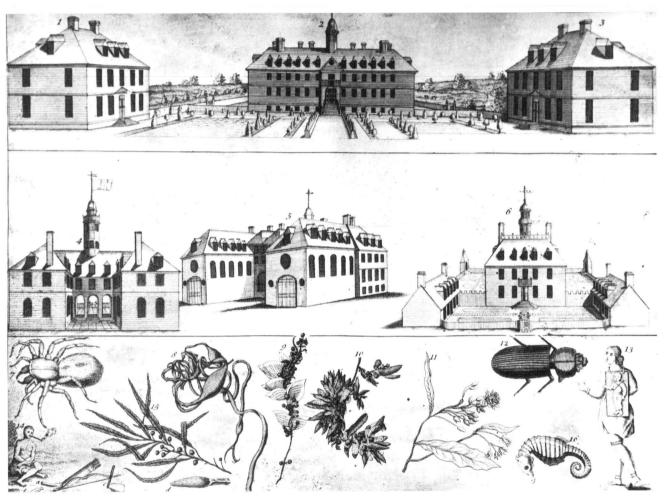

6-30. The "Bodleian Plate," engraved c. 1737. This engraving (given the name of the library wherein it was discovered) was originally prepared for a projected history of the Virginia colony; it shows (top) the College of William & Mary, (middle) two views of the Capitol, view of the Governor's Palace, (bottom) Virginia flora and fauna. (Courtesy of Colonial Williamsburg).

6-28. *Governor's Palace, Williamsburg, Va., 1706-1709. As reconstructed 1931-1934 (Photo: M. C. Donnelly).*

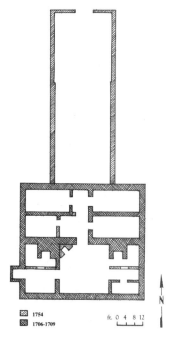

6-29. *Governor's Palace, Williamsburg, Va. Plan. (After Whiffen, Public Buildings, Figs. 15 and 16).*

included in *Vitruvius Britannicus*, and is probably the closest English parallel to the Foster-Hutchinson house.[47] Hawthorne's reference to the "twisted and intertwined pillars," or balusters, is also interesting. These were probably the spiral type that became popular in the eighteenth century and for which Moxon had given instructions in his publication of 1680.[48]

We have, then, a house built according to a marked change in fashion nearly a quarter of a century before the far more conservative Parson Barnard house a few miles away in North Andover. There is another aspect of the Foster-Hutchinson house, however, that should also be considered, and that is its possible relation to Dutch models. As Whiffen has pointed out, the garlanded pilaster capitals had appeared on Dutch houses earlier in the century.[49] If Stone was indeed the builder of Lindsey house, these capitals would have been familiar to him from his work in Amsterdam before 1613.[50] It seems therefore appropriate to avoid calling the Foster-Hutchinson house "Georgian" and instead to regard it as representing the second stage of Netherlandish fashion in the English colonies, perpetuating the mid-seventeenth-century style known as "Dutch Palladianism."

To pursue the idea of strong Dutch influence in this transitional period we may turn to the problems of the Governor's Palace in Williamsburg, built in 1706-1709, burned in 1781, demolished, and reconstructed from the ground up in 1931-1934.[51] The building we see today has the virtue of showing something of what the end of Palace Green looked like throughout most of the eighteenth century [6-28 and 6-29]. But it also has the limita-

tions of being constructed from modern materials and being at best an educated guess.

However much guesswork may have been involved, the reconstruction of the Governor's Palace was not undertaken without some knowledge of the original building. The Act of 1706 which authorized building a house for the Governor of the colony stipulated that "...the said house be built of brick, fifty-four foot in length, and forty-eight foot in breadth, from inside to inside, two story high with convenient cellars underneath, and one vault, sash windows, of sash, glass and a covering of stone slate."[52]

Henry Cary, who had already worked on the Capitol (which shall be considered later), was appointed overseer, and it was evidently he who designed the building according to the specifications. The site was excavated in 1930-1932, revealing much of the foundations, and further information was provided by a plan drawn by Thomas Jefferson. Finally, the Palace was represented in the famous "Bodleian" engraved view of Williamsburg [6-30].[53]

From all this we can see that the Palace was essentially a manor house, set back behind a fence, with one-and-one-half story buildings flanking the front garden. The house itself was brick, two-and-one-half stories high, a double pile in plan, with two chimney stacks, a balustraded roof deck, and a cupola. The ballroom and supper room wing on the north was added probably in 1754. There are some questions about the internal disposition of the rooms, which remaining accounts for payments and verbal descriptions do not entirely clarify. More than one view has been advanced as to the source of design for the Palace, whether published Dutch models, established English manor house types, or the "Governor's Castle" at St. Mary's City, Maryland, which had recently been demolished in 1694.[54]

Looking at these two grand houses, one in Boston and one in Williamsburg, we might well ask whether the accession of William III intensified taste for Dutch fashions among the comparatively wealthy in England and the colonies. As can be seen from the Parson Barnard and Hyland houses that were built later, the Dutch Palladian style certainly did not sweep the colonies. With such a variety of building types undertaken simultaneously it would perhaps be well to avoid searching for a comprehensive stylistic designation for these years.

A SIMILAR VARIETY of approaches to public buildings and churches becomes apparent when several examples of each are reviewed in chronological rather than geographical order. What happened at Annapolis is a case in point. The Act of 1694 that provided for the removal of the capital from St. Mary's City also gave instruction for a "Court House" which "Shall be Forty six foot in length, from Inside to Inside, and Twenty two foot wide from Inside to Inside, Brickwork two story high."[55] Further instructions are given for the roof, porches, the various rooms, and the materials. Colonel Casparus Herman was employed to oversee the construction. The building was completed by May, 1698, damaged by lightning a year later, and burned to the ground in October 1704. From the documentary descriptions, however, a conjectural drawing has been made [6-31]. This shows a two-story brick building, on a stone foundation, with a two-story porch, hipped roof, cupola, and end chimneys. The Assembly Room was on the ground level, with chambers for the jury, clerks, committees, and records above. Nothing remains to give any details of ornament or finish. Enough is known to show that the State House, as it soon came to be called, strongly resembled the previous State House in St. Mary's City of 1674 [5-4], and the Annapolis building was probably based on the former. Again the appearance was basically that of a large manor house.

Two years after the beginning of the Annapolis State House, in 1699, a new City Hall was begun in New York [6-32].[56] It was a two-story brick building with hipped roof and cupola and

6-31. *First Maryland State House, Annapolis, Md., 1697. Conjectural restoration drawing. (Annapolis, Hall of Records Commission).*

question must be raised as to the reason for such a comparatively sophisticated design in New York. References to Sir Christopher Wren's designs of the 1680s and 1690s do not seem appropriate,

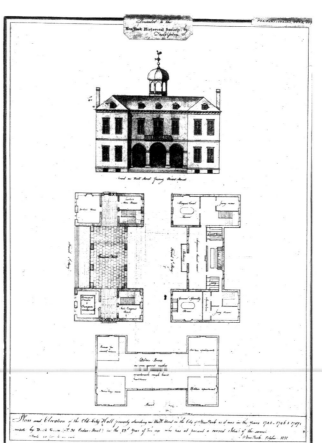

6-32. *City Hall, New York, N.Y., 1699-1700. (Courtesy of the New York Historical Society).*

end chimneys. The three central bays were setback, with an arcade at the ground level and a central balcony above. Inside were a council chamber and court room, a jury room, offices and committee rooms, and a prison in the basement. It resembled nothing so much as Somerset House in London, built 1547-1552, and after 1649 used as a residence for government officials [6-33].[57] Abbreviated, to be sure, but the connection seems unmistakable. The new City Hall in New York was clearly quite different from the State House in Annapolis, and the

for at New York there was not the two- or three-story portico contrasting with the ranks of windows that mark his designs for Hampton Court, Chelsea, and Greenwich.

SINCE IT IS PROBABLE that the builders of a new City Hall in New York would have looked to England for assistance, other likely sources of help should be investigated. One possibility is the office of William Talman (1650-1720), who became Comptroller of the Works in 1689.[58] Had the colonists appealed for help to the then Secretary of State, William Blathwayt, they might well have been referred to Talman, who was then working on Blathwayt's estate at Dyrham Park, Gloucestershire.[59] A west wing had just been completed by a French Huguenot architect, Samuel Hauduroy, who had included a second-story balcony over three bays on the ground level [6-34]. William Talman's

6-33. Somerset house, London, England, 1547-1552. Aquatint after W. Moss. (Courtesy of the British Museum, Crace Collection).

6-34. William Talman, Dyrham Park (William Blathwayt house), Gloucestershire, 1692. West range. (National Monuments Record).

6-35. *Dyrham Park. Greenhouse, 1701. (National Monuments Record).*

6-36. *Capitol, Williamsburg, Va., 1701-1705. As reconstructed 1928-1934. (Photo: M. C. Donnelly).*

greenhouse, completed in 1701, combined heavy window arcades with Tuscan pilasters [6-35]. When such details are put together with the general scheme of the Somerset House courtyard, we may speculate whether William Talman's office had provided suggestions for the City Hall in New York in 1699.

Even more enigmatic is the Capitol at Williamsburg, for which authorization was enacted in April, 1699 [6-36 and 6-37].[60] Like the Governor's Palace, the structure on the site today is a total reconstruction of the 1930s.

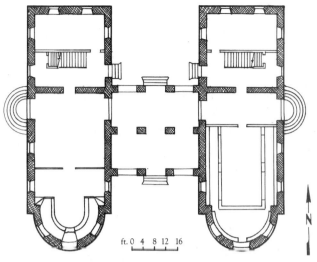

6-37. Capitol, Williamsburg. Plan. (After Whiffen, Public Buildings, Fig. 10).

The original capitol was ready for use in April 1703. It suffered heavily in a fire in 1747 and was rebuilt from the ground up in 1751 largely following the original. After the removal of the capital to Richmond in 1779 the west wing was demolished in 1793, and the east wing burned in 1832, necessitating its demolition.[61] An academy was then built over the foundations, this being demolished in 1881. Specifications in the various Acts for its original construction, the excavated foundations, and the representation on the "Bodleian Plate" formed the basis for the reconstruction, although the academic training of the restoration architects led to errors in rebuilding with the imposition of certain concepts of turn-of-the-century Beaux-Arts symmetry.[62] Again the details of finishing the interiors had to be derived from contemporary examples. Linked by an open "piazza," the east wing housed the House of Burgesses and the west wing the General Court. On the second level a conference room over the piazza lay between committee rooms on the east and the Council Chamber on the west.

The Capitol was unique in its design, and no firm attribution has been brought forward as to its designer. It was also the first building in the colonies to have the title. The role that Sir Francis Nicholson may have played in planning the building is uncertain. He became Governor of Virginia in 1698, just after the building of the State House in Annapolis,

which was a traditional and quite different building. For the second time William Talman's office might be considered, since the Capitol with two wings linked by an arcade and crowned by a cupola was in its program much like the new City Hall in New York. When the "Bodleian Plate" view of the Capitol is compared with the drawing of the City Hall, the similarities are striking indeed. These two buildings seem to set forth a new concept for a house of assembly.

By contrast, when the recently finished State House in Annapolis burned in 1704, it was rebuilt using what was left of the original walls and foundations.[63] Here too there can be only conjecture as to its appearance [6-38]. Economy seems to have dictated the essential repetition of the earlier building. Rooms for the Assembly were on the upper floor. By 1770 the building was no longer adequate and in bad repair, and it was taken down.

The last of these early legislative buildings to be considered, and the only one to survive, is the Old State House in Boston, built in 1712 as the successor to the Town House of 1657, which burned in the great fire of October 1711 [6-39]. The complex history of the building has been related elsewhere.[64] For its original state a good deal can be surmised. The designer is unknown, but the builder was William Payne. At the outset it was to be used by the Province (Royal Governor and General Assembly and Council), Suffolk County (Courts), and the Town of Boston (Selectmen), all of whom contributed to the cost of construction. It is built of brick, two stories high, with a cupola "consisting of three stories, finished according to the Tuscan, Dorick, and Ionick orders."[65] The ground level was apparently one large room, "the roof of which is supported all along the middle with a row of wooden pillars about 25 foot high."[66] The height is excessive in this description, being in fact closer to fifteen feet. A fire in 1747 was followed by rebuilding, in which the ground story was kept

6-38. Second Maryland State House, Annapolis, Md., 1705-1707. Conjectural restoration drawing. (Annapolis, Hall of Records Commission).

6-39. *Old State House, Boston, Mass., 1712. (From J. Winsor, Memorial History of Boston, 1880-1881, 2:507).*

6-40. *Dutch Reformed Church, Bushwick, N.Y., c. 1708-1711. (Long Island Historical Society).*

A VIEW OF THE LATE PROTESTANT DUTCH CHURCH in the CITY of ALBANY

6-41. *Dutch Reformed Church, Albany, N.Y., 1715. (Albany, Institute of History and Art).*

"always open, design'd as a Change," according to a description written in 1748.[67] The later description by Thomas Pemberton states that the lower floor served as a "covered walk for any of the inhabitants" and that on it were "ten pillars of the Dorick order, which support the chambers occupied by the legislature."[68]

A decade later this space was partitioned off into small shops, but the ten Doric columns fit in with the ten trusses supporting the roof. With Council Chamber, Representatives Chamber, and Court Chamber above the Exchange, the State House was in effect an extension of the English market hall tradition. But now in brick, with all the embellishments of stringcourse, sash windows, octagonal cupola, and east balcony facing down King Street toward the Long Wharf, it was a much grander building, as befitted the growing prosperity of the city. The present cupola and segmental headed balcony door, along with other details, belong to the 1748 rebuilding.

In this transitional period the churches built in the Middle Colonies by the Dutch and Swedes were among the most conservative. For the former there is the example of the Dutch Church

at Bushwick, Long Island [6-40].[69] It appears to have been built about 1708, and perpetuated the octagonal plan favored by the Dutch. If the painting is at all a correct representation, the little building of stone had a large arched window in each side, a steep roof, and open belfry. Then in Albany, New York, in 1715 a new church was built around the blockhouse church of 1656, "interrupting services for only two weeks in October while the inner walls were being torn out" [6-41].[70] This was a large square building, with entrance porch, pyramidal roof, and belfry. Doors and windows on the porch are depicted in different arrangements in different early views, but the brick mullions dividing the tall windows are consistently represented. Neither building of these two Dutch congregations is still standing, but these early views show that for them a centralized church with steep roof and belfry was still desirable.

The Dutch had, after all, a tradition of hexagonal or octagonal churches in Holland. In Sweden, on the other hand, the nave-and-chancel or simple rectangular plans had generally been the rule in parish churches. Two churches built by Swedish congregations perpetuate this type in America, both still standing. The first is the Old Swedes Church, Gloria Dei, in Philadelphia, begun in 1697 [6-42].[71] As first built, of brick laid in Flemish bond, it was simply a rectangular building with the sanctuary marked off by slanting in the north and south walls, the pulpit and altar placed against the shortened east wall. It was completed in 1700, and evidently not of sturdy enough construction, for by 1703 the heavy timber roof was causing the walls to start spreading. The entrance porch on the south (in the Swedish "vapenhus" or "weapon house" tradition) and the sacristy on the north were added to buttress the walls, and the heavy modillioned cornice was probably added then. The west tower and small belfry came later.

The other church, begun in May 1698 and completed a little over a year later, is Holy Trinity Church in Wilmington, Delaware [6-43].[72] This is built of stone, a plain rectangular building, which also developed problems with walls and roof, buttressing porches being added in 1750-1751. Additional seating was provided by a gallery in 1774, and the brick tower with its wooden belfry was added by William Strickland in 1802. Holy Trinity is arranged with the altar at the east end and the pulpit on the north side. These two buildings are among the earliest of surviving colonial churches, in brick and stone.

By this time there had been important changes in New England, and the Puritan oligarchy was no more. The Charter of the Massachusetts Bay Company was withdrawn in 1684 and a governor appointed over Massachusetts, New Hampshire, Maine, Rhode Island, and Connecticut, with New York and New Jersey added later. Sir Edmund Andros as governor incurred the wrath of his Dominion of New England and was overthrown on the accession of William and Mary in 1688. In 1691 a new charter was issued, creating a royal colony with its governor appointed by the Crown and abolishing church membership as a test for voting privileges. Times had indeed changed. The younger generation of colonists did not need to fear the religious

6-42. Gloria Dei ("Old Swedes Church"), Philadelphia, Pa., 1697-1700. (Photo: M. C. Donnelly).

6-44. King's Chapel (Anglican), Boston, Mass., 1688-89. (From F. W. P. Greenwood, A History of King's Chapel in Boston..., Boston, 1833).

6-43. *Holy Trinity Church, Wilmington, Del., 1698-1699. (Photo: M. C. Donnelly).*

persecutions of earlier in the century, and all but Roman Catholics were protected by the Toleration Act of 1689.

With the withdrawal of the old Charter came the first Anglican church in New England, introduced by Andros and first holding services in the library of the Town House in Boston, using movable pulpit, table, and seats.[73] For a permanent church a contract was drawn up in July 1688, the building being ready in June 1689. This was for a framed church, fifty-four feet long, thirty-six feet wide, and twenty feet high, to be clapboarded, the walls to be filled with brick and sealed with "lime and hair," and then whitewashed. The roof was to be boarded and shingled, with a belfry on the west end of the roof, "ten feet square and twenty feet above ye roofe." The entrance was evidently on the side, for the contract calls for five windows on the front and rear and two windows at the ends. In this first stage the church was simply a large framed structure, much like the meeting houses. The tops of the pews were finished with little balusters, and the pulpit was on the north side.

Queen's Chapel, as it was then called, was doubled in size in 1710, and this was the state of the building as depicted on the Burgis View in 1722 [6-44].[74] The pulpit was moved to be once again near the center of the north side, and the first church organ in New England installed in the west gallery in 1713 (additional galleries were built in 1729). In August 1713 it was voted "that the Pillars, Capitalls and Cornish of the Church be painted wainscot colour, before the scaffold be taken down." A further insight into color comes from the vote of April 29, 1738, "that the Governor's Pew be new lined with China, and that the Cushions and Chairs be covered with Crimson Damask, and the Curtains to the Window be of the same Damask."[75] We may be reminded of the "green velvet chair" in the chapel at Jamestown Fort. "China" at this time and in this context meant a fine watered woolen cloth.

The "housewrights" named in the 1688 contract were Stephen French, John Holebrook, and Jacob Nash, all from Weymouth, where the second meeting house was voted in December 1682. Jacob Nash had been the carpenter for the Weymouth meeting house, and was now hired in Boston.[76] How he was selected we do not know, but his skill in carpentry was apparently more important that his probable Congregational affiliation. The building that he, French, and Holebrook constructed was one of the trio that started Anglican building in New England. Shortly thereafter, a parish was founded in Newport, Rhode Island, with a church building ready for use by September 1702.[77] Records about this church, the first Trinity Church in Newport, are scanty, little being known except that in 1719 there were thirty-five pews.[78] Conjecture about its probable size, shape, and interior arrangement are based on St. Paul's Church, originally built in North Kingston, Rhode Island, in 1707, and moved to its present location in Wickford in 1800 [6-45].[79] This building could pass for a Congregational meeting house with the possible exception of the round-headed windows

6-45. St. Paul's Church (Anglican), Wickford, R.I., 1707. (Photo: M. C. Donnelly).

6-46. *Bruton Parish Church II (Anglican), Williamsburg, Va., 1711-1715. (Photo: M. C. Donnelly).*

in the lower story. These had already made the appearance in late-seventeenth-century English parish churches and were possibly requested by the clergy. The pulpit is opposite the door in St. Paul's and the tops of the pews are closed, as were those of the enlarged Queen's Chapel in Boston.

Conjecture is risky with so little known of the carpenters who built Trinity Church and St. Paul's. Of some possible significance is the building of the meeting house on Tanner Street in Newport for the First Congregational Church in 1696. Newport and nearby North Kingston thus had one or more meeting house carpenters at hand, to serve as did Jacob Nash of Weymouth in Boston. All three Anglican churches differed from the meeting houses primarily in their liturgical vessels and the fitting up of the altars, creed boards, etc. Even the pulpits were in the middle of the north sides. There is then the interesting possibility of the more or less radical meeting house form taken over by the Anglican Church in New England at the time when changes in decorative fashions were overtaking builders of both faiths.

In the middle and southern colonies this period of transition saw only comparatively modest structures built for the Anglican Church. The charter of Trinity Church in New York was signed May 6, 1697, and the contract for a church building

on June 3.[80] By March 1698 the church was ready for services, but little is known of its appearance. It was described in 1790 as having been a "small square edifice," which was enlarged in 1735 and again in 1737 and then destroyed in a great city fire in 1776.[81] The original dimensions are not known, but later records speak of the "south side" and "west end," suggesting not a square but a short rectangle, perhaps something like the New England churches.

One of the most interesting of the Anglican churches to survive is Bruton Parish Church in Williamsburg, begun in 1711 and in use by 1715 [6-46]. An addition to the east end in 1752 and the building of the tower and spire in 1769 brought it to its present size. In its original form it was one of the three cruciform churches in the colonies, and it is considered to be a major example of the use of geometrical systems for its plan and elevation.[82] Hugh Jones described the church as "a large strong piece of brickwork in the form of a cross, nicely regular and convenient, and adorned as the best churches in London."[83]

The design of Bruton Parish Church appears to have been provided by Governor Alexander Spotswood, for according to the report of the minister, James Blair, on March 1, 1711, "...he had received from the Honble. Alexr. Spotswood, a platt or draught of a Church, (whose length is 75 foot, and bredth 28

6-47. Merchant's Hope Church (Anglican), Prince George Co., Va., c. 1715. (Photo: M. C. Donnelly).

foot in the clear, with two wings on each side, whose width is 22 foot) which he Laid before the Vestry for approbation."[84] Since Williamsburg had the special functions of the capital city, paying for the church was divided between the parish (for the nave and chancel) and the colony (for the transepts). Hugh Jones's comment implies greater richness of embellishment than is actually the case. The dignity of the exterior depends on the proportions of the arched windows, the texture of the brick laid in Flemish bond, and the details of the molded brick water table and the modillioned cornice. Restorations in 1903-1907, 1939, and 1930-1942 brought the interior, with its high pulpit on the south chancel wall and the canopied Governor's seat opposite, to its present state of quiet simplicity.

From the several more conventional parish churches built in the southern colonies at this time we may note Merchant's Hope Church in Prince George County, Virginia.[85] [6-47] Built of brick laid in Flemish bond, it measures sixty feet by thirty feet, with no tower, vestry, chancel, or other projection. Although it has been thought to have been built as early as 1657, a date about 1715 seems more likely, especially with the tall round-headed windows. Several changes have been made on the interior, but the original arrangement was probably with the altar at the east end and the pulpit in the middle of the south wall.

Like the Swedish churches at Philadelphia and Wilmington, the Anglican churches of the New England and southern colonies were built to accommodate a Reformed liturgical form of worship. This was not the case with the buildings of the transitional period which were built by the Puritan, now Congregational, churches. The internal arrangement of the traditional seventeenth-century meeting house was still preferred and would in fact remain popular until well after the Revolution. Of the more than eighty such meeting houses built from 1685 to 1720 the most splendid was the "Old Brick Meeting House," the third building of the First Church in Boston [6-48].[86] Built grandly of brick by a wealthy congregation, it rose three stories high in the center of town, opposite the Town House (now the Old State House) of 1712. It was built in 1713, and like the Town House replaced its predecessor, which burned in the fire of October 1711. Measuring seventy-two feet by fifty-four feet, it was the largest house of worship then in New England. Although larger than the late seventeenth-century meeting houses, such as the one at Hingham, it perpetuated their principal features, such as the hipped roof, balustraded deck, and belfry. The town clock was added in 1716, and the meeting house had the first

6-48. First Church, "Old Brick Meeting House", Boston, Mass., 1713. The classical two-story porch was added in the 1760s. (From Winsor, Memorial History of Boston, 2:219).

6-49. First College Building, College of William and Mary, Williamsburg, Va., 1695-1700. Drawing by Francis Michel. (Bern, Stadsbibliothek [Mss.hist.helv.X.152, f. 63ʳ]).

organ ever used in one of the Congregational buildings.[87] It appears on early views and maps of Boston, the Bonner Map of 1722 [see 6-2], and remained an important landmark until the congregation moved to a new site, whereupon "Old Brick" was taken down in 1808.

A T THE TURN OF THE EIGHTEENTH CENTURY pressures were also increasing for more educational opportunity in the English colonies. We have already seen that by the 1670s Harvard College had to be furnished with a new building. In February 1693 a royal charter was signed, granting a college in Virginia to be named for William and Mary.[88] By 1700 the first college building at Williamsburg was complete enough to house the Governor and Council, pending the building of the Capital. 138 feet long, forty-six feet wide, and four stories high, it easily eclipsed Harvard Hall and would have been even grander had three other intended wings been built to complete a quadrangle. Whereas Old Harvard Hall retained a post-medieval appearance with its multiple gables, the first building of William and Mary College was far more formal, with a balustraded porch over the central entrance another on the roof, and dormers on either side of the central tower [6-49]. Use of the building had scarcely begun, however, when it burned on October 29, 1705.

Meanwhile, Stoughton College was built at right angles to Old Harvard Hall in Cambridge in 1698-1699.[89] [See 5-22.] An Indian College had been built in 1654, but the enterprise was not successful, and when the building was demolished in 1698 the bricks were available for the new hall. It was built as a dormitory, with chambers and studies, ninety-eight feet long but only twenty-three feet deep. The Burgis print shows how fashion was changing, for the steep gables and turret of Old Harvard Hall are gone, replaced by dormers. There were quoins at the corners, and the doors were framed by pilasters and segmental pediments. By the time of the Revolution, when like the other Harvard buildings it was used for the quartering of soldiers, it was already deteriorating. It was not reoccupied after the war and was taken down in 1781. For nearly a century, however, the two seventeenth-century buildings showed the close transition between old and new.

Then, after a delay of five years, rebuilding of the College of William and Mary was begun. Portions of the remaining walls and foundations were used, and the second college building was essentially completed by 1716. Our knowledge of it depends on early views and descriptions, for it burned in 1859, was rebuilt, burned again in 1862, rebuilt again, and in 1928-1931 restored to suggest its original state [6-50 and 6-51].[90] From the "Bodleian

6-50. Second College Building ("The Wren Building"), College of William and Mary, Williamsburg, Va., 1710-16. As restored 1928-31. (Photo: M. C. Donnelly).

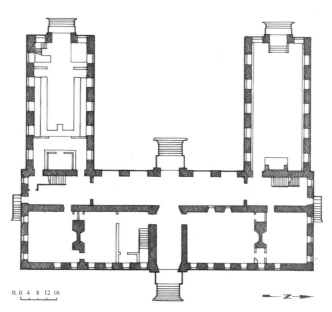

6-51. Second College Building, College of William and Mary. Plan as reconstructed. (After Whiffen, Public Buildings, Fig. 37).

Plate" and a pre-1859 daguerreotype comes the restored elevation, with three stories, central pavilion, dormers, and cupola. The rebuilding of 1710 was done under the direction of Governor Spotswood, who doubtless made use of proportional systems as he had done for Bruton Parish Church.

By this time a third college had been founded in the English colonies, at Saybrook, Connecticut, in 1701. In 1716 New Haven was chosen as a better location and a wooden college building erected there in 1717-1718. As it neared completion a gift from Elihu Yale resulted in the college's being named in his honor.[91] The master builder was Henry Caner, of Bristol, England, who had gone to Boston and had been employed in the enlargement of King's Chapel in 1710. Yale College was 165 feet long and 22 feet deep, and must have been much like an elongated Stoughton College with the addition of a belfry [6-52]. At the south end was the Hall, with library above, and suites and bedrooms that could house more than sixty students. It had been demolished by 1782.

While Yale was finishing her first building, Harvard began yet another, Massachusetts Hall, built 1718-1720 [see 5.22].[92] It too was designed as a dormitory, with chambers and studies for sixty-four students. It has survived as the oldest building at Harvard. It is built of brick, three stories high, and has an attic story under the gambrel roof. Its regular pattern with two entrances, dormers, and chimneys rising behind a balustrade may have been intended to reflect Stoughton College, to which it was placed at right angles. In length and width it was similar to Old Harvard Hall opposite. Old Harvard Hall is thought to have been designed by one of the Overseers, the second college building at William and Mary by Governor Spotswood, Yale College by Governor Saltonstall, and Massachusetts Hall by President Leverett and Benjamin Wadsworth. The time had not yet come when designs for such buildings would be sought from builders in the colonies who regarded themselves as architects. This would become a possibility in the next half century, up to the outbreak of the Revolution.

Notes to Chapter 6

1. John William Reps, *Town Planning in Frontier America* (Columbia, Mo.: University of Missouri Press, 1980), 193-194; The Rev. John Miller, *A Description of the Province and City of New York with Plans of the City and Several Parts as they Existed in the Year 1695* (London: Thomas Rodd, 1843); and John A. Kouwenhoven, *The Columbia Historical Portrait of New York* (New York: Doubleday & Co., 1953).

2. Jedidiah Morse, *The American Geography* (London, 1794), 381.

3. Edward Johnson, *Johnson's Wonder-Working Providence, 1628-1651* (New York: C. Scribner's Sons, 1910), 71.

6-52. *New Haven, Conn., Yale College. 1717-1718. Conjectural drawing. (From E. Oviatt,* Beginnings of Yale (1701-1726), *New Haven, 1926, 354).*

4. Nathaniel B. Shurtleff, *A Topographical and Historical Description of Boston* (Boston: 1871); and Walter M. Whitehill, *Boston, a Topographical History* (Cambridge: Belknap Press of Harvard University Press, 1959), 15-21.

5. Carl Bridenbaugh, ed., *Gentleman's Progress* (Chapel Hill: University of North Carolina, 1948), 12.

6. Andrew Burnaby, *Burnaby's Travels Through North America,* ed. Rufus Rockwell Wilson (New York: A. Wessels Co., 1904), 87.

7. Reps, *Town Planning,* 224-225.

8. Maurice Mathews, "A Contemporary View of Carolina in 1680," *South Carolina Historical Review* 55 (1954): 154.

9. Frederic R. Stevenson and Carl Feiss, "Charleston and Savannah," *JSAH* 10, no. 4 (December 1951): 3-9.

10. "Instructions given by me, William Penn....," in *William Penn and the Founding of Pennsylvania,* ed. Jean R. Soderland (Philadelphia: University of Pennsylvania Press, 1983), 83-85.

11. William Penn, "A Further Account of the Province of Pennsylvania," in Albert Cook Myers, ed., *Narratives of Early Pennsylvania, West New Jersey and Delaware, 1630-1707* (New York: C. Scribner's Sons, 1912), 262.

12. Thomas Holme, "A Short Advertisement upon the Scituation and extent of the City of Philidelphia and the Ensuing Plat-form Thereof," in Myers, ed., *Narratives*, 242-244.

13. Gabriel Thomas, "An Historical and Geographical Account of Pennsylvania and of West New-Jersey," in Myers, ed., *Narratives*, 317.

14. Penn, "Instructions," 85; Reps, *Town Planning*, 204-220; and Hannah B. Roach, "The Planting of Philadelphia, a Seventeenth-Century Real Estate Development," *Pennsylvania Magazine of History and Biography* 92 (1968): 3-47 and 143-194.

15. Samuel Maverick, "A Briefe description of New England and the Several Towns Therein," *Proceedings of the Massachusetts Historical Society* 1, Series 2 (1884-1885), 325.

16. Deering Davis, *Annapolis Houses 1700-1775* (New York: Architectural Book Publishing Company, 1947), 9-10.

17. William H. Browne, ed., *Archives of Maryland* 19 (Baltimore, 1899): 76-80 and 187.

18. Reps, *Town Planning*, 132-137; and, John W. Reps, *Tidewater Towns: City Planning in Colonial Virginia and Maryland* (Williamsburg: Colonial Williamsburg, 1972), 117-140.

19. Marcus Whiffen, *The Public Buildings of Williamsburg* (Williamsburg: Colonial Williamsburg, 1959), 6-15; Reps, *Town Planning*, 137-144.

20. Robert Beverley, *The History and Present State of Virginia*, ed. Louis B. Wright (Chapel Hill: University of North Carolina Press, 1947), 105; and Hugh Jones, *The Present State of Virginia*, ed. Richard L. Morton (Chapel Hill: University of North Carolina Press, 1956 [1724]), 66.

21. Beverley, *History and Present State of Virginia*, 250.

22. Whiffen, *Public Buildings*, 188-208.

23. The definitive work is Marcus Whiffen, *The Eighteenth-Century Houses of Williamsburg* (Williamsburg: Colonial Williamsburg, 1984). For general essays on building materials, crafts, tools, design, and construction, see pages 3-123. These essays include some of the matters already discussed in Chapter 3 and extend the material into the eighteenth century.

24. Ibid., 127-132. See also Paul E. Buchanan, "The Eighteenth-Century Frame Houses of Tidewater Virginia," in Charles E. Peterson, ed., *Building Early America* (Radnor: Chilton Book Company, 1976), 54-73.

25. Whiffen, *Eighteenth-Century Houses*, 107-112. See also Charles F. Montgomery, "Thomas Banister on the New Sash Windows, Boston, 1701," *JSAH* 24, no. 2 (May 1965): 169-170.

26. Whiffen, *Eighteenth-Century Houses*, 203-204.

27. Abbott Lowell Cummings, "The Parson Barnard House," *OTNE*, no. 166 (October-December 1956), 29-40; and Abbott Lowell Cummings, ed., *Architecture in Early New England* (Sturbridge, Mass.: Old Sturbridge Village, 1958), 167-168. Just how strong and conservative building traditions were in sections of New England is well illustrated by the details of the framing of the Whitman house in Farmington, Connecticut, built at the same time as the Parson Barnard house; see Chap. 4, p. 35-36.

28. Norman Morrison Isham and Albert F. Brown, *Early Connecticut Houses: An Historical and Architectural Study* (New York: Dover Publications, 1965 [1900]), 146-148. In *Early Connecticut Houses* the house is identified as the Fiske-Parmelee house.

29. Harold D. Eberlein, *The Architecture of Colonial America*, 2nd ed. (Boston: Little, Brown and Co., 1927), 175-177; and Thomas Waterman, *The Dwellings of Colonial America* (Chapel Hill: University of North Carolina Press, 1950), 117.

30. Helen Wilkinson Reynolds, *Dutch Houses in the Hudson Valley before 1776* (New York: Dover Publications, 1965 [1929]), 68; Hugh Morrison, *Early American Architecture: From the First Colonial Settlement to the National Period* (New York: Dover Publications, 1987 [1952]), 112-114; and Alan Gowans, *Images of American Living: Four Centuries of Architecture and Furniture as Cultural Expression* (Philadelphia: Lippincott, 1964), 46.

31. Bridenbaugh, ed., *Gentleman's Progress*, 72. For a more detailed discussion of the Hudson Valley Dutch houses in the early eighteenth century see Waterman, *Dwellings*, 207-224.

32. "Information and directions formerly given to such persons as went over to settle in America: but particularly to those from England, who first peopled the now flourishing province in Pennsylvania," *Pennsylvania Magazine of History and Biography* 4 (1880): 331-342.

33. George B. Tatum, *Penn's Great Town* (Philadelphia: University of Pennsylvania Press, 1961), 154.

34. Waterman, *Dwellings*, 129-131.

35. Charles Franklin Montgomery, ed., *Joseph Moxon's Mechanick Exercises; or, The Doctrine of Handy-works Applied to the Arts of Smithing, Joinery, Carpentry, Turning, Bricklaying* (London: Praeger, 1970 [1703]), "House Carpenter's Work," Plate 10, and "Bricklayer's Work," Plate 4.

36. Charles E. Peterson kindly called this drawing to my attention.

37. Frank Cousins and Phil M. Riley, *The Colonial Architecture of Philadelphia* (Boston: Little, Brown, and Company, 1920), 51.

38. Waterman, *Dwellings*, 138-141.

39. Thomas Tileston Waterman, *The Mansions of Virginia* (New York: Bonanza Books, 1945), 21-25; Hugh Morrison, *Early American Architecture: From the First Colonial Settlement to the National Period* (New York: Dover Publications, 1987 [1952]), 146-149; Stephenson B. Andrews, *Bacon's Castle* (Richmond: The Association for the Preservation of Virginia Antiquities, 1984 [rev. ed. 2001]), this discusses the history, furnishings, archaeology, and the restoration, with architectural drawings by Stephen A. Smith; and Daniel Reiff, *Small Georgian Houses in England and Virginia: Origins and Development Through the 1750s* (Newark: University of Delaware Press, 1986), 196-200.

40. Henry Russell Hitchcock, *Netherlandish Scrolled Gables of the Sixteenth and Early Seventeenth Centuries* (New York: New York University Press for the College Art Association of America, 1978), 95-98.

41. Nancy Halverson Schless, "The Province House; English and Netherlandish Forms in Gables and Chimneys," *OTNE* 62, no. 4 (Spring 1972): 114-123.

42. William Summer Appleton, "The Province House, 1928," *OTNE* 62, no. 4 (Spring 1972): 88-91.

43. Nathaniel Hawthorne, *Twice Told Tales*, 2 vols. (Boston: Desmond Publishing Co., 1900), 2:3.

44. Abbott Lowell Cummings, "The Foster-Hutchinson House," *OTNE* 54, no. 3 (January-March 1964): 59-76. See also Abbott Lowell Cummings, "The Beginnings of Provincial Renaissance Architecture in Boston, 1690-1725," *JSAH* 42 (March 1983): 43-53.

45. Howard Colvin, *Biographical Dictionary of English Architects*, 2nd ed. (London: John Murray, 1978), 787.

46. Caleb H. Snow, *A History of Boston*, 2nd ed. (Boston: Abel Bowen, 1828), 261.

47. Colin Campbell, *Vitruvius Britannicus*, 3 vols. (London, 1715-1725), Cl. Plate 16.

48. Montgomery, ed., *Joseph Moxon's Mechanick Exercises*, 231.

49. Marcus Whiffen and Frederick Koeper, *American Architecture, 1607-1976* (Cambridge, Mass.: MIT Press, 1981), 12-13.

50. Colvin, *Biographical Dictionary*, 786. Stone had met the Dutch master Hendrik de Keyser in London in 1606, went to Holland to work for him, and married de Keyser's daughter.

51. Whiffen, *Public Buildings*, 53-66, 140-144, and 208; Mark R. Wenger, "Jefferson's designs for remodeling the Governor's Palace," *Winterthur Portfolio* 32, no. 4 (Winter 1997): 223-242; and Reiff, *Small Georgian Houses*, 226-231.

52. Whiffen, *Public Buildings*, 55.

53. A copper plate found in the Rawlinson Collection of the Bodleian Library at Oxford in 1929 proved to be a view of Williamsburg in about 1737. It has been a major source of information for the restoration of the Capitol, the Governor's Palace, and the College (ibid., 205).

54. Nancy Halverson Schless, "Dutch Influence on the Governor's Palace, Williamsburg," *JSAH* 38, no. 4 (December 1969): 254-270; Reiff, *Small Georgian Houses*, 230-231; and, Henry C. Forman, *The Architecture of the Old South: the Medieval Style, 1585-1850* (Cambridge, Mass.: Harvard University Press, 1948), 112. An independent design based on the second and third possibilities seems most likely.

55. Browne, ed., *Archives of Maryland*, 18:23-25. The documents concerning the State House through its destruction are quoted in Morris L. Radoff, *Buildings of the State of Maryland at Annapolis* (Annapolis: Hall of Records Commission, 1954), 1-11.

56. Morrison, *Early American Architecture*, 551.

57. John Summerson, *Architecture in Britain 1530 to 1830* (Baltimore: Penguin Books, 1954), 17-18, 90.

58. Colvin, *Biographical Dictionary*, 803.

59. David Verey, *The Buildings of England: Gloucestershire, 1: The Cotswolds* (Harmondsworth: Penguin Books, 1970), 201.

60. Whiffen, *Public Buildings*, 34-60.

61. Ibid., 190-191.

62. The side entrances should have been centered on the total length of the side wings (including the semi-circular apses) and not simply on the length of the straight portion of the walls. Such a placement would have put the entrances directly in line with the cupola. See Carl Lounsbury, "Beaux-Arts Ideals and Colonial Reality: The Reconstruction of Williamsburg's Capitol, 1928-1934," *JSAH* 44 (December 1990): 373-389. As Lounsbury notes, all three restoration architects — Perry, Shaw, and Hepburn — took architecture degrees at Harvard or MIT (both with Beaux-Arts-based programs) and Perry and Shaw continued study at the Ecole des Beaux-Arts in Paris. The plan in 6-37 shows the building as rebuilt 1928-34, not as it is thought to have been built originally. [Ed.]

63. Radoff, *Buildings of the State of Maryland*, 12-16.

64. Sara B. Chase, "A Brief Survey of the Architectural History of the Old State House, Boston, Massachusetts," *OTNE* 68, nos. 3 and 4 (Winter/Spring 1978): 31-49.

65. Thomas Pemberton, "A Topographical and Historical Description of Boston," *Collections of the Massachusetts Historical Society* 3, series 1 (1974), 250-251.

66. Bridenbaugh, ed., *Gentleman's Progress*, 107.

67. Francis Goelet, "Journal of Capt. Francis Goelet," *New England Historical Genealogical Register* 24 (1870): 62.

68. Pemberton, "Topographical and Historical Description," 250.

69. Maud Esther Dilliard, *An Album of New Netherland* (New York: Bramhall House, 1963), Figure 55.

70. Joel Munsell, *The Annals of Albany*, 10 vols. (Albany: J. Munsell, 1850-1859), 10:194.

71. Harold Wickliffe Rose, *The Colonial Houses of Worship in America* (New York: Hastings House, 1963), 337-338.

72. Ibid., 132-133.

73. Walter Kendall Watkins, "Three contracts for seventeenth-century building construction in Massachusetts," *OTNE* 12 (July 1921): 31-32.

74. Ibid., 72-76.

75. Ibid., 126.

76. Marian C. Donnelly, *The New England Meeting Houses of the Seventeenth Century* (Middletown, Conn.: Wesleyan University Press, 1968), 128. This information comes from a transcript of the Town Records in the office of the Town Clerk, Weymouth.

77. Norman M. Isham, *Trinity Church in Newport, Rhode Island* (Boston: 1936), 15.

78. Ibid., 6.

79. Antoinette Forrester Downing, *Early Homes of Rhode Island* (Richmond, Va.: Garrett and Massie, Inc., 1937), 103-107; Hunter White, *Old St. Paul's in Narragansett* (Wakefield, R.I.: 1957); and, Peter T. Mallary, *New England Churches & Meeting Houses, 1680-1830* (New York: Vendome Press, 1985), 51-55.

80. Morgan Dix, *A History of the Parish of Trinity Church in the City of New York*, 3 vols. (New York: G. P. Putnam's Sons, 1898), 1:108-109.

81. Ibid., 2:136.

82. Whiffen, *Public Buildings*, 77-84.

83. Jones, *Present State of Virginia*, 50.

84. Whiffen, *Public Buildings*, 77.

85. James Scott Rawlings, *Virginia's Colonial Churches* (Richmond: Garrett & Massie, 1963), 27-30; and Rose, *Colonial Houses of Worship*, 462-463.

86. Morrison, *Early American Architecture*, 430.

87. Justin Winsor, *The Memorial History of Boston*, 4 vols. (Boston: James R. Osgood and Company, 1880-1881), 430.

88. Whiffen, *Public Buildings*, 4-6 and 18-33; and, Glenn Patton, "The College of William and Mary, Williamsburg, and the Enlightenment," *JSAH* 29, no. 1 (March 1970): 24-32.

89. Samuel Eliot Morison, *Harvard College in the Seventeenth Century*, 2 vols. (Cambridge, Mass.: Harvard University Press, 1936), 2:518-521; and Bainbridge Bunting, *Harvard: An Architectural History* (Cambridge, Mass.: Belknap Press of Harvard University Press, 1985), 21-22. The designer of Stoughton Hall is not known for certain, but since the building was instrumental in introducing Anglo-Dutch classical ideas in New England, its authorship is of particular interest. Rick Kennedy has suggested that it may have been Thomas Brattle, a mathematics teacher at Harvard who was a member of the building committee, spent time in England, and met with Christopher Wren and his scientific and architectural circle. See Rick Kennedy, "Thomas Brattle, mathematician-architect in the transition of the New England mind, 1690-1700," *Winterthur Portfolio* 24 (Winter 1989): 231-45. [Ed.]

90. Whiffen, *Public Buildings*, 96-107 and 193-196.

91. Edwin Oviatt, *The Beginnings of Yale* (New Haven: Yale University Press, 1926), xxviii-xxix and 356-357; and, George Dudley Seymour, "Henry Cancr, 1680-1731, master carpenter, builder of the first Yale College building, 1718, and of the rector's house, 1722," *OTNE* 15, no. 3 (1925): 99-124.

92. William C. Lane, "The Building of Massachusetts Hall, 1717-1720," *Publications of the Colonial Society of Massachusetts* 24 (1920-1922): 81-110.

7-1. St. Augustine, Fla. Castillo de San Marcos. 1672-1756. Aerial view. (Castillo de San Marcos).

7-3. Louisbourg, N.S. Fortress. 1719-1745. Aerial view. (Fortress of Louisbourg National Historic Park).

⅜ *Chapter 7* ⅝

French and Spanish Building in the Colonial Period

I N THE LAST THREE CHAPTERS we have been following the builders in the English, Dutch, and Swedish colonies during their first century or so of successful settlement in North America. We had left the Spanish and French adventurers in the early years of the seventeenth century, still in exploratory activities. By 1715-1720, however, the Roman Catholic enterprises were surrounding the Protestant colonies, now all under the English crown. Two great forts, the Castillo de San Marcos in the south and Louisbourg in the north, were like brackets at either ends of the English claims, which at best were penetrating about 300 miles inland.

Spain extended her holdings from what is now eastern Texas across New Mexico and Arizona, while France occupied the St. Lawrence and Mississippi valleys. As at the beginning of their explorations, neither country was primarily interested in developing agricultural and commercial communities, and both continued their mission activities, still seeking gold or at least trade in furs. We will look first at the two forts, then at French colonial architecture, and finally at the Spanish missions of Texas and New Mexico.

Since the landing of Ponce de León near St. Augustine in 1513 the Spanish had attempted to protect their trade passing there, having founded a town in 1565, as we have seen [7-1]. It was defended by nine successive wooden forts. Then on May 28, 1668, a raid by the English pirate Captain John Davis woke the Spanish to the growing threat from English expansion southward.[1] In 1669 the Queen Regent Mariana authorized funds to build a new fort of stone, the

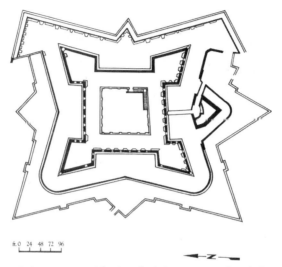

ft.0 24 48 72 96

7-2. St. Augustine, Fla. Castillo de San Marcos. Plan. (After W. B. Robinson, American Forts: Architectural Form and Function, *Urbana, Ill., 1977, fig. 4).*

wisdom of which was soon made even more clear by the founding of Charleston, South Carolina, in 1670. Under Governor Don Manuel de Cendoya, with Ignacio Daza the engineer, work was begun in October 1672 and the first stage completed by 1676.[2] The moat and outerworks were gradually added over the next fifty years [7-1 and 7-2].

Governor Cendoya and Ignacio Daza agreed to follow the plan of the previous wooden fort, and the result was the four-bastioned citadel built of the local coquina limestone. Spaniards, Indians, slaves, and even English prisoners carried out the work. The twenty-five-foot walls are fourteen feet wide at the base and taper to nine feet at the top, with a cordon projecting below the parapet, small lookouts on three bastions, and a larger watchtower on the fourth. Remodeling of the inner courtyard beginning in 1738 added the casements housing the officers' quarters, barracks, the chapel, storage chambers, and a prison. Taken by the British in 1763, retaken by the Spanish in 1783, and ceded to the United States in 1819, the fort became a National Monument in 1921. It is an excellent example of the four-bastioned type of fort popular in Europe in the seventeenth and eighteenth centuries. Daza's engineering principles are thought to have been founded on the designs of the Italian military engineer Frandesco de Marchi.

Castillo de San Marcos was planned too early for its designers to take advantage of the principles of siege and fortification developed by the great French military engineer Sèbastien Le Prestre Vauban (1632-1707).[3] His writings were, however, available when in 1713

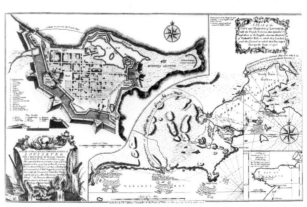

7-4. Louisbourg, N.S. Fortress. Plan by Thomas Jefferys, 1758. (Olin Library, Cornell University).

the French chose the site of Louisbourg to be fortified for the protection of their fishing and trading interests through the Gulf of St. Lawrence.[4] One-hundred-eighty settlers, who were mostly fishermen, were evacuated from Placentia in Newfoundland, which by the Treaty of Utrecht left Cape Breton Island the only French possession on the Atlantic coast. A peninsula on the east side of the island was chosen for its good harbor, and the decision for fortification was made by 1719.

As it became developed to its greatest extent by 1745, the fortress of Louisbourg, unlike Castillo de San Marcos, comprised the town as well as the defensive system [7-3 and 7-4]. On the west, or landward, side the principal works were the King's Bastion containing the Chateau St.

7-5. Quebec City. Plan by Thomas Jefferys, 1760. (Olin Library, Cornell University).

Louis or Citadel, the Queen's Bastion, the Dauphin Semi-Bastion, and the Princess Semi-Bastion. Behind these defenses the town was laid out on a grid plan, with the Place d'Armes immediately before the Citadel, and another set of walls completed the circuit around the narrow neck of land. The French military engineers Verville and Verrier based their designs on the "First System" of Vauban, and the five-sided bastions were indeed different from the older four-sided type used at the Castillo. The whole enclosure was an area of fifty-seven acres. The Citadel, 360 feet long, had well-furnished apartments for the Governor, quarters for officers and soldiers, apartments for the town administrator, and a chapel. Certain traditional fortress elements were included, such

7-6. New Orleans, La., plan by Thomas Jefferys, 1759. (Olin Library, Cornell University).

as the cordon and guard towers on the walls. Within the town most of the houses were timber, either built of uprights in palisade fashion or framed with masonry fill. In spite of the miserable climate and many difficulties in obtaining materials, the fortress was nearly complete when war between France and England broke out again in 1744.

In their eagerness to build the town walls and bastions the French engineers had not followed one of Vauban's most fundamental principles, that of analyzing the entire site with its surroundings and designing a total defensive scheme for each individual situation. Therefore the hills surrounding Louisbourg were not defended, and while the rocky coast and marshes posed threats to would-be invaders, the town was far from impervious to attack.

Under Commodore Peter Warren, commander of the Atlantic fleet, a British expedition sailed from Boston on March 24, 1745, and on June 17 the French were forced to surrender. The English occupation was short-lived, Louisbourg being returned to the French by the Treaty of Aix-la-Chapelle in 1748. Lack of materials, money, and food supplies kept the town and its inhabitants in poor condition until war between France and England was again declared in 1756. Two years later Louisbourg once more fell to British forces, and in 1760 the fortifications were blown up to prevent their ever again falling into French hands. Three years later the English gained Castillo de San Marcos by the Treaty of Paris, but here they chose to keep it for their own coastal defenses. Ironically, perhaps, of the two great European forts built against the English on the Atlantic coast it was the more modern one that fell to siege.

In this brief account of Louisbourg two features have been mentioned that require further comment. One is the gridiron plan of the town. This was characteristic of the early French towns in America. By the time Louisbourg was founded, the French missionary Father Pierre Charlevoix could say of Quebec, " ...you find yourself between two tolerably large squares; that towards the left is the place of arms, fronting which is the fort or citadel, where the governor-general resides....In the square towards your right you come first of all to the cathedral."[5] When Louisbourg fell, Quebec had grown by

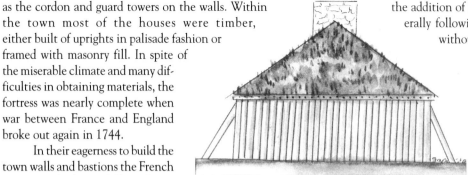

7-7. *Palisadoed structure, Louisbourg, Nova Scotia, drawing by Verrier. (Public Archives of Canada, National Map Collection).*

the addition of several gridded sections, laid out generally following the two major thoroughfares, but without adherence to a strict overall symmetrical plan [7-5]. At the southern end of the French territories grids were also used, with more planned formality for Mobile, Alabama, in 1711, and New Orleans, Louisiana, in 1721. Along the great waterways in between that were the avenues of the French fur trade and mission endeavors lay Montreal, replanned in 1721, Detroit, founded in 1701, and Kaskaskia, settled in 1703, all laid out in similarly regular patterns.[6]

In the growth of modern cities much has been lost of the original French plans and buildings. New Orleans suffered disastrous fires in 1788 and 1794, but a certain amount of the old city remains, its Place d'Armes becoming Jackson Square after the Louisiana Purchase of 1803. As planned in 1721 by the French engineers Adrien de Pauger and LeBlond de la Tour, it followed the Vitruvian principle for a harbor town, with the square beside the water, surrounded by the church and other main buildings [7-6].

The other matter is that of housing in these French towns, very little of which has survived. From the scanty structural remains and some documentary material it is possible to obtain some knowledge of how the French built their dwellings. Timber predominated, except for some of the most expensive houses, such as the town house for the engineers at Louisbourg. The timber houses were different from those of the English, depending not so much on frame construction as on a system of vertical posts from ground to roof, with or without a surrounding portico or *galerie*.[7]

For the upright timber system several approaches were used. One possibility was the palisadoed wall for a house, with a roof covered with thatch or sod. This type is known mainly from documentary references to modest dwellings in the St. Lawrence Valley and also at Louisbourg [7-7]. Another possibility was the *poteaux en terre* wall, built of vertical logs, which might be squared above ground, the spaces between filled with clay and grass (*bousillèe*) or with clay and stone (*pierrottèe*). We may recall the earthfast dwellings of the English settlers at Kingsmill in Virginia [7-8]. The obvious disadvantage of this system,

7-8. *Courthouse, Cahokia, Ill., c. 1737. (From American Magazine v. 32, 1891, courtesy of the Historical Society of Missouri, Columbia, Missouri).*

7-9. Parlange plantation, Pointe Coupèe, La., 1750. (Sandak, courtesy of the University of Georgia).

with posts liable to early rot, was avoided by the addition of a sill, giving the *poteaux sur sole* type of wall.[8]

The Cahokia, Illinois, building just illustrated has the double-pitch or pavillion roof, with the lower slope extended out to form the surrounding portico or galerie that was a distinctive element of French colonial houses. While the precise origin of the galerie is not clearly understood, there is René de Laudonnière's remark about his house in Fort Caroline in 1564, "round about which were galleries all covered."[9] An early traveler's description indicates the usefulness of the galerie in the hot and humid Mississippi valley as well as in the Caribbean: "...the heat of the climate makes porches necessary....The width of the porches offer several advantages, it prevents the sun's rays from striking the walls of the house, thus keeping them cooler; it offers a good place to walk (on the shady side), to eat, sit out in the evening with company, and often, in the warm spells of summer, to sleep on."[10] The other advantage of the galerie was to "preserve and embellish the building" by keeping rain off the walls.[11]

For the larger plantation houses that were developed especially in Louisiana the galerie provided similar conveniences. Parlange in Pointe Coupèe Parish, built about 1750, is probably the earliest extant example [7-9].[12] Here is a two-story house, the ground story of brick and the upper story of vertical cypress timbers filled with clay and Spanish moss. The galerie is in two stories on all four sides, and with doors on the second story placed opposite each other provides excellent cross-ventilation [7-10].

In such a house the lower story served as servant quarters, wine rooms, and pantry, with the main reception rooms above. The kitchen would be in a separate building. We

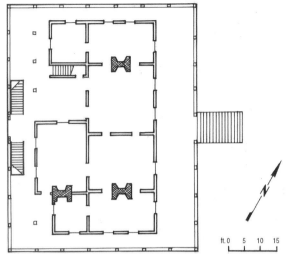

7-10. *Parlange plantation, plan. (After M. Whiffen and F. Koeper, American Architecture, 1607-1976, Cambridge, Mass., 1981, Fig. 20).*

might think of the European town house, with its merchant's or craftsman's rooms on the ground level and the living quarters above, here in another guise, adapted to the needs of the plantation establishment and the requirements of the climate. A smaller house, called "Madam John's Legacy," in New Orleans, built about 1727, shows the galerie used on a town house, and here it extends only across the front [7-11].[13]

Another possibility for French colonial timber building was framing. The poteaux sur sole houses might be considered as framed because the upright timbers are set into sills. But the French builders also used more widely spaced uprights, nogged with stone or brick. The best-known example of the latter is Lafitte's Blacksmith Shop in New Orleans, 1772-1791 [7-12].[14] Its brick-filled, or *briquetè entre poteaux*, walls also have the French type of diagonal braces, with the ends set into sills and plates.

Timber frames filled with stone or brick were also used for churches and large institutional buildings. Peter Kalm described the church at Baie St. Paul, near Quebec, as built of vertical timbers about two feet apart with an infill of black slate.[15] The first convent in New Orleans was built of briquetè entre poteaux in 1733, designed by Ignace François Broutin [7-13].[16] It was three stories high, with six bays on either side of a central portion, hipped roof, and central octagonal belfry. The drawing shows the timbers, with the patterns formed by the braces that proved insufficient to keep the building together. By 1745 the convent was in such precarious condition that Broutin, probably helped by the draftsman Alexandre de Batz, prepared designs for a new brick convent, built 1748-1752 [7-14].[17] In the later drawing the six bays on either side of a central portal were retained, but the third

7-11. *Pascal house, New Orleans, La., c. 1727. (Historic New Orleans Collection).*

99

story was reduced to dormers in the attic, the cupola was omitted, and the timbering replaced by stuccoed brick with quoins for accent at the ends and center. As with Old Harvard Hall and Massachusetts Hall, we have the change from old to new fashion.

Another analogy may be drawn between the Ursuline Convent buildings and those for the New England colleges. In both kinds of institutions the service rooms, dining rooms, etc., were on the ground floor with most of the chambers above. Peter Kalm's description of the Ursuline Convent at Quebec, rebuilt after a fire in 1686, says

7-12. Lafitte's Blacksmith Shop, New Orleans, La., 1772-1791. (Historic New Orleans Collection).

that "the cells of the nuns are in the highest story, on both sides of the long corridor…. The lowest story contains a kitchen, bake house, several butteries, etc. In the Garrets they keep their grain and dry their linen."[18] Both convents were built to accommodate schools for girls, to which the Ursuline Order was committed.

Stone was also widely used in Quebec and the Mississippi valley, though little has survived of French colonial stone buildings in the latter area.[19] As for the "black lime schist" in the Quebec region, Peter Kalm described it at some length and also noted that houses built of it were not impervious to the strength of the northeast wind: "The wind damages the houses which are built of stone, and forces the owners to repair them very frequently on the northeast side."[20] He also described the Quebec houses rather fully:

> The private houses have roofs of boards which are laid parallel to the spars, and sometimes to the eaves, or sometimes obliquely. The corners of houses

are made of a gray small-grained limestone, which has a strong smell like stink-stone, and the windows are enchased with it. This limestone is more useful in those places than the lime-slate which always shivers in the air. The outsides of the houses are generally whitewashed. The windows are placed on the inner side of the walls; for they sometimes have double windows in winter. The middle roof has two, or at most three spars, covered with boards only. The rooms are warmed in winter by small iron stoves, which are removed in summer. There are no dampers anywhere. The floors are very dirty in every house and have all the appearance of being cleaned but once every year.[21]

The tradition of stone building along the St. Lawrence left many villages with the types of stone houses brought from France in the seventeenth and eighteenth centuries [7-15]. The other major use for stone was for churches, a well-known example being the church at Sainte-Famille on the Ile d'Orleans [7-16].[22] Here the two western towers make the church somewhat grander than usual for a village church. As the New England towns were dominated by their meeting houses throughout most of the seventeenth century, so the St. Lawrence villages were dominated by their churches, architecturally and socially, a century later. The creation of eighty-two parishes in 1722 helped to populate the region with new churches, characteristically built

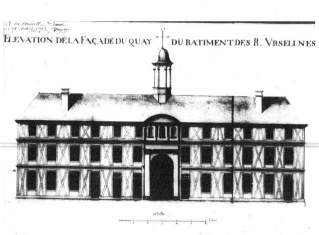

7-13. Ursuline Convent I, New Orleans, La., 1733. Alexandre de Batz drawing. (Paris, Archives Nationales).

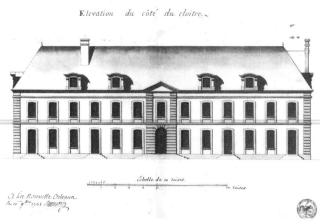

7-14. Ursuline Convent II, New Orleans, La., 1745. Alexandre de Batz drawing. (Paris, Archives Nationales).

7-15. House, Deschambault, Province of Quebec, Canada, eighteenth century. (Photo: M. C. Donnelly).

France in the interior of North America and on missions to convert the Indians to Christianity. The latter effort was confined to the Roman Catholic faith, and by law Huguenots were not permitted to settle in New France. These, especially after the revocation of the Edict of Nantes in 1698, therefore went into the English territories if they wished to venture to America. A steady increase in civilian population and domestic construction did not take place along the lines of the French outposts, and this is thought to have contributed to France's loss of her territory in 1763.[24]

If we turn to the late seventeenth and early eighteenth century building projects of the other great Roman Catholic country, Spain, we will find some similar intentions and results. The most forceful Spanish structure remaining on the east coast of the United States is of course the Castillo de San Marcos. Even more than the French, the Spanish concentrated on military posts and missions, having been lured into the Southwest and Texas by the quest for gold and finding it to no avail. They appear, however, to have been more zealous than the French in founding missions, and far more ambitious in their building projects. What remains are some striking convent churches that dominate their arid settings as do the churches in the St. Lawrence valley towns.

A certain amount is known about domestic architecture in New Mexico, to which a governor was appointed in 1609, with Santa Fe founded as the capital city.[25] The few settlers that came with the Franciscan friars built one-, two-, and three-room houses of adobe, the universal regional building material [7-17 and 7-18]. The Spaniards improved a little on native Indian techniques by using wooden forms for the sun-dried bricks instead of merely shaping them by hand. What little wood could be found was reserved for door and window frames and also the ceilings. The latter might have handsomely carved and brightly painted beams, or *vigas*, above which the thin poles, or *latias*, on which the final covering of adobe rested, would be laid closely together in herringbone patterns. The fireplace was often placed in one corner of the room.

7-16. *Church, Sainte-Famille, Province of Quebec, Canada, 1743-1746. (Photo: M. C. Donnelly).*

of stone, sometimes whitewashed or clapboarded, and by now often much altered.[23]

The scanty remains of French colonial buildings in America in part reflect the growth of cities such as New Orleans, St. Louis, and Quebec, where so many of the earliest works have given way to more recent construction. They also reflect French policies in the seventeenth and eighteenth centuries, which had concentrated on military posts to protect the vast territories claimed by

7-17. *Adobe house, Abiquiu, New Mexico, nineteenth century. (Photo: M. C. Donnelly).*

7-18. *Adobe bricks, Abiquiu, New Mexico. (Photo: M. C. Donnelly).*

Some more prosperous settlers, especially in the eighteenth century, might build a larger establishment with several rooms in single around a court, called a *placeta*, and a second court, or *corral*, around which were grouped the barns and sheds [7-19]. The whole complex, called a *hacienda*, would have a defensive function, opening to the outside only through a single door to the placeta and one to the

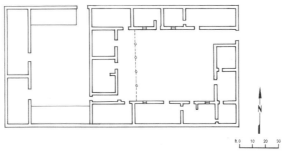

7-19. *Plan of hacienda. (After Bunting,* Early Architecture in New Mexico, *62).*

housed the chapel. The building has been remodeled several times, obscuring much of its original state. Even the sheltering portal on the plaza front is questionable, although often cited as a major element of Spanish style in the building.

corral. Windows would be used only on the inside courtyard walls [7-20].

If a community wished to defend itself, the individual houses could be built side by side around a plaza, their end walls common, and again no openings on the outside walls. While this practice was fairly widespread in New Mexico, only El Cerro de Chimayo, about 1730, remains to demonstrate it [7-21].

The major city of Santa Fe was laid out with a central plaza and a grid plan of streets as stipulated by the Laws of the Indies [7-22].[26] Not much grandeur was achieved here in the colonial period. Frey Angelico Atanasio Dominguez observed the plaza with the Governor's Palace on one side, a chapel on another, and houses on the other two, remarking that the appearance of the place was "mournful because not only are the houses of earth, but they are not adorned by any artifice of brush or other construction."[27] He was equally short with the Governor's Palace: "The government palace is like everything else there, and enough said."[28]

The palace itself remains in part, and having been built in 1610-14 it appears to be the oldest non-Indian building in the United States [7-23].[29] As first built, it was part of the whole presidio, a military enclosure 400 feet by 800 feet, which in addition to the palace included offices, barracks, storage chambers, and a prison. Towers, now disappeared, were built at each end of the palace for additional defense, and the one at the east end

This brings us to the matter of the combination of Indian and Spanish building traditions in the missions. In no other area of colonial architecture was so strong a mixture accomplished. The missions themselves grew from the daring visions of the Franciscans, who carried their heroic undertaking hundreds of miles from the Spanish center in Mexico City to remote desert outposts. The New Mexico mission development came in two stages, the first in the early-seventeenth century, with forty-three churches built by 1626, and the second in the eighteenth century, following the Pueblo Revolt of 1680 and the re-establishment of the missions beginning in 1692.[30]

As their English contemporaries were having to do in attempting to settle on the Atlantic coast, so the Spanish had to plan for very long journeys with no supplies waiting at the end. A list of tools to be provided for each friar in 1631 reads much like that recommended by Thomas Graves in 1680: "...ten axes, three adzes, three spades, ten hoes, one medium-sized saw, one chisel, two augers, and one plane."[31] Locks, hinges, a latch for the church door, and 6,000 nails were also listed, as no metalworking on the site could be expected in the first stages of construction.

On the building site the friar would lay out plans for the church and residence (*convento*) and direct the construction. The work was done by the Indians, using their custom of having women and children build the adobe walls. The men could now be provided with tools for more refined and elaborate woodwork than was possible in the pueblos. Basically the challenge was how to build a Spanish Christian church by and for people of a totally

7-20. *Antonio Severino Martinez House, Taos, New Mexico, 1824-1827. Placeta, courtyard. (Photo: M. C. Donnelly).*

7-21. *El Cerro de Chimayo, New Mexico, c. 1730. (Photo: M. C. Donnelly).*

different culture who could never be enlightened by seeing a prototype. The response was unique and forceful.

A single-nave church was the rule in these mission churches, colonnades and clerestories for aisled churches not being feasible in adobe. The polygonal shape of the sanctuary might be expressed on the exterior, or it might be concealed by squaring off the exterior. In the eighteenth century, some churches added transepts or chapels. The single entrance in the facade might be flanked by towers. Detailed measurements have revealed a number of irregularities, which have not been fully explained. The axis of the sanctuary is not always in line with that of the nave, perhaps for perspective effects. The walls of the nave are not only tapered but of uneven thickness, perhaps to give one wider wall as an aid to construction methods [7-24].

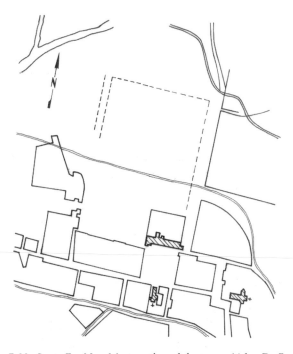

7-22. Santa Fe, New Mexico, plan of the town. (After D. P. Crouch, D. J. Garr, and A. I. Mundigo, Spanish City Planning in North America, Cambridge, Mass., 1982, Fig. 28).

los, only now with timbers more than thirty feet long which could span the wide interior space that was needed. Covered with boards or poles, then adobe, the vigas rest on corbels that could be elaborately carved or painted. Windows were few, and the friars invented an ingenious device for lighting the sanctuary. The church orientation is reversed so that it faces east. The walls of the sanctuary are higher than those of the nave, allowing a transverse clearstory window which can flood the sanctuary with the morning light [7-25].

The two missions just used to illustrate some of the characteristic features of these New Mexico buildings are among the better preserved examples of the seventeenth-century type. Founded in 1629, San Estevan at Acoma was probably completed by 1644, certainly before 1664.[32] The church with its adjoining convento occupies a dramatic site on a 100-acre mesa, 400 feet high [7-26]. Its heavy walls and twin towers echo the cliffs of its own and the surrounding mesas. Building here was unusually laborious, since all materials had to be carried up steep paths. While the convento complex with adobe walls, projecting vigas, and canales projecting to shed rainwater was composed of familiar

The most interesting structural feature of the mission church is the roof. Vaults and domes were not used in New Mexico, possibly because they would have taken too long in this technology or because of difficulty in obtaining sufficient wood for scaffolding. Instead the system of vigas was used as in the pueb-

7-23. Governor's Palace, Santa Fe, New Mexico, 1610-1614 (as rebuilt c. 1910). (Photo: M. C. Donnelly).

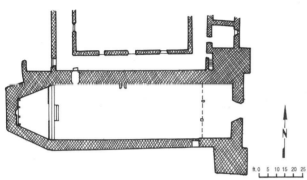

7-24. Church of San Estevan, Acoma, New Mexico, c. 1642. Plan. (After G. Kubler, Religious Architecture of New Mexico..., Colorado Springs, Co., 1940, Fig. 32).

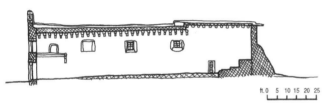

7-25. Church of San Josè, Laguna Pueblo, New Mexico, c. 1706. Longitudinal section. (After G. Kubler, Religious Architecture of New Mexico ..., Colorado Springs, Co., 1940, Fig. 16).

7-27. San Estevan, Acoma. Interior. (Photo: Courtesy of Museum of New Mexico, neg. no. 1984).

7-26. San Estevan, Acoma, New Mexico. View from the north. (Photo: Courtesy of Museum of New Mexico, neg. no. 1964).

elements, the massive church, its walls sixty feet high, must have seemed a powerful innovation to the Indians, accustomed to small spaces. The vigas for the church, forty feet long and fourteen inches square, and the elaborate corbels give the interior a closely spaced rhythm for the roof which contrasts sharply with the plain walls [7-27]. Resources could not supply the elaborate carved altarpiece of the typical Spanish Baroque church, and a painted version was substituted. Later rebuilding of the roof removed the transverse clearstory which once illuminated the interior.

The plan of San Estevan shows the choir loft at the east end. A document of 1664 states that "the paraphernalia of worship is abundant and unusual; [the church] has a choir and organ."[33] This must have been a portative organ, as the Spanish are known to have taught the Indians to make as well as to play organs and other musical instruments for use in the services of worship. Unfortunately those of this early period appear to have all been destroyed in the uprising of 1680.

At Laguna, Mission San José, founded in 1699 and administered from Acoma, the church was completed by 1706.[34] The plan is similar to that of San Estevan, but here there are no flanking towers. Instead the facade rises to a stepped gable with

7-28. San José, Laguna Pueblo, New Mexico. Exterior view. (Photo courtesy of Museum of New Mexico, neg. no. 55494).

7-29. San José, Laguna Pueblo, New Mexico. Interior. (Photo courtesy of Museum of New Mexico, neg. no. 68911).

7-30. *Church of Santo Tomás, Las Trampas, New Mexico, c. 1760. (Photo: M. C. Donnelly).*

bell openings [7-28]. The outward appearance of San José is otherwise similar to that of San Estevan, the plaster covering providing wide plain surfaces and rounded edges, but the walls are of rough stone laid in thick adobe mortar. The interior is among the most astonishing among the mission churches. Again there is the roof with vigas and corbels and an elaborate painted *reredo*. But along the nave walls are colorful friezes of Indian symbols, such as sun and rain, boldly painted in black and earth colors [7-29]. Not only were the Indian structural methods perforce adopted, but the inclusion of Indian religious symbols in the Christian context recalls the admonition of Gregory the Great to the missionaries in Britain in the sixth century. In its most successful expeditions to convert unbelievers over the centuries the Church often had had the wisdom to assimilate rather than to overturn long-held traditions.

At Las Trampas the church of Santo Tomás was built probably about 1760.[35] Here the plan is more elaborate, as was the case with many of the eighteenth-century mission churches. The church faces south rather than east, probably because of the terrain beside the road where it is placed. Buttress-like spurs of

the nave wall form a portico with a gallery on the south facade, and a baptistery projects from the east wall of the nave [7-30]. Then there are transepts projecting before the sanctuary, with a sacristy opening off the west transept.

By the early years of the nineteenth century the original missionary fervor was gone and the churches often falling into disrepair. They were further modified under Bishop Lamy after the American occupation of 1846.[36] More repairs and restorations have been made in the present century, with greater sensitivity to the original intentions of the builders. Although much has been lost, what remains is the legacy of one of the most creative episodes in the history of American building.

The Spanish colonial accomplishment in Texas was different.[37] Explorations in the sixteenth and seventeenth centuries aroused little interest in mission activity, to say nothing of colonization. Toward the end of the seventeenth century the presence of the French on the Mississippi stimulated the founding of some missions in East Texas, but the area was too hostile, and they were eventually abandoned. On the other side El Paso was the center of some development since it lay on the supply route

107

7-31. *Mission church of Nuestra Señora de la Purisima Concepción, San Antonio, Texas, c. 1740-1755. (San Antonio, National Historic Parks).*

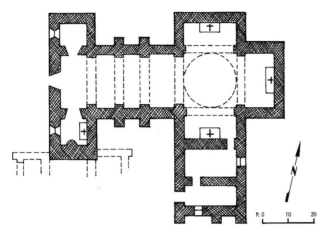

7-32. *Nuestra Señora de la Purisima Concepción, San Antonio. Plan. (After R. Newcomb*, Spanish-Colonial Architecture in the United States, *New York, 1937, Plate 18)*.

from Mexico City to Santa Fe. Its importance increased when it became a major refuge for the Spanish after the Pueblo Revolt.

The most important and lasting Spanish settlement was in and around San Antonio, founded in 1718. The five mission churches which remain, at least in part, are clearly in the established Spanish tradition, but they differ from those of New Mexico in several important respects.[38] The earliest appears to be the church of Mission Nuestra Señora de la Purisima Concepción, founded in 1716, moved to its present site in 1731, with the present church built from 1740-1755 [7-31 and 7-32].[39] Like the other San Antonio missions it is built of tufa limestone coated with stucco and has details carved from sandstone. There being no local strong Indian building tradition, the friars undoubtedly brought trained workers with them to build and finish as was done for the churches in Mexico. The plan of La Purisima Concepción is a Latin cross with twin towers on the west facade. The nave is covered by a tunnel vault with transverse ribs and salient buttresses on the exterior. The crossing is covered by a dome raised on a circular drum. Detail is confined to the mouldings of door, window, and belfry openings, the equilateral triangle above the west portal seeming discordant. The portal opening itself is octagonal-headed and is flanked by carved pilasters carrying an entablature [7-33]. A description of 1890 suggests a very different appearance from what is seen today:

> The front of the Mission Concepción must have been very gorgeous with color, for it was frescoed all over with red and blue quatrefoil crosses and with large yellow and orange squares to simulate great, dressed stones. This frescoing is rapidly disappearing, and from but a little distance the front looks to be merely gray and undecorated stone.[40]

For the church at Mission San Antonio de Valero, the historic shrine of Texas known as "The Alamo," a similarly ambitious building program was undertaken in 1756.[41] A stone church begun in 1744 had been completed, but poor construc-

tion caused it to fall almost immediately. The present building was never entirely finished either [7-34]. It too was planned with twin towers, a vaulted nave, and a transept with a dome over the crossing. Another collapse in 1762 left it a ruin, further damaged in the siege of 1836. Concern for its historic importance led to its subsequent repair. Only the unfinished facade actually remains, and it may be compared with that of La Purisima Concepción. Here the fundamental motif of the portal was clearly the triumphal arch, spread by pattern books all over Europe in the eighteenth century. The Alamo portal has flanking niches for statuary, with additional niches suggesting a proposed second tier above, and a rich treatment of the surfaces.

If this increasing elaboration of the portals suggests a rivalry among the builders, the first two portal builders were outclassed at Mission San José y San Miguel de Aguayo, begun in 1768 [7-35].[42] The west portal has niches for statues on the first level, with an oval window flanked by more statues above, the whole crowned by a short entablature on corbels. The portal bristles with scrolls, shells, floral motifs, and the like. Again there are two west towers, only the south one completed. The nave is covered with groin vaults and ends in a sanctuary covered by a high dome, there being no transept. The baptistery on the south

7-33. *Nuestra Señora de la Purisima Concepción, San Antonio. West portal. (Photo: M. C. Donnelly)*.

7-34. *Mission Church of San Antonio de Valero ("The Alamo"), San Antonio, Texas, 1744-1757. (Photo: M. C. Donnelly).*

side of the nave is lit by an almost excessively elaborate window. Nineteenth-century descriptions report paintings on the facade here as well.

Detailed descriptions of the convento buildings of Spanish missions in New Mexico and Texas have not been included in this account. Residences for the friars and their Indian workers for cooking, grinding corn, gardening, etc., were attached to the churches in the manner of the European monasteries. They might be planned as cloisters or courtyards, as at Acoma, or as single wing extensions, as at Mission San José. Since the secularization of the missions beginning in 1794 many of these buildings fell into disrepair or disappeared altogether.

For secular residential building in eighteenth-century Texas there are scant remains. In San Antonio the Governor's Palace, as it is now called, represents the grandest to which one could aspire [7-36].[43] It was completed in 1749 as the residence of the *presidio*, or fort, commander, then became the palace of the Spanish governors, eventually was used for various shops and even a school, and was restored by the City of San Antonio in 1931. In addition to the regular living rooms there was an office, a chapel, and a ballroom, as well as a patio garden. The exterior is plain, as at the similar palace in Santa Fe, except for the Hapsburg coat of arms carved on the keystone over the main door. The building's thick stone walls with their deep door and window openings and the massive horizontal timbers of the roof as restored give the house a rugged quality. There is nothing here of the rich ornament lavished on some of the mission churches.

7-35. *Mission Church of San José y San Miguel de Aguayo, San Antonio, Texas, 1768-1782. (Photo: M. C. Donnelly).*

WITH THIS WE SHALL LEAVE the history of Spanish colonial building and return to the record of building on the Atlantic seaboard as the English colonies moved from settlement toward separation from the mother country. The missions of Arizona and California will not be discussed here. The present buildings date from after 1776. Although such churches as San Xavier del Bac in Tucson, Arizona, and San Carlos Borromeo and Santa Barbara in California have individually interesting histories and notable architectural features, they do not add significantly to understanding of the Spanish colonial enterprise. The long difficult journeys through desert land, the founding of missions with minimal facilities, success and troubles with the Indians, the achievement of a certain splendor in prosperous times and eventual decay, with or without restoration following, form histories parallel to those of New Mexico and Texas.[44]

Notes to Chapter 7

1. Albert C. Manucy, *The Building of Castillo de San Marcos* (Washington D.C.: United States Government Publishing Office, 1942), 1-8; and Willard B. Robinson, *American Forts* (Urbana: University of Illinois Press, 1977), 15-23.

2. Manucy, *Building of Castillo de San Marcos*, 8-26.

3. Daniel Halevy, *Vauban: Builder of Fortresses,* trans. Cecil J. C. Street (New York: Dial Press, 1925).

4. Katherine McLennan, *Fortress of Louisbourg National Historic Park* (Ottawa: N.P. 1963); Fairfax Downey, *Louisbourg: Key to a Continent* (Englewood Cliffs, N.J.: Prentice-Hall, 1965); Richard B. Lane, "The Fortress at Louisbourg," *Archaeology* 19, no. 4 (October 1966): 258-267; John Lunn, "Louisbourg—the Forgotten Fortress," *Antiques* 97, no. 6 (June 1970): 872-879; and John Fortier, *Fortress of Louisbourg* (Toronto: Oxford University Press, 1979).

7-36. *Governor's Palace, San Antonio, Texas, c. 1749. (City of San Antonio, Parks and Recreation Department).*

5. Pierre François Xavier de Charlevoix, *Journal of a Voyage to North America*, quoted in John William Reps, *Town Planning in Frontier America* (Columbia, Mo.: University of Missouri Press, 1980), 75-76.

6. Reps, *Town Planning*, 74-105.

7. The principal writings on French housing in the Mississippi Valley are by Charles E. Peterson, "French Houses of the Illinois Country," *Missouriana* 1, no. 4 (August/September 1938): 9-12; "Early Ste. Genevieve and its Architecture," *Missouri Historical Review* 35, no. 2 (January 1941): 207-232; "Notes on Old Cahokia," *The French American Review* 1, no. 3 (July-September 1948): 184-225; and "French Landmarks along the Mississippi," *Antiques* 53 (April 1948): 286-288. For French upright timber construction see Shane O'Dea, "The Tilt: Vertical Log Construction in Newfoundland," *Perspectives in Vernacular Architecture* 1 (1982): 55-64.

8. Peterson, "Notes on Old Cahokia," 206. The courthouse was originally a dwelling and converted to a courthouse and prison in 1793. It was moved to the St. Louis Fair in 1904, then to Jackson Park in Chicago, and returned to Cahokia for re-erection on the original foundations in 1939.

9. Richard Hakluyt, comp., *The Principal navigations, voyages, traffiques & discoveries of the English Nation, made by sea or overland to the remote and farthest distant quarters of the earth at any time within the compass of these 1600 years* (London: J. M. Dent and Sons, LTD, 1927-28), 9:18.

10. C. C. Robin, quoted in Peterson, "Houses of French St. Louis," 20.

11. Governor Vaudreuil, quoted in Leonard Victor Huber and Samuel Wilson, Jr., *Baroness Pontalba's Buildings, their Site and the Remarkable Woman who Built them* (New Orleans: New Orleans Chapter of the Louisiana Landmarks Society, 1964), 12.

12. J. Frazer Smith, *White Pillars* (New York: William Helburn, Inc., 1941), 186-189.

13. Hugh Morrison, *Early American Architecture: From the First Colonial Settlement to the National Period* (New York: Dover Publications, 1987, 1952), 259.

14. Ibid., 260.

15. Adolph B. Benson, rev. and ed., *Peter Kalm's Travels in North America* (New York: Dover Publications, 1966), 2:483.

16. Samuel Wilson, Jr., "An Architectural History of the Royal Hospital and the Ursuline Convent of New Orleans," *The Louisiana Historical Quarterly* 29, no. 3 (July 1946): 572-602; Samuel Wilson, Jr., "Louisiana drawings by Alexandre de Batz," *JSAH* 22, no. 2 (May 1963): 76-78; and Samuel Wilson, Jr., "Religious Architecture in French Colonial Louisiana," *Winterthur Portfolio* 8 (1973): 91-97.

17. Wilson, Jr., "Architectural History," 603-611. The second building has survived, having undergone some alteration and restoration. For the seventeenth-century Ursuline convents in France on which Broutin's plans were probably based, see Joan Evans, *Monastic Architecture in France* (Cambridge: Cambridge University Press, 1964), 88-93.

18. Benson, ed., *Peter Kalm's Travels*, 2:444-445.

19. Charles E. Peterson, *Colonial St. Louis: Building a Creole Capital* (Saint Louis: Missouri Historical Society, 1949), 30-33.

20. Benson, ed., *Peter Kalm's Travels*, 2:506-507 and 456.

21. Ibid., 2:430.

22. Alan Gowans, *Church Architecture in New France* (New Brunswick: Rutgers University Press, 1955), 149.

23. Ibid., 66-88.

24. Alan Gowans, *Images of American Living* (Philadelphia: J. B. Lippincott Company, 1964), 29-45.

25. Trent Sanford, *The Architecture of the Southwest* (New York: W. W. Norton and Company, 1950), 91-93; and Bainbridge Bunting, *Early Architecture in New Mexico* (Albuquerque: University of New Mexico Press, 1976), 59-79.

26. Reps, *Town Planning*, 56-60; and Dora P. Crouch, Daniel J. Garr, and Axel I. Mundigo, *Spanish City Planning in North America* (Cambridge, Mass.: MIT Press, 1982), 69-115.

27. Fray Angelico Atanasio Dominguez, *The Missions of New Mexico, 1776*, trans. Eleanor B. Adams and Fray Angelico Chavez (Albuquerque: University of New Mexico Press, 1956), 40.

28. Ibid.

29. Sanford, *Architecture of the Southwest*, 90-91; and Bunting, *Early Architecture in New Mexico*, 80-81.

30. The fundamental study of the New Mexico missions is George Kubler, *The Religious Architecture of New Mexico*, 4th ed. (Albuquerque: University of New Mexico Press, 1972). Other accounts are in Cleve Hallenbeck, *Spanish Missions of the Old Southwest* (Garden City, N.Y.: Doubleday, Page and Company, 1926), 17-37; Rexford Newcomb, *Spanish-Colonial Architecture in the United States* (New York: J. J. Augustine, 1937), 29-31; Sanford, *Architecture of the Southwest*, 94-118; Morrison, *Early American Architecture*, 185-199; William Harvey Pierson, *American Buildings and their Architects* (New York: Oxford

University Press, 1986), 157-193; and Bunting, *Early Architecture in New Mexico*, 52-59. Since these accounts depend primarily on Kubler's original publication in 1940, references for the individual missions will be made only to Kubler.

31. France V. Scholes, "The Supply Service of the New Mexico Missions in the Seventeenth Century," *New Mexico Historical Review* 5, no. 1 (January 1930): 103-104.

32. Kubler, *Religious Architecture*, 92-95.

33. France V. Scholes, "Documents for the History of the New Mexico Missions in the Seventeenth Century," *New Mexico Historical Review* 4, no. 1 (January 1929): 49. The use of organs in the Spanish missions is discussed in Orpha Ochse, *The History of the Organ in the United States* (Bloomington: University of Indiana Press, 1975), 3-7.

34. Kubler, *Religious Architecture*, 110.

35. Ibid., 104-105.

36. Ibid., 141.

37. Newcomb, *Spanish-Colonial Architecture*, 26-28; Hallenbeck, *Spanish Missions*, 48-60. Sanford, *Architecture of the Southwest*, 151-171; Morrison, *Early American Architecture*, 199-208; and Pierson, *American Buildings*, 173-185.

38. Marion A. Habig, *The Alamo Chain of Missions* (Chicago: Franciscan Herald Press, 1976), 17-27.

39. Ibid., 118-155.

40. William Corner, *San Antonio de Bexar: A Guide and History* (San Antonio: 1890), quoted in Habig, *Alamo Chain of Missions*, 150.

41. Habig, *Alamo Chain of Missions*, 28-77.

42. Ibid., 83-116.

43. Sanford, *Architecture of the Southwest*, 160.

44. There is a large body of literature especially on the California missions, ranging from Rexford Newcomb, *Old Mission Churches and Historic Houses of California* (Philadelphia: J. B. Lippincott Company, 1925) to Paul C. Johnson, ed., *The California Missions: A Pictorial History* (Menlo Park, Calif.: Lane Magazine and Book Company, 1968), the latter with extensive bibliography. For the Arizona missions a new authoritative study is badly needed. They are listed, with some commentary, in Newcomb, *Spanish-Colonial Architecture*, 38-47, and San Xavier del Bac in Tucson is discussed in Sanford, *Architecture of the Southwest*, 172-180. For Arizona and California see also Morrison, *Early American Architecture*, 207-252, and Pierson, *American Buildings*, 185-204.

8-1. MacPhaedris-Warner house, Portsmouth, New Hampshire, 1716-1723. (SPNEA).

Chapter 8

18th-Century Housing in the English Colonies: The Georgian Period

I<small>N</small> C<small>HAPTER</small> 6, <small>ATTENTION WAS</small> <small>FOCUSED</small> on building in the years 1680 to 1720, when the forces of conservatism and innovation were intermingled and the results defy stylistic classification. There was perhaps more consistency in the next fifty to sixty years as ornamental vocabularies based on current English models were applied to building types now firmly establishing themselves in the English colonies. Not that traditions were wholly abandoned, as will be apparent in the next chapter with the public buildings and churches. But an increased population, becoming more prosperous and more confident of its own capabilities, built with an increased interest in taste for its own sake, and the result was the only moment of real coherence in American architecture on the Atlantic seaboard, the Georgian period.

8-2. MacPhaedris-Warner house, Portsmouth. Doorway. (Photo: M. C. Donnelly).

possible variations. An important aspect of the eighteenth-century building scene was the vast increase in printed sources of design, and this too will be discussed, along with the changing perception of the builder as "architect" in the English colonies.

The assurance of the successful early eighteenth-century New England merchant is clearly expressed in the MacPhaedris-Warner house in Portsmouth, New Hampshire, built 1716-1722, and surviving with change [8-1].[2] It is built of brick laid in Flemish bond, two stories high, with dormers lighting the attic. The roof is the only part of the house to have had a major change. It originally had two gables parallel to the street with a valley between them. The New England climate evidently proved too severe for this kind of roof, and indeed in the seventeenth century some of the cross-gabled meeting house roofs had

T<small>HE TERM</small> "Georgian," like "Elizabethan" and "Jacobean," is a political rather than stylistic designation, and refers to English and American art from the reign of George I beginning in 1714 to midway in the reign of George III about 1800. By the latter date many changes in taste were taking place on both sides of the Atlantic, so that the last twenty-five years of the eighteenth century were ones of survival of earlier colonial building traditions as well as of innovation. By the outbreak of the American Revolution the ideas of planning and ornament of the Georgian styles in architecture had been fully explored and developed. Change was inevitable.

Accounts of this period in American building have sometimes been prefaced with general descriptions of its stylistic elements and their English prototypes.[1] Here the approach will be to begin with some of the early examples in New England with which the basic principles can be demonstrated. The later New England houses and those of the Southern and Middle Atlantic colonies have been chosen to illustrate some of the many

required repairs to their valleys.[3] The old shingles were left in place when a new center roof was put on the Warner house, giving it a gambrel shape; and a new cupola was built; the break in the roof line was marked with a new balustrade. In this case the exterior trim is modest, consisting of segmental arches above the first floor windows, a brick belt course between stories, a modillioned cornice, alternating triangular and segmental pediments on the dormers, and a pilastered and pedimented doorway (a replacement of the mid-eighteenth century) [8-2]. Here the pediment is a segmental arch, one of several possible types. Such doorways had long been used in England, and in the colonies they were the single most distinctive feature of eighteenth-century houses [8-3].

Regularity of plan was also characteristic of the eighteenth-century house. The symmetrical five-bay facade of the Warner house with its chimneys in the end walls and its central cupola, suggests a central hall within [8-4]. The front door opens into this hall, with the parlors to the right and what would be called

115

8-3. Grammar school, Dedham, Essex, England. 1732. (Photo: M. C. Donnelly).

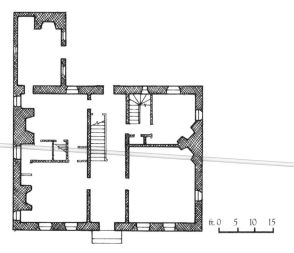

8-4. MacPhaedris-Warner house, Portsmouth. Plan. (After Great Georgian Houses of America, New York, 1933-37, 2:253).

8-5. Ropes mansion, Salem, Mass., 1719. (Photo: M. C. Donnelly).

today the dining room to the left. The stair occupies the rear portion of the hall. A chamber with its own stair is behind the parlor, and the kitchen, also with its own stair, is behind the dining room. A scullery was added back of the kitchen. There is a similar arrangement of hall and chambers on the second floor. This is the "double-pile" plan, two rooms deep and two rooms high on either side of a central hall. Already established in England, it became the basic formula for the Georgian house in America, and we shall see that there were possibilities for variations on the theme.

8-6. *Thomas Hancock house, Boston, Mass., 1736. (SPNEA).*

The more usual building material for the New England Georgian town house and farm house alike was wood. Contemporary with the Warner house and not far from it is the Ropes mansion in Salem, Massachusetts, begun in 1719 [8-5].[4] This is again a five-bay double pile, built with an oak frame filled with bricks and clay. The gambrel roof here is original. The Ropes mansion differs from the Warner house in having but three dormers in the attic and the chimney stacks placed within the house, each serving front and rear rooms. Although the door is embellished with columns and pediment it is not original, having been rebuilt and recessed in 1804.

A much grander house was begun by Thomas Hancock on Beacon Hill in Boston in 1736 [8-6].[5] In this case the building is known from early drawings and illustrations and fragments, it having been taken down in 1863. It was a five-bay double pile house, with end chimneys, gambrel roof with balustrade, and three dormers in the attic. Granite for the walls came from the quarries at North Commons in Braintree. For the corner quoins, door, and window trim Hancock had fine-grained sandstone shipped from Thomas Johnson's quarry near Chatham, Connecticut. The mason was Joshua Blanchard, who had been the mason for the South Meeting House in Boston and who would later do Faneuil Hall. The roof was tiled.

Thomas Hancock had two enthusiasms which he shared with many prosperous New England home owners. One was for his lands and gardens. In 1736 he wrote to London ordering trees and shrubs, saying that he did not intend "to Spare any Cost or pains in making my Gardens Beautifull or Profitable."[6] This recalls Parkinson again: "What Herbes and Fruits were fit...for Use or for later Delight."[7] A century later Thomas

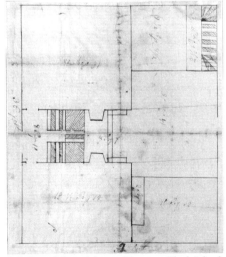

8-7. *Daniel Ayrault house, Newport, Rhode Island, 1739. Plan by Richard Munday and Benjamin Wyatt. (Newport Historical Society).*

Hancock had an even greater flood of garden literature to assist him if he wished, and the work of John James particularly gave instructions for building terraces and capitalizing on views.[8] A similar landscape was undertaken on the nearby estate of Governor William Shirley at Roxbury, Massachusetts, in 1746, perhaps inspired by Hancock's accomplishment.[9]

The other enthusiasm was for wallpaper. Thomas Hancock was a bookseller and stationer, and he imported wallpapers from England. In 1738, as work was progressing on his house, he wrote to John Rowe, his agent in London, regarding papers that he hoped to acquire, "If they can make it more beautiful by adding more Birds flying here and there, with some Landskips at the Bottom, Should like it well."[10] In addition to more extensive use of interior paneling in early Georgian houses came the application of sheets of hand-colored paper hangings to walls above paneled dadoes.[11] Later in the century printed papers were manufactured in the colonies as well as being imported. And if paper hangings were too costly, paintings directly on the walls were another solution.[12]

The name of Thomas Hancock's mason, Joshua Blanchard, has already been mentioned. It was, however, one matter to do the actual work or supervise it in the laying up of brick or stone walls. It was quite another to determine the plan and elevation of the building they were to form. We have seen that the early buildings of Harvard and Yale were planned not by architects but by those involved in the administration of the colleges. So it was with homeowners, especially those of means and education, in the early Georgian period. The professional architect was not yet on the scene in the English colonies.

A good example, and one of the earliest surviving, is a drawing for a house for Daniel Ayrault in Newport, Rhode Island, by Richard Munday and Benjamin Wyatt in 1739 [8-7]. Together with the specifications for the house in a contract, such a drawing would suffice to confirm the division into rooms, the location of fireplaces, and other particulars, and the competent carpenter or mason needed little more.[13] In *Mechanick Exercises* Joseph Moxon described such a drawing: "Their measure the length and breadth of the ground-plot they note down upon a piece of paper, and having considered the situation of the Sides, East, West, North and South, they draw on paper their several Sides accordingly, by a small Scale, either elected, or else made for that purpose."[14] He went on to tell how the measurements and drawing should be made, including a perspective view if possible, "for then he may, on a single piece of paper, describe the whole Building, as it shall appear to the Eye at any assigned Station."[15]

Returning to the Hancock House and Joshua Blanchard the

8-8. Ebenezer Gay house, Suffield, Conn., 1742. (Photo: M. C. Donnelly).

mason, we can find similar instructions for bricklayers in the *Mechanick Exercises*. Here the advantage of a good drawing or actual model is held to be that then "there will be no need of Alterations, or Tearing and pulling the Building to pieces after it is begun," thereby making the building "lame and Deficient." The passage concludes with an illuminating statement: "The drawing of Draughts is most commonly the work of a Surveyor, although there be many Master Workmen that will contrive a

Building, and draw the Designs thereof, as well, and as curiously, as most Surveyors: Yea, some of them will do it better than some Surveyors; especially those Workmen who understand the Theorick part of Building, as well as the Practick."

The sketchy nature of the drawing for the Ayrault House shows clearly that Munday and Wyatt came under Moxon's definition of "Master Workmen," and he made the distinction between them and "Architects," saying, "Architecture is a Mathematical Science, and therefore different from my present Undertakings, which are (as by my Title) Mechanick Exercises."[16]

The work of those who at least considered themselves to be "architects" will concern us later, but first we should observe some of the other possibilities that were introduced in New England Georgian houses. The special ornamenting of the front door has already been noted at the Warner house. Not the main

8-9. Rooth house, Surrey, England. Elevation. (From C. Campbell, Vitruvius Britannicus, London, 1717, v. 2, Plate 49).

door itself but the second floor hall window above it was given a different and more elaborate pattern at the Hancock house, just visible in the drawing, squeezed beneath the cornice. This scroll pediment, another familiar motif in England, was made for Hancock in Connecticut, where it became especially popular in the Connecticut River valley.[17] The Ebenezer Gay house in Suffield, Connecticut, 1742, is a good example of a frame house, double-pile, conservatively retaining the central chimney, with a handsome door flanked by pilasters carrying a scroll pediment that is well set off against the otherwise unpretentious facade [8-8].

By the time of the Hancock and Gay houses the scroll pediment and other motifs for door and window openings and other details were readily available in the various kinds of pattern books that were now beginning to flood the market. The scroll pediment, for example, appears on Rooth house, Surrey, illustrated by Colen Campbell in *Vitruvius Britannicus*, published 1715-1725 [8-9].[18] It is also to be found in

8-10. *"A Frontispiece and Door of the Composite Order." (From W. Salmon,* Palladio Londinensis, *London, 1734, plate 26).*

William Salmon's *Palladio Londinensis* of 1734 [8-10].[19] Whether elegantly printed volumes on notable buildings (already built or projected like the former) or more modest handbooks of sources for carpenters like the latter, these publications served to spread ideas to owners and builders alike, as do the many illustrated journals of our own day.[20] Further examples of the use of these books will be found in many of the buildings remaining to be discussed.

For a house in a small town such as Suffield, a pedimented front door might satisfy any desire for fashionable ornament. In the larger New England towns and cities, however, more elaboration was often required. This was the case when Major John Vassall built his house in Cambridge, Massachusetts, in 1759 [8-11].[21] It is of wood, double-pile in plan, with chimneys between the front and rear portions and a central hall with front and rear stairs, and the basic formula is complete with its symmetrical five-bay facade. It is raised on a terrace above the street level, and

8-11. *Major John Vassall house, Cambridge, Mass., 1759. (Photo: M. D. Ross).*

8-12. Wentworth-Gardner house, Portsmouth, New Hampshire, 1760. Although the door itself is original, a Victorian porch addition destroyed the original door surround; around 1915 Wallace Nutting restored the door surround, copying a Salem, Massachusetts, example, with an elegant scroll pediment, preserved in the Essex Institute. (Photo: M. C. Donnelly).

8-13. Richard Derby house, Salem, Mass., c. 1761. (National Park Service).

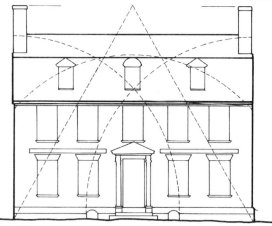

8-14. Derby house, Salem. Elevation diagram showing proportional relationships.

an attempt to give it further grandeur was made by applying four Ionic pilasters to the facade, rising the full height of the building. The two central ones frame the front door and second-story hall window, and then a pediment is added to the attic above. The hip roof has a balustrade surrounding the central portion and chimneys. The piazzas at either side were added later.

By contrast the Wentworth-Gardner house in Portsmouth, New Hampshire, 1760, built on the same general plan with but one staircase, has neither pilasters, pediment, nor balustrade [8-12].[22] Instead the wood siding is scored to imitate stone, and the corners are emphasized with heavy quoins. All this was later covered with clapboard, and its discovery and restoration by Wallace Nutting, who owned it, was one of the early preservation efforts in New England. Nutting also recovered the original staircase, which had been removed to another house. Nutting also restored the missing front door surround. There is extensive paneling throughout the house, with pilasters and entablatures, Corinthian on the first floor and Ionic on the second.

The Wentworth house is on the waterfront in Portsmouth, and so is another seaport house, the Derby house in Salem, Massachusetts, begun a little later, about 1761 [8-13].[23] It is built

of brick, an early example in Salem, and like the Warner house in Portsmouth has end chimneys. It has a gambrel roof. The simplicity of the front doorway, with its Tuscan pilasters and triangular pediment, is consistent with the smooth surface of the exterior, accented only by the bands of stringcourse on either side. The contrast to its close contemporary, the Wentworth house, is striking.

By this time the Palladian movement was well underway in England, set into motion by the publication of the first volume of *Vitruvius Britannicus* and an English translation of Palladio's *I quattro libri dell' architettura* in 1715.[24] Supported by the Whig aristocracy, the architects of this new force in England had turned from the richness of the English Baroque to the cooler and, to them, more rational manner of Palladio and his English follower, Inigo Jones. Now the Derby house was certainly not derived from any designs by Palladio or Jones; that had already been accomplished in the Southern colonies, as we shall see. But the restraint of its surfaces is certainly a departure from the Baroque manner that was still fashionable in New England.

Furthermore, the elevation of the Derby house seems to have been derived from geometrical principles such as those already described for the Galt and Bracken houses in Williamsburg. If an equilateral triangle is drawn with the length of the house at ground level as its base, the apex is in line with the chimney tops [8-14]. The height from ground to eaves is half the width. Radii centered at the outside corners and window openings intersect to establish the structural top of the lower slope of the roof. The system is not in itself Palladian, but this kind of orderly approach is in the spirit of the Palladian movement. The only builder in the New England area at that time who is known to have deliberately used Palladian sources is Peter Harrison, then at work on Christ Church in Cambridge.[25] Could the wealthy Richard Derby have appealed to Harrison for the basic principles that would guide his mason?

To discover how such geometrical systems were used in building eighteenth-century New England houses would be a study in itself. The particular system described for the Derby house was clearly not used for the other two great seaport houses in the area. Requiring additional living quarters prompted some of the owners to build higher than the normal two stories. The Moffatt-Ladd house in Portsmouth, 1760-64, is built of wood, five bays wide and three stories high, with a hip roof and balustraded Captain's Walk [8-15].[26] Like the Wentworth house it has quoins at the corners, but the covering is simply clapboard. There is a Tuscan portico before the front door, and the second floor is strongly emphasized with scroll pediments over the windows, the center one being larger than the others. Then come the smaller windows of the third story.

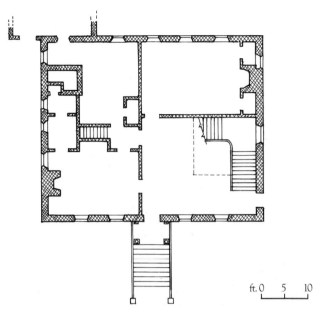

8-16. *Moffatt-Ladd house, Portsmouth. Plan. (After Great Georgian Houses, 2:249).*

8-15. *Moffatt-Ladd house, Portsmouth, New Hampshire, 1763. (SPNEA).*

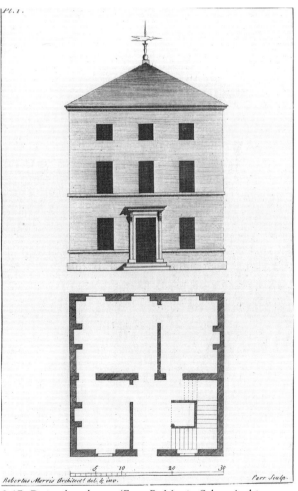

8-17. *Design for a house. (From R. Morris, Select Architecture, London, Plate 1).*

121

8-18. *Moffatt-Ladd house. Portsmouth. Stair hall. (SPNEA).*

8-19. *Colonel Jeremiah Lee house, Marblehead, Mass., 1768. (SPNEA).*

The plan is different from the standard Georgian plans of the other houses in that there is no central hall [8-16]. Instead the front door opens into a large hall with the staircase against the window wall to the right. The dining room is to the left, with a service stair between it and the kitchen, and the drawing room or parlor is at the back of the house. This plan may well have come from Robert Morris's *Select Architecture of 1757*, Plate 1 [8-17].[27] A fine Georgian staircase is here, now open-string, with ample possibilities for panels and carving on the ends of the steps. The balusters are turned, sometimes as here using three patterns, one example of each on each step. The handrail curves to an ornamental newel post may be echoed by a dado against the wall. The underside of the second run in the Moffatt-Ladd house is elaborately paneled, and the landing window is framed with pilasters [8-18].

Within five years another wealthy merchant, Colonel Jeremiah Lee, began his "mansion" in Marblehead, Massachusetts [8-19].[28] Built of wood, three stories high, with quoins at the corners, the Lee mansion has some features different from those at the Moffatt-Ladd house, and these tend to greater elaboration. The wood siding is scored to imitate masonry, the front portico is Ionic rather than Tuscan, and the house is seven rather than five bays wide. The three central bays projecting slightly are crowned by a pediment with a semi-circular window, above which rises a cupola in the center of the roof. In neither house was achieved the balance of proportions for a three-story house

that would be the special contribution of Salem builders after the Revolution.

For the interior of the Lee mansion the central hall plan with chimneys between the front and rear rooms was used. Rather than a drawing room there is a spacious entertaining room to the left at the front, with library, office, and storage rooms behind. Across the hall are the family dining room and kitchen. The stair is among the finest in New England [8-20]. It is quite broad, with unusually low risers, and again paneling on the dado and under the second run. An even greater effort in carving is the chimneypiece of the banquet room, a tour-de-force in carved pine, based on Plate 51 of Swan's *British Architect* of 1745 [8-21].[29]

In less than a decade following the completion of his mansion, Jeremiah Lee died of exposure after his work with compatriots in the Continental Congress on the night of April 18, 1775. His house is a witness to the economic and social status and the self-confidence attainable in New England in the second half of the eighteenth century.

MEANWHILE THERE HAD BEEN vigorous and different building activities in the Southern colonies. The plantation economy was still dominant, with only a small number of towns of much importance.

Since the time of Bacon's Castle the plantation houses were taking on new guises, and in these houses we may see variants on some of the Georgian elements that we have observed in the

8-20. *Lee house, Marblehead. Stair hall. (SPNEA).*

New England examples. We may then see how some of the build-ers of southern town houses responded to the Georgian style.

William Byrd II planned a large plantation house around 1729, but the present well-known house, Westover, was in fact built by his son, William Byrd III, soon after a fire in 1749. It stands on the banks of the James River in Charles City County, Virginia [8-22].[30] While by no means the earliest of the plantation houses where Georgian ideas appear, it is so well proportioned and retains so much of its original detail that it is generally considered one of the finest. Like the Lee mansion it is seven bays wide, but only two stories high and therefore appears less cramped. The end chimneys bracket the steep hipped roof and its dormers. Apart from the segmental brick arches of the first floor window heads and the modillioned cornice there is no exterior ornament except for the north and south doors, of white Portland stone set against the brick laid in Flemish bond. The scroll pediment of the south door we have already met, and this was chosen for the side facing the water, the original principal facade. The north door has a segmental pediment, based on Salmon's Plate 25 [8-23].

The plan of Westover is a variant on the double-pile [8-24]. The staircase hall is not centered, but includes the doors and the first west window bays. The two rooms on the east were accordingly one bay larger than the two on the west.[31] This gives more light to the hall than could come directly from transom windows in the doors. The interior was finished with paneling, marble chimneypieces, and ornamental plaster ceilings, especially fine in the drawing room.

When William Byrd II planned building Westover, he was in his mid-fifties, wealthy and prominent. Educated in England, he had already served twenty years on the Governor's Council for Virginia and was shortly to found the city of Richmond. His library included a number of books on architecture. Either he or his master mason, whose name is not known, made use of the equilateral triangle in the design of the elevation of Westover in the same manner as that of the Derby house. When completed the whole establishment was one of the finest fully developed plantations of its day. The house was originally free-standing, the earlier kitchen on the west and another dependency on the east, the latter burned during the Civil War and rebuilt in 1901. At that time were also built the passages connecting the depen-dencies to the main house. The north side of the grounds are entered through an extraordinary wrought iron gate, made in London, and possibly one of Byrd's first imports for his estate. That his efforts aroused admiration from his contemporaries is evident from the comment of William Beverley, who spoke of the garden as "the finest in that country."[32]

For all its grandeur, Westover was essentially conservative. When the land at Westover was purchased by William Byrd I in

8-21. Lee Mansion, Marblehead. Chimneypiece. (SPNEA).

8-22. William Byrd III house, Westover, Charles City Co., Va.. c. 1750. (Richmond, Division of Historic Landmarks).

8-23. "A Frontispiece and Sash-Door of the Corinthian Order." (From W. Salmon, Palladio Londinensis, London, 1734, Plate 25).

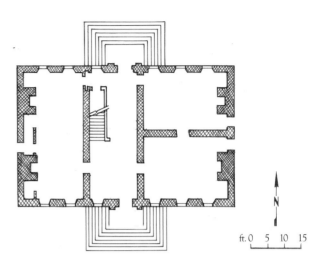

8-24. Westover, Charles City Co. Plan of main house. (After Great Georgian Houses, 1:64).

8-25. Uppark, Sussex, England, c. 1690. (National Monuments Record).

8-26. *John Drayton house, Drayton Hall, outside Charleston, South Carolina, c. 1738-1742. (Courtesy of Drayton Hall).*

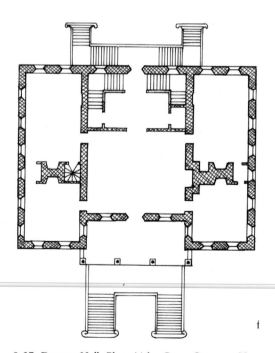

8-27. *Drayton Hall. Plan. (After Great Georgian Houses, 1:25).*

1688, houses such as Uppark, Sussex, c. 1685-1690, were already being built [8-25].[33] The first major Palladian work in the Southern colonies came soon after Westover, not in Virginia, but in South Carolina on the Ashley River, where John Drayton built Drayton Hall in 1738-1742 [8-26].[34] Perhaps as a member of the King's Council John Drayton knew William Byrd and was prepared to build something less old-fashioned, if less splendid, than Westover. The plan of Drayton Hall is close to Colen Campbell's house of Chester-Lee-Street, published in *Vitruvius Britannicus* in 1717 [8-27 and 8-28].[35] This is a variant of the double-pile plan, for the west door is recessed behind a portico, then there is a large vestibule three bays wide and a hall for a double stair on the west side. The chimneys are set within the house between the east and west rooms. The basement is high, containing the kitchen and servants' quarters, and the space above the vestibule on the second floor became the large drawing room. On the east front, the front facing the river, the double staircase inside appears also on the exterior, where there is a pedimented central doorway but no portico.

The west front appears to be the earliest of the double porticoes in the colonies, Doric below and Ionic above. The source is clearly Leoni's translation of Palladio's treatise [8-29].[36] The breezy second level outside the drawing room must have seemed desirable in the South Carolina climate. As originally built, the main house was framed by dependencies, similar to those of Chester-Lee-Street, which are now gone. These put the whole complex of the house into the orbit of the Palladian villa, whence Campbell had derived his inspiration. One more detail demonstrates the connection with the Palladio-Jones revival. Amid the extensive fine paneling of the interior is the chimneypiece in the vestibule, taken from William Kent's *Designs of Inigo Jones* of 1727 [8-30 and 8-31].[37]

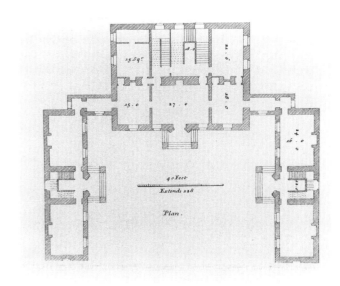

8-28. *Chester-Lee-Street house, County Durham, England. (From C. Campbell,* Vitruvius Britannicus, *London, 1717, v. 2, Plate 88).*

8-29. *Design for a villa. (From A. Palladio,* Four Books, *Book II, London, 1715, Plate 61).*

8-30. *Drayton Hall. Hall chimneypiece. (Courtesy of Drayton Hall).*

With Westover and Drayton Hall we can see the southern plantation owners turning either to long-standing English Baroque ideas or to the currently fashionable Palladian revival motifs for the planning and embellishment of their great houses. The same diverse choices would be made for similar houses during the next forty years or so before the American Revolution. Many have now been lost altogether, some extensively altered, and some have retained enough of their original character that their contributions to the American Georgian traditions can still be observed.

Carter's Grove in James City County, Virginia, begun at mid-century in 1750, is a case in point [8-32].[38] As originally built the roof was lower, without dormers, and the dependencies were detached, their roofs also lower and without dormers, the changes having been begun in 1928. The building is of brick laid in Flemish bond, with a wood modillioned cornice and rubbed brick accents at the corners and windows. Especially interesting are the pilasters and pediments of the north and south doors, which are brick rather than stone or wood [8-33]. From this front the view is across former gardens and fields towards the James River [8-34]. The house was placed on a rise between two wooded ravines; excavations have revealed a fenced garden with terraces,

8-31. *Design for a chimneypiece. (From W. Kent,* Designs of Inigo Jones, *London, 1727, Plate 64).*

8-33. *Carter's Grove. South door. (Photo: M. C. Donnelly).*

8-32. *Carter Burwell house, Carter's Grove, James City Co., Va., 1750-1754. South front. (Photo: M. C. Donnelly).*

8-34. *Carter's Grove. Excavations of garden. (Photo: M. C. Donnelly).*

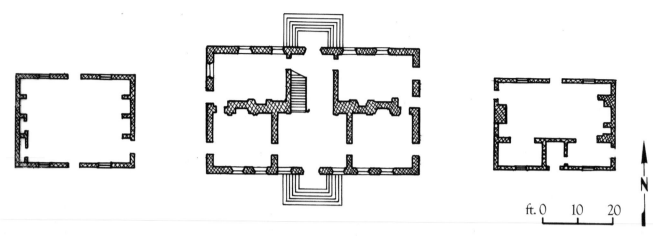

8-35. *Carter's Grove. Plan of main house and dependencies. (After Great Georgian Houses, 1:101).*

8-36. *Carter's Grove. Entrance hall. (Colonial Williamsburg Foundation).*

8-37. *John Arris, Colonel John Taylor house, Mount Airy, Richmond Co., Va., Richmond, 1758-1762. (Richmond, Division of Historic Landmarks).*

which could well have comprised a flower garden before the house and a vegetable garden beyond.

The plan of the house may be another derivation from Palladio's Book II, Plate 61 [8-35]. It is another variant on the double pile, with the chimneys between the front and rear rooms. Here the entrance hall is three bays wide, as at Drayton Hall, but the staircase opens directly from it, framed by an elliptical arch resting on simple mouldings which is in turn framed by the Ionic order that panels the entire hall [8-36]. The original builder, Carter Burwell, hired a Williamsburg mason, David Minitree, for the brick construction of the house. For the interior woodwork, generally considered among the finest in the colonies, he brought an English craftsman, Richard Bayliss. The paneling in the hall and elsewhere in the house is of walnut and pine and has been variously painted over the years. The most recent approach was to remove the paint on the first floor, leaving a natural waxed finish, and to paint the woodwork in the upper stories. The effect on the first floor is a rich glow of the waxed wood, but probably all but the walnut stair itself was originally also painted.

From Carter's Grove we may turn to another Virginia plantation house, Mount Airy on the Rappahannock River in Richmond County [8-37].[39] The name of the builder is not known with certainty. On stylistic grounds and circumstantial evidence John

Arris, 1720-1799, has been proposed, who is known to have been active in Virginia at this time.[40] This brings up two important matters. One is that according to an advertisement in the *Maryland Gazette*, May 22, 1751, Arris regarded himself as more than a master carpenter or mason.[41] He said he was prepared to undertake buildings in "either the Ancient or Modern Order," showing that he intended to work from theory, which would place him within Moxon's definition of an "architect."

Whether Arris was the "architect" of Mount Airy or not, his advertisement also speaks of a specific publication that he used, and that publication was indeed used in the design for Mount Airy: This is a *A Book of Architecture*, published by James Gibbs in London in 1728.[42] It was, according to its writer, designed "as a pattern book for the use of country gentlemen in districts remote from architectural advice," and so Arris announced himself ready to use it on such a gentleman's behalf. This is not the place to enlarge on the career of Gibbs, who died in 1754.[43] Suffice it to say that he combined elements of the late English Baroque, Jones-Palladianism, and Italian Mannerism as he had encountered it in his travels to form a highly individual style that turned out to have wide appeal. As we shall see, Arris was not the first American designer to make use of ideas from Gibbs, but apparently the earliest to use them in overall planning.

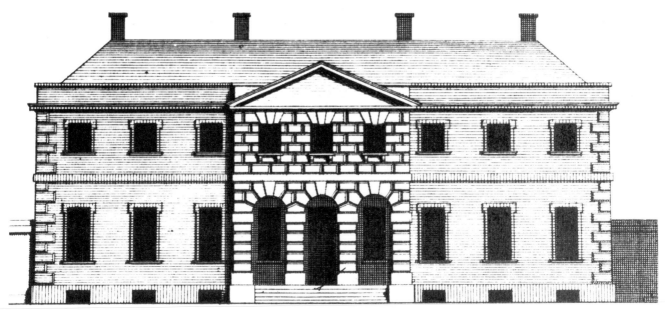

8-38. *Design for a villa. (From J. Gibbs,* A Book of Architecture, *London, 1728, Plate 58).*

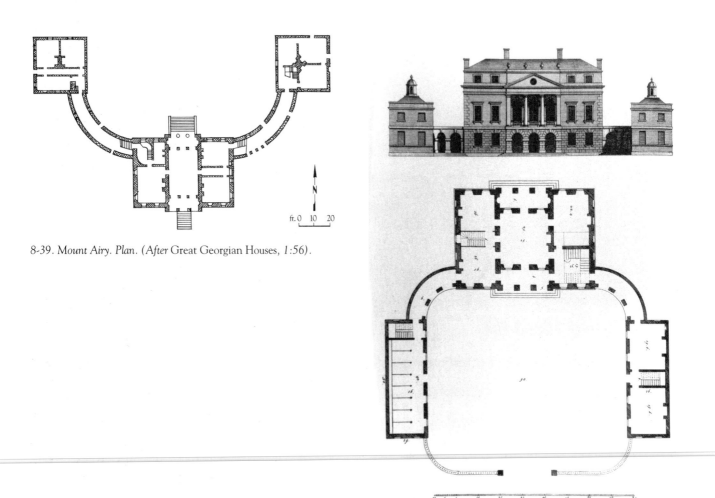

8-39. *Mount Airy. Plan. (After Great Georgian Houses, 1:56).*

8-40. *Plan for a villa. (From Gibbs,* A Book of Architecture, *Plate 55).*

To return to Mount Airy, its materials are interesting to begin with, for instead of brick it is built of dark sandstone with lighter limestone for trim. Comparison with the Wentworth house of the same date is instructive as to the effect of different materials on similar designs. The three central bays of the south front of Mount Airy project slightly and are laid up in rusticated limestone, a triple arcade below, three windows in the second story, and a pediment above. The source of Plate 58 is Gibbs's *A Book of Architecture* [8-38]. Plate 43 was used for the north front. These central elements, the hip roof, and chimneys set into the body of the house suggest the double pile again, and this is nearly the case. The central hall is a square behind recessed porticoes, and the stair is in one of the rooms on one side. The main house is connected to dependencies by curved passages, and again there is reference to Gibbs, this time to Plate 55 [8-39 and 8-40]. A disastrous fire in 1844 destroyed the interiors of Mount Airy. They were probably finished with a dignity similar to that of Carter's Grove.

A MUCH MORE EXUBERANT spirit prevailed in the work of William Buckland at Gunston Hall in Fairfax County, Virginia [8-41].[44] Situated on a smaller estate, the house is a one-story brick building with sandstone trim, two rooms deep with central hall and chimneys. It was already under construction when Buckland, who had been born and trained in England, was brought to America as an indentured carpenter and joiner in 1755. Buckland was then twenty-one years old, and the builder of the house, George Mason, thirty. Which of the two young men made the choices for the interior woodwork may not be determined: the result was richness to the point of over-elaboration. Perhaps the most exotic is the woodwork of the Chinese room, where a variety of sources appears to have been used, including motifs from Thomas Chippendale's *Gentleman and Cabinet Maker's Guide* of 1754.[45] [8-42]. This introduces a hint of romantic taste for the Chinese, from a treatise that was to be widely influential in American furnishings.

8-41. *George Mason house, Gunston Hall, Fairfax Co., Va., 1755-1758. (The Board of Regents of Gunston Hall).*

8-42. William Buckland, Gunston Hall. Chinese room. (The Board of Regents of Gunston Hall).

HALL
NORTH ELEVATION

8-43. Gunston Hall. Hall, elevation drawing. (The Board of Regents of Gunston Hall).

In the drawing room at Gunston Hall the gentleman and his cabinet maker appear to have been rather carried away. The upper part of the room is almost menacing with broken pediments over doorway and cupboards and pilasters carrying heavy entablatures surrounding the windows. The source is in Abraham Swan's *Collection of Designs in Architecture* of 1757.[46] The Doric of the hall is more sober [8-43]. Buckland was adapting from these books rather than copying them precisely, and it is now known that his designs were carried out by trained carvers. If at Gunston Hall the woodwork seems to overpower the small interior, Buckland's later work at Annapolis shows him in a more temperate light.

A number of buildings in and around Annapolis have been attributed to Buckland, and he has been associated with Whitehall, on Chesapeake Bay, near Annapolis, begun in 1764 [8-44].[47] The identity of the original designer of Whitehall is not certain, although it may have been one Joseph Horatio Anderson, then active in Annapolis. The owner was Governor Horatio Sharpe, who had no suitable official residence in Annapolis. For a house that would accommodate official gatherings a plan differing from the double pile was chosen [8-45]. The main block is only one room deep, with a two-story reception hall in the center, drawing rooms on either side, and

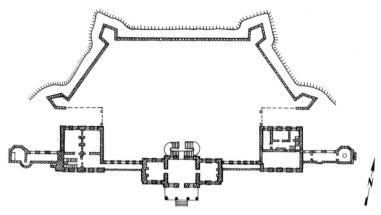

8-45. *Whitehall. Plan. (After C. Scarlett, Jr., "Governor Horatio Sharpe's Whitehall,"* Maryland Historical Magazine 46 [March 1951]: 17).

east and west galleries leading to dependencies with additional chambers. These latter were built after the original main block. This departure from the standard Georgian plan was shared by several other Virginia houses of the time and seems to have been founded on a design by Robert Morris in his *Select Architecture* of 1757 [8-46].[48]

At first the bedrooms at Whitehall were in an earlier house on the estate, and their eventual connection to the main house in the west wing, with the kitchen in the east wing, was evidently

8-44. *Joseph Horatio Anderson, Governor Horatio Sharpe house, Whitehall, outside Annapolis, Md., 1764-1765. South front. (Photo: M. C. Donnelly).*

not felt the most convenient arrangement by later owners. The two drawing rooms were originally one story high, with the reception hall rising between them. These were raised to two stories about 1793, bedrooms being built in the second stories, and a gable roof built to cover the whole. Although this made the living quarters more compact, the central hall prevented communication between the rooms on the second level. Finally in 1957 this second level was removed and the present appearance attained, based on as much structural evidence of the original as could be found.[49]

The great Corinthian portico on the south front is the earliest domestic use of the full height temple front in the English colonies. Its effectiveness in creating a monumental principal entrance is far greater now that the second stories over the drawing rooms have been removed. For the details of the Corinthian entablature, a book more in the nature of a carpenter's handbook seems to have been consulted, *The Modern Builder's Assistant* by William Halfpenny.[50]

On the north side, facing the lower garden, a curved double flight of stairs led up to the entrance to the reception hall. A prototype is the design for Lowther Hall by Colen Campbell in *Vitruvius Britannicus* [8-47].[51] On this side there are now the remains of another curious feature, a defense consisting of ramparts and bastions, built in apprehension of Indian attack, even

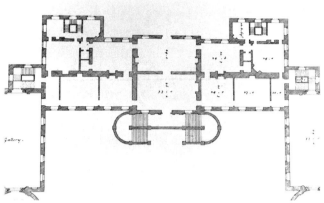

8-47. *Lowther Hall. Plan (detail). (From C. Campbell,* Vitruvius Britannicus, *v. 2, Plate 78).*

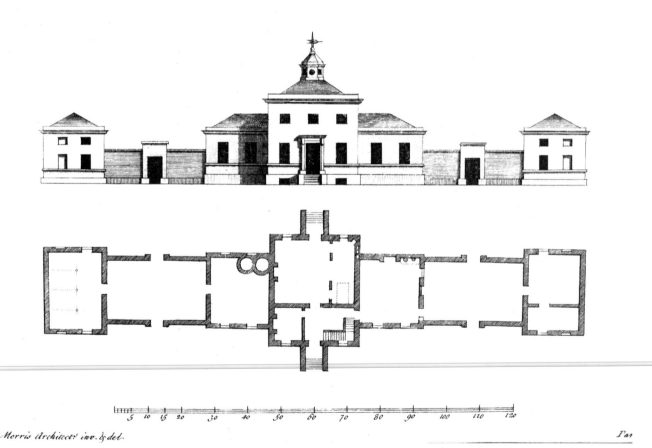

8-46. *Robert Morris, Design for a House, Plate III, from* Select Architecture, *London, 1757. (Courtesy of the British Architectural Library/RIBA).*

8-49. Nathaniel Harrison house, Brandon, Prince George Co., Va., 1765. (Photo: M. C. Donnelly).

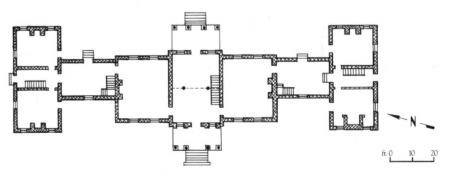

8-50. Brandon. Plan. (After Great Georgian Houses, 1:107).

8-48. Whitehall. Entrance hall, doorway.
(Photo: M. C. Donnelly).

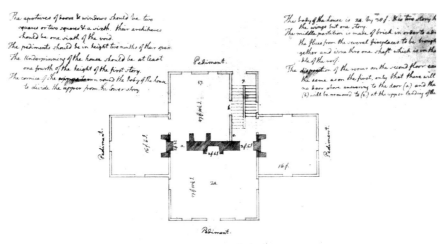

8-51a. Thomas Jefferson (designer and draftsman), Monticello, Charlottesville, Va., begun 1768. Revised plan for first version, based on Plate 37 in Morris, Select Architecture, 1755. (Massachusetts Historical Society, Coolidge Collection, K24).

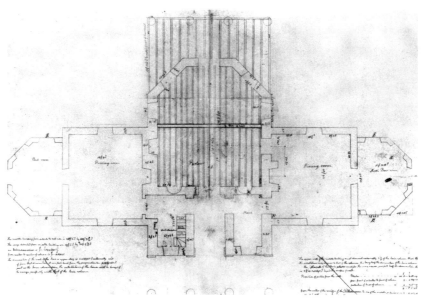

8-51b. Thomas Jefferson (designer and draftsman). Revised plan for Monticello, with semi-octagonal projections, about March, 1771. (Massachusetts Historical Society, Coolidge Collection, K24).

after the Treaty of Paris of 1763. The mountains to the west were still a potentially dangerous frontier.

The interior details at Whitehall, attributed to Buckland, have been restored, and are carried out with greater overall restraint than those of Gunston Hall [8-48]. If this is his work, it would appear that his skills were better suited to buildings on a larger scale.

The same plate from *Select Architecture* by Robert Morris was used, with modifications, for Brandon, in Prince George County, Virginia, begun in 1765 for Nathaniel Harrison, a friend of Thomas Jefferson [8-49 and 8-50].[52] The central portion is one room deep, the entrance hall flanked by drawing room and dining room. These are connected by lower rooms to the two-story end buildings for the chambers. The pattern of central block, lower connecting portions, and two-story end buildings reproduces the Morris drawings more faithfully than does that of Whitehall, and there is no monumental portico. The staircase is not set off as a separate architectural feature, but occupies one corner of the entrance hall.

THROUGHOUT THESE discussions of colonial housing it has been apparent that the builders of early America, whatever their national origins, made use of traditional designs and methods, interpreting them to be appropriate in the colonies. That some

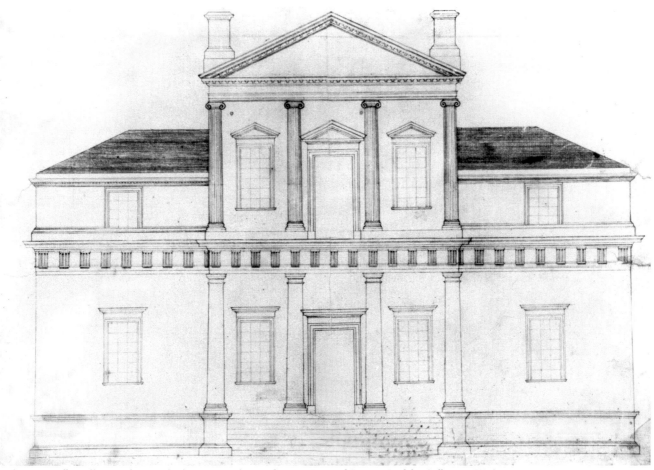

8-52. Monticello. Jefferson's elevation for first version. (Massachusetts Historical Society, Coolidge Collection, K23).

on occasion made use of published designs is also apparent, and again the results were, as at Whitehall and Brandon, interpretations rather than precise imitations.

The most notable product of such interpretation was brought about by one whose career, far more than Peter Harrison's, went beyond architecture to activities and responsibilities of extensive national and international significance. In 1768 Thomas Jefferson began to plan a house to crown "Monticello," a hill near Charlottesville that he inherited from his father. Here was begun a building history that would last far beyond the colonial period and hold his affection, if not always his full attention, during his years as statesman and architect to the new state of Virginia.

It was long thought that the original house of Monticello was also based on Plate 3 of *Select Architecture*, but recent study indicates that Jefferson's development of the plan was more complicated and more original.[53] His first intention appears to have been to build a square house with porticoes on all sides, with separate outbuildings as the nucleus of his farm and gardens, and for this he had a model in Gibbs's *Book of Architecture*, Plate 4. Practical considerations led him to change this to a cruciform design with central two-story portion and lower wings [8-51]. To this scheme he added the extended service wings below the level of the main house which replaced the originally planned outbuildings. By 1772 he had settled upon an elevation for the east facade of the house, using a double portico for the central portion and extending the entablature of the lower order around the wings [8-52]. Here he depended more upon Palladio for the details, which he adjusted to suit himself.

The farm and gardens were of equal and in fact not separate concern for Jefferson. That is a story in itself, but it may be noted here that he planned a series of terraces after the manner of John James's *Theory and Practice of Gardening*, much as Governor Shirley had done twenty years earlier. Excavations have shown the extent to which these plans were carried out and how the whole property developed into a nearly self-sufficient village, as the Frenchman had observed at Bacon's Castle. From the beginning of construction according to the first scheme in 1769, house, farm, and gardens were to undergo many changes, and the remaining account of these belongs to the history of American architecture after the Revolution.[54]

8-54. Mount Vernon. West front. (Photo: M. D. Ross).

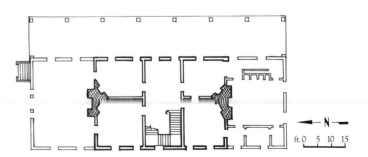

8-53. George Washington, Mount Vernon, Fairfax Co., Va., begun 1730. Plan. (After Great Georgian Houses, 1:73).

8-55. Mt. Vernon. North side. (Courtesy of The Mount Vernon Ladies' Association).

8-56. Venetian window of the Tuscan Order. (From B. Langley, The City and Country Builder's... Treasury of Designs, London, 1741, Plate 51).

MONTICELLO HAS BECOME a national shrine, and so has the home of another early American statesman, George Washington. When he inherited the estate of Mount Vernon in Fairfax County, Virginia, Washington had a one-and-one-half story house, with end chimneys and two rooms on either side of a central hall [8-53].[55] Three major campaigns of rebuilding brought the house to completion [8-54]. In 1757-1758 Washington had the height raised to two and one-half stories, much renovation done, and four dependencies added. Then in 1773-1778 he enlarged the house by adding a library on the south and a banquet room on the north. To this period belong many details of decoration based on pattern books, such as the window of the banquet room [8-55], from Batty Langley's Treasury of Designs of 1740 [8-56].[56]

Before all this expansion of Mount Vernon was finished the Revolutionary War began. The final addition was the two-story portico overlooking the Potomac that Washington built after his return from the war in 1783. The original dependencies had by this time been replaced by the present ones, linked to the main building by curved arcades. And as at Monticello, the full story of Mount Vernon includes Washington's extensive planning and work for his farm and gardens.[57]

IN THE MAJOR SOUTHERN TOWNS, Williamsburg, Charleston, and Annapolis particularly, similar use was made of the printed sources, especially for ornamental details. Of particular interest is the George Wythe house in Williamsburg, built 1752-1754 by Richard Taliaferro, who had worked on the ballroom wing added to the Governor's Palace in 1749-1751. He built the house for himself but moved to another property that he owned, Powhatan, when his daughter married George Wythe in 1755, and the young couple settled in the bride's home. All this is a matter of some historical consequence, as George Wythe, who became professor of law at the College of William and Mary, also gave instruction in law to Jefferson, who came to the College in 1760. Jefferson's interest in architecture may have been encouraged by meeting Taliaferro there.

The house itself has much the character of the original Carter's Grove [8-57].[58] There is no pedimented doorway, but the same geometrical system was used for the elevation. In fact the study of several Virginia houses for their stylistic properties and the family relationships of their owners has given rise to the speculation that Taliaferro was the architect for them all.[59] The Wythe house is a double pile, with chimneys between the front and rear rooms, and it is dignified in its simplicity as it faces on the Palace Green. As could be the case with a town house on

sufficient property, it presides over a miniature plantation, with separate kitchen, other outbuildings, and a kitchen garden.

Not so much space was available for the house of Miles Brewton at 27 King Street, Charleston, South Carolina, built about 1769 and generally considered to be the finest eighteenth-century house in that city [8-58].[60] In the heart of the old city, the Brewton house is a nearly square double pile, with central stair hall. Here instead of the plain facade of the houses in and near Williamsburg there is a two-story Doric and Ionic portico, as at Drayton Hall. The carver is known, Ezra Waite, who described himself in 1769 as coming from London, a "Civil Architect, House-builder in general, and Carver," who spoke of his house, also in King Street, "where architecture is taught by a peculiar method never published in any book extant."[61] Waite died in 1769, and we do not know whom he may have taught in what must have been a short period of time. This, along with Ariss and Taliaferro is another instance of a builder designated in contemporary terms as an "architect," and it may be the earliest instance in America of a builder proposing to give instruction in "architecture" as he perceived it.

Waite's carvings for the interior of the Brewton house are of a richness comparable to those in Gunston Hall, using motifs from Swan and Chippendale. They are more appropriately scaled

8-57. Richard Taliaferro, George Wythe house, Williamsburg, Va., 1752-1754. (Photo: M. C. Donnelly).

8-58. Ezra Waite, Miles Brewton house, Charleston, S.C., 1765-1769. (Photo: HABS).

to the sizes of the rooms. The house is raised on a high basement, and the major drawing room, with its pilastered and pedimented doorways and elaborate chimneypiece, was planned to catch the breezes, as often done in Charleston houses.

Several fine brick homes were built in Annapolis in the middle of the century, among which is the James Brice house, 1767-73 [8-59].[62] Although Buckland is known to have worked on the interiors, the house was probably designed by the master mason. It is a mini-plantation house in the city, with a main block and low passages connecting to one-and-one-half story dependencies on either side. The plan is similar to that of the Moffatt-Ladd house, the hall widening out with parlor behind, and in this case a tiny office built in one corner at the front. The exterior is plain except for the rather astonishing ornament of the central second-story window and the cornice. Otherwise the Brice house appears even more severe than the Derby house, lacking pedimented doorway, belt course, and dormers. It is closer in spirit to the original Carter's Grove and to the Wythe house, suggesting a current of more severe taste in the third quarter of the eighteenth century, running parallel to the more elaborate preferences expressed in the Brewton house. Buckland did contribute to the finishing of the interior, some of the details coming from Swan's *British Architect*.

The last, and by no means the least, of the eighteenth-century houses in the Southern colonies to be discussed is also in Annapolis, designed completely by William Buckland. Built for

8-59. James Brice house, Annapolis, Md., 1767-73. (Photo: M. C. Donnelly).

8-60. *William Buckland, Hammond-Harwood house, Annapolis, Md., 1773-1774. (Photo: M. C. Donnelly).*

Matthias Hammond in 1773-1774, the Hammond-Harwood house is now a museum [8-60].[63] That Buckland was the designer of the building as a whole is apparent from the portrait by Charles Wilson Peale, showing him with a plan and elevation of the house [8-61]. One might be skeptical of this portrait for securing the attribution to Buckland were it not for the eighteenth-century tradition of portraits of architects holding drawings of their designs.[64] While yet another in the group of houses that were designed from *Select Architecture*, the Hammond-Harwood House shows some variation from the plans we have seen thus far. The Palladian formula of central block, connections, and attached dependencies all in one line appears, but the plan of the main house here is two rooms deep. The double-pile plan is further modified by having a short, narrow entrance hall, leading to the dining room, and the stair in a separate room to one side, actually in one of the smallest spaces for this element in any of the Georgian houses. The effect seems pinched, in comparison to the great sweep of the stairs at Carter's Grove, especially on the second level.

The splendor of the Hammond-Harwood house lies in Buckland's masterful design and carving of the woodwork through-

8-61. *Charles Wilson Peale, William Buckland, 1789, oil on canvas. (Yale University Art Gallery, Mabel Brady Garvan Collection).*

out. From the Ionic front door, with carved roses in the spandrels above the fanlight, to the chimneypiece and richly carved lintels of the dining room, Buckland's mastery of his technique is evident [8-62]. Fortunately surviving when many fine eighteenth-century houses have perished or been altered beyond recognition, the Hammond-Harwood house is eloquent testimony to the aspirations of the owners and the skill of the builders in colonial Virginia and Maryland.

THE ELEMENTS OF PLAN and ornament that were used in numerous variations in the New England and Southern colonies were of course also used in the eighteenth-century houses of the Middle Atlantic colonies.[65] An especial richness prevailed, particularly in the Philadelphia area, achieved in part by some use of stone rather than wood or brick. Two of the grander houses that have survived illustrate these houses at their richest development.

The first is Mount Pleasant, built in 1761-1762 by a wealthy Scottish sea captain named John McPherson [8-63].[66] It is placed on a rise above the Schuylkill River in what is now Fairmount Park, and the whole estate included gardens, barns, and dependencies in the manner of the plantations of the South. The barns are now gone, but the house

8-62. Hammond-Harwood house. Dining room. (Photo by M. E. Warren, Annapolis, Md.).

8-63. *Captain John McPherson house, Mount Pleasant, Philadelphia, Pa.. 1761-1762. (Photo: M. C. Donnelly).*

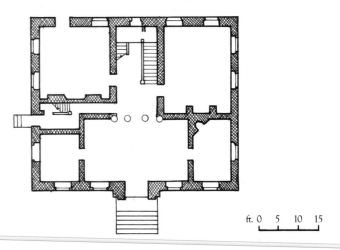

86-66. *Cliveden. Plan. (After F. Kimball, Domestic Architecture of the American Colonies and of the Early Republic, New York, 1927, fig. 47).*

8-64. *Mount Pleasant. Second floor window. (Photo: M. C. Donnelly).*

has been spared encroachment from the city and is more a country house than a merchant's town house.

The two-story five-bay facade, end chimneys, hip roof, and balustrade make up a standard formula for the east front. The richness of the whole scheme is at once apparent. The house is built of stone and the walls covered with stucco, leaving the details of quoins, lintels, and the belt course to stand out against it. The central bay projects slightly, with pedimented door, Venetian window, and pediment above. The chimney stacks pierced with arches are especially notable.

In plan Mount Pleasant is not a conventional double pile. There is a central hall, but the parlor occupies the full width of the house on the north side, and the stair is in a hall directly to the left of the east door, with the dining room behind it on the south side. The interior is extensively fitted with woodwork, Doric on the first floor and Ionic above for the pilasters. Philadelphia was wealthy, and her homeowners could call upon craftsmen for such woodwork as finished the eighteen-inch-thick openings of the Venetian window [8-64].

In nearby Germantown two years later a Philadelphia lawyer, Benjamin Chew, began his country house, finished in 1767 [8-65].[67] This time the facade is of ashlar, in a warm color that sets off the pedimented door, the modillioned cornice, and the central pediment. The other sides are again covered with stucco. The chimneys are set into the house, the dormers are similar to those of Mount Pleasant, and there are five rather startling stone urns adorning the roof.

The plan of Cliveden, as the Chew house is known, is a modified double pile [8-66]. The wide entrance hall is screened from the stair hall by a Tuscan colonnade. As at Mount Pleasant the kitchen was originally in a wing, but later additions have altered the service areas at the rear of the house. Although built as a country house, it does not have the plantation house character of Mount Pleasant.

One other house in the Middle Atlantic colonies may be included here, the William Corbit house in Odessa, Delaware [8-67].[68] Built in 1772-1774, it is of brick, with stone lintels and string course, a hip roof with dormers and balustrade, and the

8-65. *Benjamin Chew house, Cliveden, Germantown, Pa., 1763-1767. (Photo: M. C. Donnelly).*

147

8-67. *William Corbit house, Odessa, Del., 1772-1774. (Photo: M. C. Donnelly).*

chimneys set into the house. The central bay is not projected as on the more elaborate Philadelphia houses. The pedimented door has the fan light carried up into the pediment, a motif that was to become popular in the Middle States after the Revolution and made one of its early appearances here.

The plan of the Corbit house is a double pile, with central staircase hall and four rooms on the first floor. The original kitchen was in the cellar, the present wing having been added later. The house has been described as "square."[69] This is not correct, however, as it is actually rectangular, the length falling just short of being equal to the diagonal of a square constructed on the width [8-68]. The woodwork was done by the local firm of Robert May, and it is elaborate for the comparative modesty of the exterior. The ornamental details closely resemble designs in Swan's *British Architect* that had evidently been used in several Philadelphia houses a few years earlier. William Corbit had served as an apprentice tanner in Philadelphia from 1765 to 1767. Whether Corbit or May had knowledge of these houses and sought to emulate them, or whether Swan's designs were the sole source of inspiration is not clear.[70] There was unmistakably a desire for a splendid interior, and the outcome gave Delaware a fine town house with much the exuberant spirit of Gunston Hall.

W E HAVE NOT TOUCHED UPON the eighteenth-century houses of New York and New Jersey. While some fine examples have survived, they can show little more than further variations on the American Georgian style.[71] We shall now instead turn to the churches and public buildings of this period to see how the elements of this style were used in other contexts.

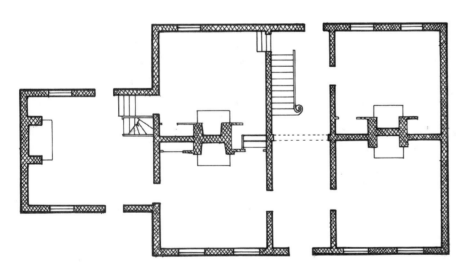

8-68. Corbit house. Plan. (After J. A. H. Sweeney, Grandeur on the Appoquinimink: The House of William Corbit at Odessa, Delaware, *Newark, Del., 1959, 41).*

Notes to Chapter 8

1. For these discussions see especially Hugh Morrison, *Early American Architecture: From the First Colonial Settlement to the National Period* (New York: Dover Publications, 1987, 1952), 270-313; William Harvey Pierson, *American Buildings and their Architects* (New York: Oxford University Press, 1986), 61-73; and Marcus Whiffen and Frederick Koeper, *American Architecture, 1607-1976* (Cambridge, Mass.: MIT Press, 1981), 53-59. Fiske Kimball, *Domestic Architecture of the American Colonies and of the Early Republic* (New York: Dover Publications, 1966 [1922]), treats separately the elements of plan, doorway, staircase design, etc.

2. Morrison, *Early American Architecture*, 478-480.

3. Town Records of Ipswich, Massachusetts, February 19, 1655, ". . . make the Meetinghouse Tite, where shingles were removed by him [George Norton]. occasioned by the puting in of the gutters."

4. Nellie Stearus Messer, "The Ropes Memorial at Salem, Massachusetts," *OTNE* 17, no. 4 (April 1924): 146-163.

5. Walter Kendall Watkins, "The Hancock House and its Builder," *OTNE* 17, no. 1 (July 1926): 3-19; and Kimball, *Domestic Architecture*, 268.

6. Watkins, "The Hancock House," 7.

7. John Parkinson, *Paridisus in Sole* (London: 1629), 3.

8. John James, *The Theory and Practice of Gardening* (London: 1712, reprinted, Farnborough: Gregg, 1969), 116-127. The numerous reprint editions of eighteenth-century treatises on architecture and gardening, some with editorial commentary, have greatly facilitated studies of early American architecture and gardening. For the latter see Ann Leighton, *American Gardens in the Eighteenth Century* (Boston: Houghton Mifflin Company, 1976). Reference to a visitor named "John James" in one of Hancock's letters led to the opinion in some of the earlier literature that the visitor was the English architect and writer. That this was simply a coincidence was suggested by Priscilla Metcalf, "Which John James was in Boston in 1736," *OTNE* 43, no. 2 (October/December 1952): 54-56.

9. Frederic C. Detwiller, "The Evolution of the Shirley-Eustis House," *OTNE* 70, no. 257 (1980): 17-30; and Danella Pearson, "Shirley-Eustis House Landscape History," *OTNE* 70, no. 257 (1980): 1-16.

10. Walter Kendall Watkins, "The Early Use and Manufacture of Paper-Hangings in Boston," *OTNE* 12, no. 3 (January 1922), 112.

11. Catherine Lynn, *Wallpaper in America* (New York: W. W. Norton and Company, 1980), 17-20 and 107-119.

12. Nina Fletcher Little, *American Decorative Wall Painting 1700-1850* (Sturbridge, Mass.: Old Sturbridge Village, 1952).

13. Antoinette Forrester Downing, *Early Homes of Rhode Island* (Richmond, Va.: Garrett and Massie, Inc., 1937), 213-214. The contract accompanying this drawing was published, with commentary, by George C. Mason in *American Architect and Building News* 10 (August 20, 1881): 83-85.

14. Charles Franklin Montgomery, ed., *Joseph Moxon's Mechanick Exercises; or, The Doctrine of Handy-works Applied to the Arts of Smithing, Joinery, Carpentry, Turning, Bricklaying* (London: Praeger, 1970 [1703]), 126.

15. Ibid., 128.

16. Ibid., 253 and 117.

17. Kevin M. Sweeney, *Mansion People: Kinship, Class, and Architecture in Western Massachusetts* (n.p., 1984), 235-245.

18. Charles B. Wood, "A Survey and Bibliography of Writings on English and American Architectural Books Published before 1895," *Winterthur Portfolio* 2 (1965): 127-137; and Campbell, *Vitruvius Britannicus*, 3 vols. (London 1715-1725), Cl. Plate 40.

19. William Salmon, *Palladio Londinensis* (London: 1734), Plate 26.

20. For builder's manuals see: Helen Park, *A List of Architectural Books Available in America Before the Revolution* (Los Angeles: Hennessey and Ingalls, 1973); and also Janice G. Schimmelman, *Architectural Treatises and Building Handbooks Available in American Libraries and Bookstores through 1800* (Worcester, Mass.: American Antiquarian Society, 1986); Rudolf Wittkower, *Palladio and Palladianism* (New York: George Braziller, 1974), 95-112; William B. O'Neal, "Pattern Books in American Architecture, 1730-1930," in *Building by the Book*, Mario di Valmarana, 3 vols. (Charlottesville, Va.: The University of Virginia Press, 1984), 1:47-74; and Warren J. Cox, "Four Men, the *Four Books* and the Five-Part House," in *Building by the Book*, di Valmarana, 2:117-146; John Harris, "The Pattern Book Phenomenon," in *Building by the Book*, di Valmarana, 2:101-116.

21. Henry W. L. Dana, "The Longfellow House, Cambridge, Massachusetts," *OTNE* 37, no. 4 (April 1948): 82-98. The house is variously named in the literature, having at one time been owned by Andrew Craigie and later by Henry Wadsworth Longfellow.

22. Charles Cornelius, "Wentworth-Gardner house," *Metropolitan Museum of Art Bulletin* 14 (February 1919): 24-31.

23. Edwin W. Small, "The Derby House," *OTNE* 47, no. 4 (April-June 1957): 101-107.

24. John Summerson, *Architecture in Britain 1530 to 1830* (Baltimore: Penguin Books, 1954), 197-208.

25. Carl Bridenbaugh, *Peter Harrison* (Chapel Hill: University of North Carolina Press, 1949), 112-117.

26. Philip Dana Orcutt, *The Moffatt Ladd House* (Portsmouth: N. H. Society of Colonial Dames of America, 1935); and Thomas Waterman, *The Dwellings of Colonial America* (Chapel Hill: University of North Carolina Press, 1950), 269-294.

27. Robert Morris, *Select Architecture; being regular designs of plans and elevations well suited to both town and country* (New York: Da Capo Press, 1973 [1757]), Plate 1.

28. Hannah Tutt, *The Lee Mansion* (Marblehead: Marblehead Historical Society, 1911); Pauline Soroka Chadwell, "The Colonel Jeremiah Lee Mansion," *Antiques* 48 (December 1945): 353-355; and Morrison, *Early American Architecture*, 497-499.

29. Abraham Swan, *The British Architect* (London: 1745, reprint, New York: Da Capo Press, 1967), Plate 51.

30. Thomas T. Waterman, *The Mansions of Virginia* (Chapel Hill: University of North Carolina Press, 1945), 149-153; and William M. S. Rasmussen, "Architectural Drawings and Design in the Virginia Colony," in *The Making of Virginia Architecture*, eds. Charles E. Brownell, et al. (Richmond: Virginia Museum of Fine Arts, 1992): 138-139. See also Richard Guy Wilson, ed., *Buildings of Virginia: Tidewater and Piedmont* (New York: Oxford University Press, 2002): 356-357. [Ed.].

31. The plan in Figure 24 shows the present arrangement. The wall between the two west rooms on the first floor was removed about 1900. The plan was not unique, having been used in England and elsewhere in Virginia (Waterman, *Mansions of Virginia*, 141-142).

32. Ibid., 149.

33. I. A. Nairn and Nikolaus Pevsner, *Buildings of England: Sussex*, by Ian Nairn and Nikolaus Pevsner [Harmondsworth, Middlesex]: Penguin Books, 1965), 358-360.

34. Samuel Gaillard Stoney, *Plantations of the Carolina Low Country* (Charleston: The Carolina Art Association, 1966), 142-165; Frederick D. Nichols, "Drayton Hall, plantation house of the Drayton family," *Antiques* 97, no. 4 (April 1970): 576-583; and Mills Lane, *Architecture of the Old South* (New York: Abbeville Press, 1993), 44-54.

35. Campbell, *Vitruvius Britannicus*, 2, Plate 88.

36. Andrea Palladio, *The Four Books of Architecture*, trans. Giacomo Leoni, 2 vols. (London, 1715): 2, Plate 61.

37. William Kent, *Designs of Inigo Jones and Others* (London: 1727), Plate 64. The same plate had been used for the chimneypiece in Governor Wentworth's house at Little Harbor, New Hampshire (Kimball, *Domestic Architecture*, 124-127).

38. Waterman, *Mansions of Virginia*, 183-192; Mary A. Stephenson, *Carter's Grove Plantation: A History* (Williamsburg: 1964), 25-54 and 157-171; Ivor Noël Hume, *Digging for Carter's Grove* (Williamsburg: Colonial Williamsburg, 1974); and Marcus Whiffen, *The Eighteenth-Century Houses of Williamsburg* (Williamsburg: Colonial Williamsburg, 1984), 263-274.

39. Waterman, *Mansions of Virginia*, 253-260; and William M. S. Rasmussen, "Palladio in Tidewater Virginia: Mount Airy and Blandfield" in di Valmarana, ed., *Building by the Book*, 3:75-110.

40. Waterman, *Mansions of Virginia*, 243-248.

41. Ibid., 244.

42. James Gibbs, *A Book of Architecture* (London: 1728, reprinted, New York: Benjamin Blom, 1968).

43. An extensive, probably definitive, study of Gibbs is Terry Friedman, *James Gibbs* (New Haven: Yale University Press, 1984). The influence of *A Book of Architecture* and Gibbs's other book, *Rules for drawing the Several Parts of Architecture* (London: 1732), is discussed pages 272-282. Summaries of Gibbs's life and work are in Summerson, *Architecture in Britain*, 209-215, and in Howard Colvin, *A Biographical Dictionary of English Architects 1600-1840*, 2nd ed. (London: John Murray, 1978), 337-354.

44. Waterman, *Mansions of Virginia*, 223-230; Fiske Kimball, "Gunston Hall," *JSAH* 13, no. 2 (May 1954): 3-8; Rosamond Randall Beirne and John Henry Scharff, *William Buckland* (Baltimore: The Maryland Historical Society, 1958), 22-30; Luke Beckerdite, "William Buckland and William Bernard Sears: The Designer and the Carver," *Journal of Early Southern Decorative Arts* 8 (November 1982): 7-40; and Thomas J. Colin, "Solving the Mystery of Gunston Hall," *Historic Preservation* 36, no. 3 (June 1984): 41-45.

45. Thomas Chippendale, *The Gentleman and Cabinet Maker's Guide* (London: 1754, reprinted, New York: Dover, 1966), Plate 26.

46. Abraham Swan, *A Collection of Designs in Architecture* (London: 1757, reprinted, Farnborough: Gregg, 1972).

47. Charles Scarlett, Jr., "Governor Horatio Sharpe's Whitehall," *Maryland Historical Magazine* 46, no. 1 (March 1951): 8-26; and Barbara Brand, "The Work of William Buckland in Maryland" (Master's thesis, George Washington University, 1979), 73-75.

48. Robert Morris, *Select Architecture* (London: 1757), Plate 3.

49. Beirne and Scharff, *William Buckland*, 60-61.

50. William Halfpenny, *The Modern Builder's Assistant* (London: 1742), Plate 18.

51. Campbell, *Vitruvius Britannicus*, 2:78-79.

52. Waterman, *Mansions of Virginia*, 364-373; and Calder Loth, "Palladio in Southside Virginia: Berandon and Battersea," in Mario di Valmarana, ed., *Building by the Book*, 1:25-46.

53. The literature on Thomas Jefferson is of course enormous. The earliest major work on his architectural contributions is Fiske Kimball, *Thomas Jefferson, Architect* (Cambridge: Riverside Press, 1916), Plate 5, which includes the fundamental list of Jefferson's drawings in the Coolidge Collection of the Massachusetts Historical Society. Books and articles published by 1968 are listed in Frank John Roos, *Bibliography of Early American Architecture: Writings on Architecture Constructed before 1860 in Eastern and Central United States* (Urbana: University of Illinois Press, 1968). Among the recent publications are Buford Pickens, *Mr. Jefferson as Revolutionary Architect* (Philadelphia: Society of Architectural Historians, 1975); William B. O'Neal, *Jefferson's Fine Arts Library for the University of Virginia, with Additional Notes on Architectural Volumes Known to Have Been Owned by Jefferson* (Charlottesville, University of Virginia Press, 1956) and the expanded second edition published as *Jefferson's Fine Arts Library: His Selections for the University of Virginia, Together with his own Architectural Books* (Charlottesville: University Press of Virginia, 1976); Frederick Nichols and James Bear, *Monticello* (Monticello, Va.: Thomas Jefferson Memorial Foundation, 1967); and Thomas Jefferson, *Thomas Jefferson's Architectural Drawings*, ed. Frederick Nichols (Boston: Massachusetts Historical Society, 1978). The revised analysis of Jefferson's use of sources is in Gene Waddell, "The First Monticello," *JSAH* 46, no. 1 (March 1987): 5-29, which should be consulted for the documentary sources.

54. Edwin M. Betts, *Thomas Jefferson's Farm Book* (Philadelphia: The American Philosophical Society, 1944); Edwin M. Betts and Hazlehurst B. Perkins, *Thomas Jefferson's Garden Book* (Philadelphia: The American Philosophical Society, 1944); Edwin M. Betts and Hazlehurst B. Perkins, *Thomas Jefferson's Garden at Monticello* (Charlottesville: University of Virginia Press, 1971); and Frederick Nichols and Ralph Griswold, *Thomas Jefferson, Landscape Architect* (Charlottesville: University Press of Virginia, 1978), 90-120. For the later stages of the house see Pierson, *American Buildings*, 356-367, and Waddell, "The First Monticello," 25-27.

55. Morrison, *Early American Architecture*, 356-367; Elswyth Thane, *Mount Vernon Is Ours: The Story of its Preservation* (New York: Duell, Sloan and Pearce, 1966).

56. Batty Langley, *The Builder's and Workman's Treasury of Designs* (London: 1740), Plate 52. This publication was one of several by Batty Langley, together with his brother Thomas, which went into successive editions and became popular sources for such details.

57. Leighton, *American Gardens*, 247-269; and, Elizabeth de Forest, *The Gardens and Grounds at Mount Vernon: How George Washington Planned and Planted Them* (Mount Vernon, Va.: Mount Vernon Ladies' Association of the Union, 1982).

58. Waterman, *Mansions of Virginia*, 214-220; and Whiffen, *Eighteenth-Century Houses*, 174-176.

59. Waterman, *Mansions of Virginia*, 103-107; Morrison, *Early American Architecture*, 347-349; and Eric S. McCready, "The Architecture of Richard Taliaferro" (Master's thesis, University of Oregon, 1968), n.p.

60. Beatrice Ravenel, *Architects of Charleston* (Charleston: Carolina Art Association, 1945), 47-48; Morrison, *Early American Architecture*, 416-418; Carolyn W. Dixon, "The Miles Brewton House: Ezra Waite's Architectural Design Books and Other Possible Sources," *South Carolina Historical Magazine* 82 (April 1981): 118-52; and Mills Lane, *Architecture of the Old South: South Carolina* (Savannah, Ga.: Beehive Press, 1984), 63-68.

61. Morrison, *Early American Architecture*, 416-418.

62. Deering Davis, *Annapolis Houses 1700-1775* (New York: Architectural Book Publishing Company, 1947), 34-39; Morrison, *Early American Architecture*, 393-395; Beirne and Scharff, *William Buckland*, 96-98; and Michael F. Trostel, "The Annapolis Plan in America," in di Valmarana, ed., *Building by the Book*, 2:10-11.

63. Davis, *Annapolis Houses*, 41-65; Morrison, *Early American Architecture*, 398-400; Beirne and Scharff, *William Buckland*, 90-94; Trostel, "The Annapolis Plan in America," 11-14.

64. An interesting study could be made of the portraits of architects in early America.

65. Morrison, *Early American Architecture*, 525-526.

66. Waterman, *Dwellings*, 178-182; Morrison, *Early American Architecture*, 526-528; and Helen Comstock, "Mount Pleasant, the most elegant seat in Pennsylvania," *Connoisseurs* 156 (August 1964): 226-231.

67. Waterman, *Dwellings*, 175-177; Margaret B. Tinkcom, "Cliveden: The Building of a Philadelphia Countryseat, 1763-1767," *Pennsylvania Magazine of History and Biography* 88, no. 1 (January 1964): 2-36; and Raymond J. Shepherd, Jr., "Cliveden," *Historic Preservation* (July-September 1972): 4-11.

68. Morrison, *Early American Architecture*, 532; and John A. H. Sweeney, *Grandeur on the Appoquinimink: The House of William Corbit at Odessa, Delaware* (Newark: University of Delaware Press, 1959), 39-66.

69. Ibid., 42.

70. Ibid., 49-57.

71. Morrison, *Early American Architecture*, 556-565; and Waterman, *Dwellings*, 190-234.

9-1. St. Philip's Church, Charleston, S.C. 1711-1723. Drawing by William Birch, 1820. (Courtesy of the Henry Francis du Pont Winterthur Museum).

◄ *Chapter 9* ►

18th-Century American Churches and Public Buildings

THE HOUSES THAT have survived from the eighteenth century in the English colonies, whether modest or downright extravagant, demonstrate how their builders both perpetuated and modified what they knew of English building, and it was entirely right and natural that they should do so. When it came to building churches, town halls, colleges, and other public buildings, the decisions about plans and details were more those of building committees than of individuals, but the methods and procedures were similar. Again many of these buildings have

9-2. St. Philip's Church. View of the interior. Painting by Thomas Middleton. (Courtesy of Charleston, S. C., St. Philip's Church).

survived, and because more copious records were usual in the case of institutions a great deal is also known about those which have not.

CHURCHES FORM a large body of material which can only be summarized here.[1] With the colonies all under the English crown in the eighteenth century, buildings of the Church of England will be reviewed first, then the Congregational churches that still dominated New England, and finally the buildings of other Protestant sects, including those of the Society of Friends.

Perhaps the most astonishing of the American Anglican churches of the eighteenth century was St. Philip's Church in Charleston, begun about 1711 [9-1].[2] Although begun earlier than the Georgian period proper, it is included here because it was clearly a harbinger of things to come. The church, destroyed in 1835, was more than 100 feet long and 62 feet wide. An octagonal tower in three stages rose above the vestibule, and the west, north,

9-3. St. Philip's Church, Birmingham, Warwickshire, 1709-1715. (Birmingham Reference Library).

and south doors were covered by giant Tuscan porticoes of four columns each. These were the first known, and for a long time, the only such porticoes in the English colonies. An early account describes St. Philip's as having been modeled after St. Ignatius in Antwerp, which burned in 1718, but it also resembled the city churches of London. The tower has been compared to that of St. Magnus in London, built by Wren in 1671-1687.[3]

Two paintings of the interior, owned by the church, show a five-bay nave with a cove ceiling and galleries behind a giant arcade with Corinthian pilasters [9-2]. This was the scheme of St. Lawrence Jewry in London, also by Wren, 1670-1687. These paintings confirm a description of 1820: "Each Pillar is now ornamented with a piece of Monumental Sculpture, some of them with Bass-relief figures, finely executed by some of the first Artists in England."[4] Such sculptures, mounted in cartouches, are certainly not characteristic of the Wren churches, but do appear against the square pillars of St. Philip's Church in Birmingham by Thomas Archer, 1709-1715 [9-3]. Having a long nave with galleries behind a giant order, St. Philip's, Charleston, is much more like St. Philip's, Birmingham, its precise contemporary, than it is like St. Lawrence Jewry. Archer was appointed one of the Commissioners of the Act for Building Fifty New Churches in 1711, and he could well have been consulted by the "Supervisors" appointed in Charleston. It is perhaps noteworthy that neither of the St. Philip churches was originally built with a separate chancel, that in Birmingham having been added in 1883-1884.[5]

The prospect of moving from coincidence to attribution is always enticing, as witness the speculations about Richard Taliaferro. Unless such proposed attributions are clearly stated to be conjecture and not fact, however, a great disservice is done to a proper understanding of the building in question. Attempts to force the work of Sir Christopher Wren into American colonial buildings, whether built in his lifetime or not, have become almost venerable. The variety and ingenuity of Wren's interiors and steeples were undoubtedly influential, but when the first fully developed American churches, with rectangular body, tower, and spire, were being built it was not Wren himself but the next generation of English architects who were active and likely to be consulted from the colonies. When St. Philip's in Charleston was begun Wren was seventy-nine years old and long since past his years of church-building. He wrote advice to his fellow commissioners for the Fifty New Churches, but they were built by his younger successors. Whatever of his ideas were employed in the design of American churches, they were most likely already re-interpreted by architects in London as well as in America.

Christ Church in Boston is probably the one most frequently held to exemplify Wren's churches in the colonies [9-4].[6] To the extent that it has a main body, tower, and spire, this is correct; and a parallel with Wren's St. James, Piccadilly, 1680-1684, may be seen in that the proportions of length to width to height are approximately the same in both buildings: four to three to two. The problem is immediately apparent. More than forty years separate the two, during which churches built by Wren's contemporaries and successors had gone up all over England. Were these proportions unique to St. James and Christ Church, or were they part of the stock-in-trade of how to build a church? As at the first King's Chapel, the tower of Christ Church projects fully on the west front. The separate levels of the tower are marked by stringcourses, as had been done on English churches since the Middle Ages,

9-4. Christ Church, Boston, Mass., 1723. (From J. Winsor, Memorial History of Boston, 2:509).

and there is no need to search for a prototype here. An element which is different is the projecting semicircular apse on the east, not to be found elsewhere in the colonies until the enlargement of Trinity Church in New York in 1735. It was also rare in England at this period, but a recent example was Whitchurch, Shropshire, built in 1712-1713 by William Smith of Warwick.[7]

The Burgis Print of 1726 shows Christ Church as originally built, with simply a tall octagonal spire rising above the brick tower. The elaborate upper tower and spire seen in the illustration were added in 1741. Here is where the oft-repeated erroneous attribution of the church to the printmaker William Price comes in. Price provided the design for the tower in 1740, not the church itself. The illustration shows it with pyramids at the base, a quoined inner square base, then two square stages, the lower Doric with two arched openings and the upper Ionic with one, and finally a spire. This blew down in 1804 and was rebuilt with help and alterations from Charles Bulfinch. It blew down again in another hurricane and was rebuilt in 1954. The original illustrated here in the print seems far closer to Gibbs than to Wren.

For the interior of Christ Church a reflection of some of Wren's designs is more plausible. There is a high nave with a curved ceiling and galleries on either side, supported by square pillars below and the bays marked by fluted square posts above [9-5]. This two-story arrangement was used by Wren several times, the closest parallel being St. James, Piccadilly, whereas at Christ Church the gallery bays are separated by entablatures perpendicular to the nave, each with its own curved ceiling. St. James, rebuilt since World War II, is of course far richer. Wren made his preference for St. James as an ideal church design known to the Commissioners in 1711, and this could have been known to the unidentified architect who supplied the designs for Christ Church.[8] The interior of Christ Church is, however, almost

9-5. Christ Church, Boston. Interior. (SPNEA).

9-6. *Richard Munday, Trinity Church, Newport, R.I., (Newport Histori-cal Society).*

austere in comparison with St. James. While the structural formula is similar, the aesthetic is not. The bold projection of the abaci and the cornices of the entablature blocks, for example, are closer to those of All Saints, Derby, by James Gibbs in 1723-1725, and speak of a new generation of architects in England.

The discussions of St. Philip's and Christ Church should serve to illustrate how imperfect is our knowledge of some of the major building projects in the American colonies. This will be evident for some of the other colonial churches. Closest to Christ Church in time and design is Trinity Church in Newport, Rhode Island, built in 1725-1726 [9-6].[9] A little more is known here, primarily that the master carpenter was Richard Munday, builder of the Ayrault House.[10] This was a much larger undertaking. Trinity Church, built of wood, was clearly modeled after Christ Church in Boston. It was originally only five bays long and was lengthened to seven in 1762. The upper parts of the tower and

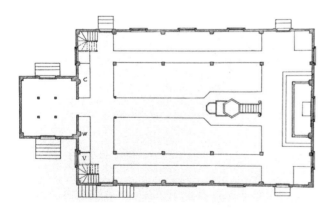

9-7. *Trinity Church, Newport. Plan in 1726. (From N. Isham, Trinity Church in Newport, Rhode Island, Boston, 1936, 37).*

9-8. *Sir Christopher Wren, St. James Piccadilly, London, 1676-1684. Interior. (National Monuments Record).*

spire were not built until 1741 and were copied from those of Christ Church, so precisely, in fact, that the same drawings may have been used for both. The interior is similar except for the position of the pulpit and reading desk in the center aisle instead of to one side. Christ Church is thought to have had the pulpit in a similar location at the beginning, but the interior there has been altered many times. A comparison is possible between a conjectural plan of Trinity Church before its enlargement and a plan of St. James, Piccadilly, published sometime after 1709 [9-7 and 9-8].[11] The possibility that both churches were inspired by a copy of this print seems very strong. This gave New England two fine city churches, but nothing to rival St. Philip's.

A year after the completion of Trinity Church a new building was begun for Christ Church in Philadelphia [9-9].[12] The first church of 1695 had been enlarged in 1710. The designer of the new church remains unknown. As at Christ Church and Trinity Church the rectangular building is preceded by a full west tower, the whole built of stone faced with brick. The plan was standard enough, the nave and aisles separated by rows of columns and the east end subdivided into sanctuary, sacristy, and vestry. The round-headed windows of both stories are framed by Doric pilasters in two stories, and the walls are crowned by a balustrade with urns. This system is a close parallel to St. Mary-le-Strand in London by James Gibbs, 1714-1721. If this was the

9-9. Christ Church, Philadelphia, Pa. Begun 1727. Painting by William Strickland, 1811. (Historical Society of Pennsylvania).

9-10. James Gibbs, St. Mary-le-Strand, London, 1714-1721.
(J. Gibbs, Book of Architecture, London, 1728, Plate 21).

9-11. Christ Church, Philadelphia. Interior. (Courtesy of Christ Church).

9-12. James Gibbs, St. Martin-in-the-Fields, London, 1720-1726.
Interior. (National Monuments Record).

prototype for Christ Church, there was no need for the builders in Philadelphia to wait for it to be published in 1728 [9-10].[13] The east end of Christ Church has a Venetian window framed by pilasters, much like the second-story motif of the west front of St. Mary-le-Strand.

The interior is also related to Gibbs, having a giant Doric order with galleries, similar to the arrangement with the Corinthian order used by Gibbs for St. Martin-in-the-Fields in London, 1720-1726 [9-11 and 9-12].[14] As on the exterior, for Christ Church the Doric rather than the Corinthian order was chosen, and here again can be noticed proportions of capitals and entablature blocks similar to those of All Saints, Derby [9-13]. When Wren wanted a two-story aisle, on the other hand, he either used two levels of piers and columns, as at St. James, Piccadilly, or two levels of square piers, as at St. Andrew-by-the-Wardrobe, 1685-1695.[15] We have already seen the giant order with galleries at St. Philip's, Birmingham, and St. Philip's, Charleston. In connection with the interior of St. Martin-in-the-Fields, attention has been drawn to the same system

9-13. James Gibbs, All Saints, Derby, Derbyshire, 1723-1725. Interior. (National Monuments Record).

illustrated by Claude Perrault in his translation of *Vitruvius* in 1684.[16] Perhaps in St. Philip's and Christ Church we can see the first faint hints of the interest in Roman architecture as such that was to have so powerful an impact on American building after the Revolution.

However that may be, the next major church in the English colonies was designed by one who made a singular impact on American building in the middle years of the eighteenth century. When it came time to replace the first King's Chapel in Boston in 1749 an invitation was sent to Peter Harrison in Newport, who was then completing a library for a philosophical society in that town.[17] To this we shall return. Harrison had been born in York, England, in 1716, and with his older brother, Joseph, trained as a merchant seaman at Hull. In 1740 he obtained command of a ship being built to sail out of Newport, having by then made several voyages and established connec-

tions there. For the next few years he was engaged in shipping, interrupted by capture and imprisonment at Louisbourg in 1744. His knowledge of surveying and interest in fortification enabled him to make a detailed map of the site, which was of great help to the British forces in the attack of 1745. But Harrison was also interested in architecture. By 1748 he was starting to build the largest collection of architectural books in the American colonies.[18]

For King's Chapel Harrison appears to have turned to Gibbs's design for Marylebone Chapel, Plate 24 in *A Book of Architecture*, at least for the pattern of windows on the flank [9-14 and 9-15].[19] But he kept the west tower separate, intending it to be finished with belfry and spire, using a hip rather than a gable roof over the main body of the church [9-16].[20] An Ionic colonnade surrounds the base of the tower. Having sailed into Charleston, Harrison would have known St. Philip's and may well have decided that Boston should have a monumental portico

9-14. *Peter Harrison, King's Chapel, Boston, Mass., 1749-1752. (J. Winsor,* Memorial History of Boston, *2·498).*

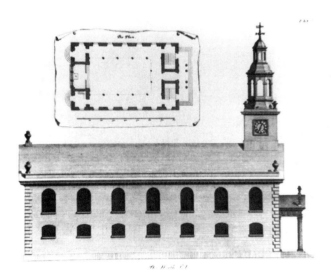

9-15. *James Gibbs, Marylebone Chapel, London. (From J. Gibbs,* Book of Architecture, *Plate 24).*

9-16. *King's Chapel, Boston. Conjectural drawing of planned tower and spire. (Drawing: David Powers).*

9-17. *Nicholas Hawksmoor, St. George, Bloomsbury, London, 1716-1731. (National Monuments Record).*

too. The balustrade above the colonnade was intended to be carried all around the church and would have relieved the austere granite of Boston's first stone church.

The relation between tower and roof on King's Chapel has no clear prototype in English churches. Attention has been called to the separation of tower from roof at St. Paul's, Deptford, 1712-1730, by Thomas Archer, where a cylindrical tower and spire rise above the flank of the church rather than at the west end, thus clearing the roof.[21] The tower also rises independently of the roof at Nicholas Hawksmoor's St. George, Bloomsbury, 1716-1731, where the ridge runs from north to south [9-17].[22] Another strong resemblance between King's Chapel and St. George is on the interior [9-18].[23] The nave of King's Chapel is divided from the aisles and galleries by four pairs of full height coupled

161

9-18. King's Chapel, Boston. Interior. (SPNEA).

9-19. St. George, Bloomsbury, London. Interior.
(National Monuments Record).

Corinthian columns with entablature blocks. The two columns in each set are placed in line with the gallery front, not perpendicular to it, and together with the long line of the flat ceiling give a strong horizontal impetus toward the east end. At St. George there is a similar pairing of Corinthian columns and entablature blocks [9-19]. These are placed east-west, and when Harrison could have seen the church before its altar was moved to the north in 1781, the columns were in line with the principal axis from the west entrance to the altar. Harrison, then, would appear to have looked to Hawksmoor as well as to Gibbs for ideas for the Boston church.[24] The finely wrought Corinthian capitals and entablatures were done under the direction of carver William Burbeck, who may have been among those who worked at the Wentworth house in Portsmouth a short time later.[25]

The influence of Gibbs was strong in other colonial churches at mid-century. A second major church was built in Charleston in 1752-1761, and while the master builder is known, Samuel Cardy, there is no certain attribution for its design [9-20].[26] Built of brick covered with stucco, the reference here seems to be to the exterior of St. Martin-in-the-Fields [9-21]. St. Michael's is in two stories, with a full Doric portico, and has a massive tower rising not from the front but from the west end of the body of the church. This tower is one of the most remarkable of colonial structures. It is of brick not only through the square base, as at Christ Church in Boston, but on up through the octagonal stages of belfry and clock chamber. Only the open arcade, used as a watch tower, and the spire are of wood.[27] The details of the tower come from no obvious source, and considering the daring and originality of its construction it is unlikely that they should. By this time the Ionic and Corinthian pilasters and the rusticated surrounds of the windows could have been found in any number of publications and simply applied here.

St. Michael's is perhaps a lesson that much more study could be made of colonial engineering. According to a petition for more funds for the tower in 1755:

> That the Steeple is carried up on a Massy Foundation to such an Height, as besides being an Ornament to Charlestown the Metropolis of this Province, it is of extraordinary Use to the Navigation on our Coast. It is so high as to be descerned at Sea before the Land is seen, & is so properly situated as to be a plain leading mark for the Bar of this Harbour, and therefore effectually answers the Purpose and Intention of building a Beacon, which expence may be thereby saved to this Pro[vince].[28]

THE BODY OF THE church had already been covered with a slate roof. Upon the completion of the roof it was apparent that the timbers were sufficiently strong to support the slates, and therefore the brick foundations for the intended interior colonnade were removed. The galleries are supported on Ionic columns, and the space above them is open the full width of the church. Cardy used modified queen-post trusses to span the width.

9-20. St. Michael's Church, Charleston, S.C., 1752-1761. (Photo: Wayne Andrews, ESTO).

9-21. St. Martin-in-the-Fields, London. Exterior view. (National Monuments Record).

His obituary called Cardy "the ingenious Architect, who undertook and completed the Building of St. Michael's Church."[29]

The tower of St. Michael's, Charleston, bears comparison to the tower of Christ Church, Philadelphia, which was being embellished with its tower at the same time that that of St. Michael's was rising. When Peter Kalm had visited Philadelphia in 1748, he had observed: "The English established church stands in the northern part of the town, at some distance from the market, and is the finest of all. It has a small, insignificant steeple, in which a bell is rung, when it is time to go to church, and at burials."[30] By 1754, however, this had been replaced by something much more splendid, the present steeple, 196 feet high [9-9].[31] It was completed by the Philadelphia master carpenter Robert Smith and clearly based on one of the steeples that Gibbs had published in his *Book of Architecture*, Plate 30 [9-22]. These steeple designs were among several proposed for finishing St. Martin-in-the-Fields, and the one chosen for Christ Church is perhaps closest to the one actually built.

The last of the major Anglican city churches to be built in the English colonies before the Revolution was St. Paul's Chapel in New York City, 1764-1766, to which the spire and eastern portico were added thirty years later, in 1794 [9-23].[32] The body of the church is of mica-schist, and the quoins, belt course, and window trim are of brownstone. The windows are arched in both stories, there is a balustrade around the roof, and the tower rises from the body of the church, but set slightly forward. The interior is closer to St. Martin than is King's Chapel [9-24]. The Corinthian columns separating nave and aisles are single, not coupled, and the plaster vaults rise to a curved ceiling. The church is attributed to a Scottish architect named Thomas McBean, whose career otherwise remains unknown.

MEMBERS OF THE Church of England in the smaller communities also needed houses of worship in the eighteenth century. Three may be chosen to illustrate briefly some of the possibilities. The first is the second building of Christ Church in Lancaster County, Virginia, built with funds provided by Robert Carter in 1732 [9-25].[33] It is built on a cross plan, seventy feet overall, with the nave slightly longer than the transepts and sanctuary. The bricks are laid in Flemish bond, and the pilasters and pediment of the door are also of brick, as at Carter's Grove. The windows are arched, with rubbed brick trim, and there is an especially rich cornice under the slight flare of the roof. The interior is undivided, the ceiling formed into a groin vault at the crossing. However wealthy its patron, the church is a simple country building. The proportions and handling of detail seem to link to the builders of the great Carter family mansions, but no firm attribution is yet possible.

About fifty years later the Anglican church in Brooklyn, Connecticut, illustrates how the same requirements could be met in wood. Trinity Church was also built with most of the funds coming from a parishioner, the merchant Colonel Godfrey Malbone. He not only organized the parish and put up the money

9-22. *James Gibbs, designs for steeples.* (Gibbs, Book of Architecture, Plate 30).

9-23. *Thomas McBean, St. Paul's Chapel, New York, 1764-1766. Painting by C. Milbourne, 1798. (New York Historical Society).*

9-24. *St. Paul's Chapel, New York. Interior. (M. Dix et al.,* A History of the Parish of Trinity Church in the City of New York, *New York, 1898).*

9-25. *Christ Church, Lancaster Co., Va., 1732. (Richmond, Division of Historic Landmarks).*

9-26. *Trinity Church, Brooklyn, Conn., 1770. (Photo: M. C. Donnelly).*

but designed the church and saw to the procuring of the timber [9-26].[34] The building is not large, measuring forty-six feet by thirty feet, built of wood, two stories high with a hipped roof and having no tower or spire. The door is framed by plain Roman Doric pilasters and a pediment. Malbone had been born and brought up in Newport, where his family attended Trinity Church. In designing the interior of the church at Brooklyn Malbone imitated Trinity in Newport as much as possible. The galleries are supported by square pillars in two stories, and the pews were planned to allow for a central pulpit and reading desk, now in different positions. And so nearly a century after Wren began St. James, Piccadilly, a distant descendant was built in a small Connecticut town.

A year earlier it had been decided to erect a new building for Pohick Church in Fairfax County, Virginia.[35] The parish had been formed under another name in 1700 and included Mount Vernon and Gunston Hall. In 1769 George Washington and George Mason were both on the vestry and appointed to the building committee. Washington apparently drew a plan, and the contractor was the mason Daniel French. As might be expected, Pohick Church is much grander than Trinity Church in Brooklyn [9-27]. It is of brick laid in Flemish bond with sandstone trim. There is no tower, and there are two entrances on the west end. There is also a central south door, and the interior (restored after destruction in the Civil War) is arranged with the pulpit on the north, as at St. Paul's in Wickford.

CONTEMPORARY WITH the Anglican churches were of course those of the other Protestant sects. The Congregational churches predominated in New England, and among these can similarly be found different degrees of elaboration and grandeur. One of the most familiar is the Old South Meeting House in Boston, the second building of the Third Church of Boston, which had been formed in 1669 [9-28].[36] The builder was Joshua Blanchard, whom we have already met at the Hancock house.[37] Old South, as it is familiarly called, 1729-1730, is a large two-story building of brick with tower and spire on the west. The arched windows in both stories and the stringcourses marking the levels of the body of the church and the tower are similar to those of Christ Church, which may have provided some model.

9-27. George Washington, Pohick Church, Fairfax Co., Va., 1769-1770.(Richmond, Division of Historic Landmarks).

9-28. *Joshua Blanchard (builder), Old South Meeting House, Boston, Mass., 1729. (J. Winsor,* Memorial History of Boston, *2:516).*

9-29. *Captain Judah Woodruff (builder), First Church of Christ, Farmington, Conn. 1771-1772. (Photo: M. C. Donnelly).*

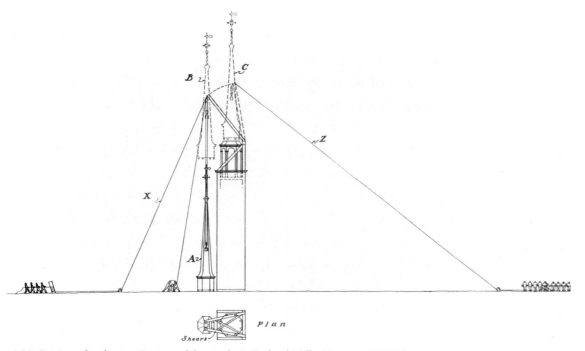

9-30. *Raising a church spire. Conjectural drawing by J. Frederick Kelly. (Courtesy SPNEA).*

The belfry and spire were not the first on a Congregational meeting house, but were the most elaborate to date and were imitated several times later.

On the interior the meeting house retains the seventeenth-century orientation, approached through the entrance porch on the south, with the pulpit in the center of the north side. There are galleries on east, south, and west, with a second tier that may have been added later. After several episodes of damage and restoration the building was taken over as an historical museum by the Old South Association in 1876.[38]

The change to the "church-like" appearance of Old South as distinct from that of the Old Brick Meeting House of sixteen years earlier was adopted by several other New England congregations. Among them was the one at Farmington, Connecticut, where in 1769 it was voted to build a new meeting house, the third, which was begun in 1771 and completed in 1772 [9-29].[39] In addition to the main body of the church and the tower and spire on the north there is an original two-story stair porch at the south. The west door was replaced and a Greek Revival porch added in 1834. On the interior the pulpit is in the center of the east side, with galleries on the south, west, and north. The present pulpit is modern, and behind it has been built an alcove to house the organ.

The builder at Farmington was Captain Judah Woodruff, who had served in the British forces during the French War and who returned to Farmington to build a number of houses as well as the meeting house. He was apparently a fine carver, for it was said of him that his "carving on the front of the pulpit,

representing vines of the English ivy, was greatly admired."[40] This is now lost, having been replaced in 1834.

The graceful spire remains, however, of somewhat lighter proportions than that of Old South, which it clearly imitated. The Farmington example has been chosen in part because early references raise the problem of whether the spire was assembled from within the tower or on the ground beside it and then raised. One solution as to how the latter might have been accomplished with windlass and tackle has been suggested [9-30].[41] A similar spire was built for the Congregational meeting house in nearby Brooklyn also in 1771, whereas at Wethersfield, Connecticut, the spire of 1761 was an imitation of that of Old North.[42] Woodruff may have consulted with his fellow builders Daniel Tyler at Brooklyn and John Chester at Wethersfield, but what techniques they used for raising their spires has not yet been fully determined.

Not all the eighteenth-century Congregational meeting houses were so grand, and the one built at Sandown, New Hampshire in 1774 is a good example of a more modest approach [9-31].[43] It is built of wood, two stories high, with the gallery stairs inside in the corners instead of in stair porches or towers. The seventeenth-century plan was still used here, the main entrance on the south side and the pulpit opposite. Although comparatively plain at first glance, the Sandown meeting house has a certain richness of detail. A modillioned cornice is carried across the north and south sides, with short returns at the ends. The doors on the south and west show how the pattern books were used by country builders, for they come from *The Builder's*

9-32. Karlslunde Church, Karlslunde, Zealand, Denmark, 1668. Detail of altar carving. (Photo: M. C. Donnelly).

9-31. Sandown Meeting House, Sandown, New Hampshire, 1773-1774. (Photo: M. C. Donnelly).

9-33. *Thomas Dawes, Brattle Square Church, Boston, Mass., 1773-1774. Conjectural drawing. (Frederic C. Detwiller).*

9-34. *Joseph Brown, First Baptist Meeting House, Providence, R. I., 1774-1775. (SPNEA).*

Jewel by Batty and Thomas Langley.[44] On the interior all the pews were once spindle-topped, some still remaining in the gallery. The pulpit is a "two-decker," with the wineglass panel between the minister's desk and the deacon's pew. The pilasters of the pulpit and those framing the window behind are marbleized. The Sandown meeting house appeared just before the Revolution, and this type continued in use into the Federal period.

The marbleizing at Sandown is one of the few surviving examples of color used in the eighteenth-century churches and meeting houses of New England. From documentary accounts, however, it is clear that the exteriors might be painted yellow, orange, red, green, or blue, with evidently some regional concentrations of color.[45] In addition the pulpits, canopies, gallery panels, etc., might as at Sandown be marbleized, of painted blue, green, or brown.[46] Even the carvings might be painted, as recalled by Harriet Beecher Stowe, writing of the meeting house in Litchfield, Connecticut: "How I did wonder at the panels on either side of the pulpit, in each of which was carved and painted a flaming red tulip, with its leaves projecting out at right angles, and then at the grape-vine, in bas-relief, on the front, with exactly triangular bunches of grapes at exact intervals."[47] We may wonder whether the pulpit that Judah Woodruff made for the Farmington meeting house was similarly painted.[48]

Further notes and legends refer to religious motifs, particularly cherub heads, on the interiors of churches and meeting houses alike.[49] This came from the North European traditions of liturgical carvings. There are English precedents, but one might also compare village churches of Denmark where numerous examples of vines, grapes, and cherub heads may be found on pulpits and especially altars, such as those carved on the altar for the church at Karlslunde, Zealand, by Caspar Lubbeke in 1668 [9-32]. While only a few fragments remain from these New England carvings, they are enough to indicate that it is no longer possible to assert that the New England churches were totally austere.

While the Sandown meeting house was under construction, another church was built in Boston which has only recently received significant attention. In 1772 a new building was needed for the church in Brattle Square, and a competition for the design was won by Thomas Dawes, master mason and architect.[50] Whereas at the Congregational meeting houses just described the tower, if any, was placed at the end of the long axis, at right angles to the axis from entrance to pulpit, Dawes placed the tower on the short side, with the pulpit opposite. In addition he widened the two lower stories of the tower to form a larger vestibule and made it a frontispiece with a Doric doorway, Venetian window in the second story, the whole crowned by a pediment, and the square tower rising above [9-33]. On the interior the meeting house arrangement was retained, with a giant order of Corinthian columns before the galleries. The church was demolished in 1872-1874, but several measured drawings and a number of photographs were made beginning in 1866.

The influence of this church on Charles Bulfinch, whose father was a member of the congregation, and on Asher Benjamin belongs to the post-Revolutionary period in American architecture. In its own time, however, it seems to have inspired some of the plans for another major New England city church, the First Baptist Meetinghouse in Providence [9-34].[51] The designs of both churches owed much to Gibbs's drawings of Marylebone Chapel, especially the interior in Plate 24. In Providence the merchant Joseph Brown was on the committee designated to "make a Draught of a House 90 by 70 feet together with a Tower and Steeple," and sent to Boston "to view the different churches and meetinghouses . . . to make a memorandum of their several dimensions and forms of architecture."[52] Brown was active in building projects in Providence and is usually credited with the design of the Baptist Meetinghouse. We now know that one of the carpenters of the Brattle Square Church, James Summer, was chosen to work in Providence, where the design for the new building now appears to have been less original than was previously thought.[53]

That the Boston church was known to the Providence builders is evident in the similarity of the frontispiece, the two bays instead of the usual one on either side of the tower, and the orientation of the pulpit across from the tower. The Baptist Meetinghouse is raised on a basement story, with the entrance at the lower level, probably because of its hilly site. Its portico comes from Gibbs's elevation of Marylebone Chapel, Plate 25, and Dawes seems to have used a similar one on the east side of the Brattle Square Church, later removed. At Providence the Doric Order was chosen, but otherwise the interior was much like that in Boston. A difference between the two is of course that no spire was ever provided for the Brattle Square Church, whereas a copy of Gibbs's spire on Plate 30 of the Book of Architecture was built rather aggressively on the Providence church.

Two major innovations seem to have been made in Boston. One was the placement of the tower in line with the pulpit in a Congregational church. In this connection we might recall that the predecessor of the Brattle Square Church, built in 1699, was the earliest of the Congregational meeting houses known to have had a full tower and spire and also the earliest to be described in contemporary documents as a "church." The other was the elaboration of the tower base into a pedimented frontispiece, above which the tower and spire would rise independently. These two ideas were to be exploited all over New England by the next generation of church architects. In addition, Dawes used a Venetian window over the main door and reflected it in part on the inside with the round-headed window over the pulpit, a relationship not up to then attempted in the English colonial

churches. The same was done at Providence in the first state of the interior, but it was plastered over in 1846.[54] Later, Charles Bulfinch carried this out much more explicitly in his Congregational Church at Pittsfield, Massachusetts, 1790-1793, which Asher Benjamin imitated in The Country Builder's Assistant of 1797, Plate 27.

With the First Baptist Meetinghouse we encounter a building for one of the other branches of Protestantism in colonial America. These were stronger in the Middle Atlantic colonies, and for most the types of buildings erected show little sectarian distinction. Another Baptist congregation moved to Imlaystown, New Jersey, about 1720 in order to escape Puritan persecution. The first meeting house burned and was replaced by the present building in 1737.[55] There are two doors in the gable end, with the pulpit at the opposite end, and a side door near the pulpit. There is also a gallery at the entrance end. Known as the "Old Yellow Meeting House," with its shutters painted blue, it is a good, albeit faded, example of the colorful nature of these buildings. In New Jersey as well as in New England the ceiling of a church or meeting house might be painted, as for the Presbyterian Church in Trenton in 1726, "painted in a sort of clouded style, blue and white, intended to represent the sky and clouds."[56]

At Daretown, New Jersey, the Pittsgrove Presbyterian congregation built a "meeting house" in 1740 and replaced it with a two-story brick building in 1767 [9-35].[57] It is rectangular, with two entrances on one long side, galleries on three sides within, and a wine-glass paneled pulpit opposite the doors. Restorations were undertaken in 1939. The plan is similar to that of the Congregational meeting houses. There was no use made of stylish motifs from pattern books, the composure of the building coming from its broad proportions, the restrained pattern of the lintels over first-story doors and windows, and the fine brickwork, which is characteristic of southern New Jersey.[58]

IN CONNECTION WITH these New Jersey buildings the matter of heating may be raised. This subject is scarcely mentioned in discussions of New England churches and meeting houses, Kelly indeed having asserted that until the nineteenth century "meetinghouses were without stoves or other means of supplying artificial warmth."[59] Such does not appear to have been the case in New Jersey, for several instances are recorded where pits or trays for burning charcoal provided heat for the congregation, and also noxious fumes. A description of the Lutheran Church at German Valley, built in 1747, ends with noting that "the preacher, from his exalted position, nearly over the burning mass, received a double portion of gas to mix with his sermon."[60]

Then there is the church built by Evangelical Lutheran Palatines near Nelliston, New York, in 1770 [9-36].[61] Major interior changes were made in 1870, but the body of the church remains, limestone, with round-headed windows, gambrel roof, and belfry. Originally arranged for the liturgy of Lutheran worship, the little church is a remainder of strong German settlement here in the Mohawk and Schoharie river valleys.[62]

9-35. *Pittsgrove Presbyterian Church, Daretown, N.J., 1767. (Photo: M. C. Donnelly).*

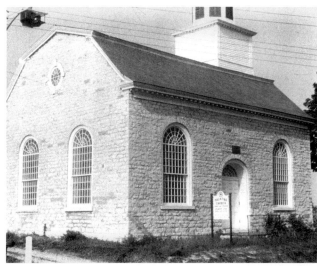

9-36. *Palatine Evangelical Lutheran Church, near Nelliston, N.Y., 1770. (Photo: M. C. Donnelly).*

9-37. *Friends Meeting House, Lahaska, Pa., 1768. (Photo: M. C. Donnelly).*

9-38. *Friends Meeting House, Crosswicks, N.J., 1773-1776. (Photo: M. C. Donnelly).*

Finally there are the Friends Meeting Houses, a special group of houses of worship in the eighteenth century. Several fine examples can be found in eastern Pennsylvania and southern New Jersey. Two have a specific relationship, the ones at Lahaska, Pennsylvania, 1768, and Crosswicks, New Jersey, 1773-1776. At Lahaska the meeting house is built of stone, two stories high, with two doors having gabled hoods, a generous cove cornice, and a gable roof [9-37].[63] The masonry is rather heavy and random, with segmental arches above the first-story windows and irregular quoins at the corners. On the interior there is no altar or pulpit, but rather tiers of benches facing the wall opposite the doors and a smaller number of "facing benches" for the elders along that wall. There is a gallery on three sides of the building, and it can be divided by shutters into separate sections for men and women. This interior arrangement is appropriate for the Friends Meeting, which does not involve a liturgical form of worship.

The meeting house at Lahaska was evidently much admired, for in 1773 the Society of Friends at Crosswicks decided to build a new meeting house and pattern it after the one at Lahaska.[64] The Crosswicks meeting house is built of brick, relieved only by the stringcourse dividing the first and second stories [9-38]. Otherwise it is very much like the one at Lahaska and one of the finest of the brick Friends meeting houses of New Jersey.

All of these churches and meeting houses were built for members of the Christian faith. There is a place of worship for members of another faith, however, that returns us to urban fashion and the use of pattern books. In 1759 Rabbi Isaac Abraham Touro settled in Newport, where there had been a

9-39. Peter Harrison, Newport, R.I. Touro Synagogue. 1759-1763. (Photo: M. C. Donnelly).

Jewish community for over a hundred years.[65] Under his leadership a proper synagogue was begun, whereas services up to then had been held in private houses. Peter Harrison had already built the Redwood Library, and a number of members of the society for which it was built belonged to the Newport Sephardic Jewish congregation. He was asked to provide a design for a synagogue, and the outcome was the only colonial purpose-built synagogue in America [9-39].[66] The exterior of the building is unassuming, brick stuccoed and painted, windows round-headed in both stories, a modillioned cornice and the Ionic porch the only ornament. The interior is another matter entirely [9-40]. Harrison was guided by Rabbi Touro in the requirements of the Jewish liturgy, which were met in ways resembling the Sephardic Synagogue in Amsterdam, whence Rabbi Touro had come. Seats for

9-40. Touro Synagogue, Newport. Interior. (Newport Historical Society).

the men run around the walls on three sides, with a gallery for the women above. The large balustraded pulpit is in the center of the floor toward the west end, while the Ark of the Covenant is at the east end. To carry out all this with elegance of detail Harrison made extensive use of the printed sources at his command. Harrison's biographer made the intriguing observation that in this unique building a devout Anglican, working for a congregation practicing an oriental faith, devised a building interior based on ancient Greek and Roman motifs.[67] An important exception to our understanding of Harrison's work appears to be that the Ark of the Covenant as we see it now is probably more a result of repairs and remodeling than of his original design.[68] If this is indeed the case, the restorer took pains to use the English models in much the manner of Harrison himself.

IN ADDITION TO the numerous religious buildings from which these few examples have been chosen many public and specialized buildings have also survived from the eighteenth century. Of the greatest national significance is undoubtedly what is now called Independence Hall in Philadelphia, scene of the adoption of the Declaration of Independence in 1776 and the Constitutional Convention in 1787 [9-41].[69] Begun as a State House for the Provincial Assembly in 1729, the building has undergone additions, changes, and restorations, and as a National Historic Site has been in the custody of the National Park Service since 1951. Here we will be concerned with its pre-Revolutionary state as seen in the illustration. Construction was begun in 1732 according to plans drawn by the master carpenter, Edmund Woolley, under the direction of the Speaker of the Assembly, Andrew Hamilton. The State House was completed for use in the winter of 1748, except for the tower and belfry. These were added by

9-42. State House ("Independence Hall"), Philadelphia. South front, tower as rebuilt by William Strickland, 1828. (Photo: M. C. Donnelly).

Edmund Woolley in 1750-1753, the belfry removed because of deterioration in 1781 and replaced by the present steeple by William Strickland in 1828.

With no inkling of the dramatic future of the State House, Woolley and Hamilton built what was a generous but normal place of assembly for its day. It is brick, two stories high and nine bays wide, with a hall on the first floor between the Assembly and Court chambers. A chamber for the Provincial Council, a committee room for the Assembly, and a "long gallery" for banquets and other entertainments were on the second floor. Arcades on each end led to wings which provided additional office space. The north facade was finished with marble quoins and a double stringcourse with panels in the center, breaking the height of the first story of an otherwise essentially domestic-appearing exterior. This was appropriately a "house" for the Province, or State, as were those of Jamestown and Annapolis before it. The tower

INDEPENDENCE HALL, PHILADELPHIA, 1776.

9-41. Edmund Woolley (builder), Pennsylvania State House ("Independence Hall"), Philadelphia, Pa., 1731-1748. Lithograph from painting by Charles Willson Peale, c. 1779. (Philadelphia Free Library).

9-43. Richard Munday, Colony House, Newport, R.I., 1739. (Photo: HABS).

9-44. Court house, Williamsburg, Va., 1770. View from rear showing cross plan. (Photo: M. C. Donnelly).

projecting on the south side has a Venetian window in the second story and two stories marked with brick pilasters above [9-42]. On the interior the Roman Doric order was used for the central hall and the Assembly and Court chambers.

While the State House in Philadelphia was under construction, Richard Munday, the builder of Trinity Church, was called upon in 1739 to build a new Colony House for Newport, the old wooden one of 1687 needing to be replaced [9-43].[70] This time the building was to be of brick, "eighty feet in length and forty in breadth, and thirty feet stud," as his contract reads. It is two stories high, with gambrel roof, dormers, balustrade, cupola, and end chimneys. This is another house-like design for a place of assembly, similar to the Old State House in Boston in having a colonnaded hall on the first floor and the Council Chamber and Chamber of Deputies on the second. The Ionic order was used for the square columns of the first floor and the Corinthian for the pilasters of the Council Chamber. The doorway, balcony, and scroll pediment over the balcony door are strikingly like the ensemble on the Hancock house in Boston, built three years previously. The Colony House differs from the State House in Philadelphia only in scale and detail. The fundamental concepts are the same.

For local divisions within the colonies or provinces the court houses could be more modest, and in Virginia particularly a number of distinctive ones were built in the eighteenth and early-nineteenth centuries.[71] At Williamsburg in 1770 such a court house was built in the center of town on the Market Square [9-44].[72] Seen across the Green the T-plan often used for Virginia court houses can be seen, the courtroom projecting and rooms on either side for justices and jury. On the street side an unusual porch having no supports projects eight feet, sheltering the door. Two chimneys and a central cupola rise above the roof. The interior has been altered so much that the original fittings are unknown. The building as a whole seems to have been designed

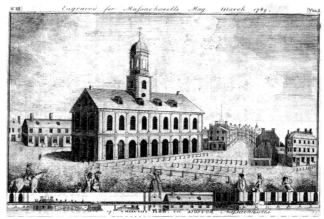

9-45. *John Smibert (designer), Faneuil Hall, Boston, Mass., 1740-1742. Engraving by Samuel Hill, 1789. (Massachusetts Historical Society).*

9-46. *Royal Exchange, London, as rebuilt 1671. (British Museum, Crace Collection).*

according to geometrical principles, as we have seen in other buildings in Williamsburg.

For the commercial as well as the legislative interests of the colonies, shops and market houses were needed, the former often as part of the owners' dwellings and the latter similar to those familiar in England.[73] In the larger cities the market houses might become substantial civic ornaments, as was the case in Boston and Newport. In Boston the demand for a civic market hall had been growing amid contention and violence when in 1740 a wealthy merchant, Peter Faneuil, proposed that a market house should be built at his personal expense.[74] A stormy town meeting in the Brattle Square Church ended in a vote of acceptance. From designs by the painter John Smibert, with Samuel Ruggles the master carpenter and Joshua Blanchard the master mason, a two-story brick building, 100 feet by 40 feet, was constructed and named for its donor [9-45].[75] Faneuil Hall was completed in 1742, and two years later Dr. Alexander Hamilton described it as an "elegant building of brick, with a cupola on the top."[76] Smibert took the unorthodox course of using Doric pilasters in both stories, marking the open arcades below and the windows of the offices and a large hall above.

Smibert was born in Scotland, studied painting in Italy, and went to Boston in 1729, setting himself up as a portrait painter. His design for Faneuil Hall, while misunderstanding a "proper" use of the Orders, was evidently based on the Royal Exchange in London as rebuilt in 1671 [9-46]. There, on a much more elaborate building, were arcades below, a pilastered story above, and a great tower carrying the grasshopper weathervane, symbol of Sir Thomas Gresham, the original founder in 1566. Significantly, the weathervane on Faneuil Hall is a copy of it in copper by Shem Drowne, done in 1742.

If a more academic reference for a market hall was desired, Peter Harrison provided one for the Brick Market in Newport, 1761-1772 [9-47].[77] When the Proprietors of the Long Wharf called upon Harrison for a design, he could hardly repeat the Royal Exchange. While Somerset House in London was then a royal residence, the New Gallery, attributed to Inigo Jones, built in 1661, also had an arcaded lower story and pilasters above, this time running through two stories with coupled pilasters at each end [9-48]. This was illustrated in Harrison's copy of *Vitruvius Britannicus*, Volume I, Plate 16. By substituting the more feasible Ionic order for the Corinthian and building in brick rather than stone, Harrison provided Newport with a market house worthy of her commercial ambitions, and in terms of fashion far outclassing the Colony House.

AMONG THE OTHER principal public buildings in the colonies some of the colleges have already been described. The basic formula for these buildings did not change during the pre-Revolutionary period, as illustrated by the design for New Harvard Hall in Cambridge [9-49].[78] The building of 1677 burned in January 1764 and was rebuilt according to the instructions of the governor, Sir Francis Bernard. As the central college building it needed the cupola for the college bell, a chapel, whose round-headed windows appear in the illustration, library, kitchen, dining room, and a "philisophical chamber" for scientific apparatus. The many gables of Old Harvard Hall were not forgotten but transformed to a pediment at each end of the roof and over the three central bays on the main facade. Details of windows, cornices, and belfry could now come from handbooks. The master mason was Thomas Dawes, who had also worked on Hollis Hall in 1762, and while given the overall plan to be followed, he probably supplied such details as the pediments, for example, from his copy of Gibbs's *Book of Architecture* [9-50].

Two buildings of special function should also be noted. One is the Redwood Library in Newport, which was actually the earliest of the works that were to bring Peter Harrison into prominence as an architect [9-51].[79] In 1747 a local merchant, Abraham Redwood, gave funds for purchasing books for a library in

9-47. *Peter Harrison, Brick Market, Newport, R.I., 1761-1772.* (Photo: HABS).

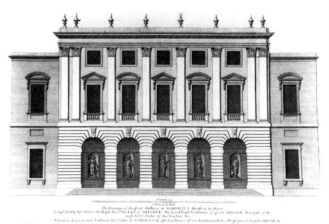

9-48. *Inigo Jones, Gallery, Old Somerset House, London, England, 1661.* (C. Campbell, Vitruvius Britannicus, *London, 1717, v. 1, Plate 16*).

Newport.[80] This was for the use of a "Society for the Promotion of Knowledge and Virtue by a Free Conversation," of which Redwood was a member. Harrison was then in England, but his brother Joseph was appointed to a committee to raise funds for a library building. It is Joseph who is named in the building contract of August 1748, and he may have contributed some of the original ideas. On Peter's return to Newport, however, he became in charge, and the details of the library as completed are generally credited to him. Three additions, in 1858, 1878, and 1915, have obscured the original lines of the building. The Redwood Library was originally planned as a tetrastyle Roman Doric temple with wings (or "outshots" as they are called in the contract) for offices. The most likely source for the front elevation is the headpiece to Book IV of the Hoppus edition of *Palladio*.[81] [9-52]. Other details can be found in some of the books owned by Harrison. The interior followed the pattern of libraries of that time, being simply a square room lined with shelves, with seats below the windows, all specified in the contract. For an additional touch of monumentality the exterior wood was planked and rusticated to imitate stone.

In 1770 the members of the Carpenters' Company of Philadelphia raised the funds for a building for themselves, Carpenters' Hall [9-53 and 9-54].[82] The architect was Robert Smith, who had been the builder for Christ Church. The hall is in the tradition of English guild halls, a compact two-story building with a cupola. It is brick, with the strongly emphasized trim of doors and windows characteristic of the Philadelphia region. The plan is cross-shaped, and the interior was apparently first divided into two large rooms and a hall on the first floor. Just after the Revolution the Carpenters' Company put out their famous *Rules of Work*, in 1784, in which their hall is illustrated. Founded probably in 1724, the Company had had much to do with building Philadelphia into one of the most splendid of the colonial cities, and it is altogether fitting that their hall should still attest to their contribution.

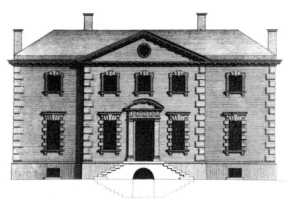

9-49. *Thomas Dawes (builder), New Harvard Hall, Harvard College, Cambridge, Mass. (J. Quincy,* The History of Harvard University, *Boston, 1860, 2:122).*

9-50. *James Gibbs, design for a country house. (J. Gibbs,* Book of Architecture, *Plate 65).*

9-51. *Peter Harrison, Redwood Library, Newport, R.I., 1748. (Photo: M. C. Donnelly).*

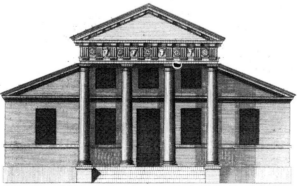

9-52. *Edward Hoppus, Frontispiece to Book IV,* Andrea Palladio's Architecture in Four Books, *trans. Edward Hoppus, London, 1733. (Courtesy of Yale University Library).*

SCHOOLS, HOSPITALS, PRISONS, and the like are also known from the colonial period and merit studies in themselves. They are not likely to illustrate much that is different from the building practices already described. Because much valuable contemporary observation has come to us from eighteenth-century travelers, however, some mention of the various taverns and inns where they sought shelter seems appropriate. Williamsburg was of course a principal place for hostelries because of legislators going there for assemblies. Wetherburn's Tavern, for example, appears to have started as a one-and-one-half story frame dwelling of central-hall plan, perhaps in the early 1730s [9-55].[83] It was later enlarged by a "Great Room" on the east, having its own chimney. Excavations begun in 1965 revealed not only the locations of the kitchens and dairy but evidence of the early stages of the building itself.[84] Among the many artifacts were found fragments of mugs, plates, decanters, and even bottles still filled with brandied cherries, all attesting to the busy life of the tavern in its heyday [9-56].[85]

Two other colonial inns which are essentially domestic in character are the London Town Publick House in Edgewater, Maryland, and the Sheldon Tavern in Litchfield, Connecticut [9-57 and 9-58]. The former, built about 1744-1750, is a two-story brick building high on a bluff overlooking the South River. The three central bays of the entrance front are projected slightly and topped with a pediment, and a curiously patterned cornice surrounds the building. Otherwise the inn is very plain, inside as well as out. The Sheldon Tavern, on the other hand, is another example of New England elaboration in wood. Built in 1760, it was altered to receive its rather heavy hip roof in 1790. The five-bay facade has the central bay projecting, an Ionic portico below, and a Venetian window above, the whole covered by a pediment.

9-53. Robert Smith, Carpenters' Hall, Philadelphia, Pa., 1770-1771. (Photo: M. C. Donnelly).

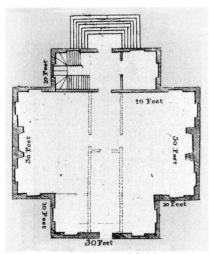

9-54. Carpenters' Hall, Philadelphia. Plan. (Courtesy of Carpenters' Company).

9-55. Wetherburn's Tavern, Williamsburg, Va., c. 1730. (Colonial Williamsburg Foundation).

It might be thought of as a New England version of the central motif of Mount Pleasant. Such were the lodgings that could be found in the cities and towns along the coast and major rivers.

IN AN EARLIER CHAPTER the years between about 1680 and about 1720 were described as being a time of mixed continuation and change in building types and fashions. In a broader view much the same can be said for the eighteenth century as a whole. The homes, churches, and other buildings of the Georgian period attest to confidence and a desire for permanent expression of status. But that was not all that was going on. Certain enterprises were undertaken that foreshadowed important cultural and architectural developments that would take place after the Revolution and on into the nineteenth century.

One was the migration to Ephrata, Pennsylvania, of Conrad Beissel, a German Pietist mystic, and his communal Society. This was a much more tightly-contained community than even the theocratic commonwealth of Massachusetts Bay. There was a brotherhood and a sisterhood, both celibate, and a married order of householders. Three major buildings, the Saal or community house, the Saron or sisters' house, and the Bethania or brothers' house (demolished about 1900) were built from 1741-1746 [9-59]. These were built from memories of German home buildings, plain two-story wooden structures with high gabled roofs and shed-roof attic dormers. In the Saal was the principal meeting room with plain tables, benches, and lectern, and also a kitchen and dining room. Nowhere were the classically-derived motifs that were in use elsewhere. Peter Kalm made an interesting

9-56. Brandied cherry bottles found in excavations of Wetherburn's Tavern, Williamsburg. (Colonial Williamsburg Foundation).

9-57. London Town Publick House, Edgewater, Md., 1744-1750. (Photo: M. C. Donnelly).

9-58. *Sheldon Tavern, Litchfield, Conn., 1760. (Photo: M. C. Donnelly).*

9-59. *The Cloisters, Ephrata, Pa., 1741-46. (Photo: M. C. Donnelly).*

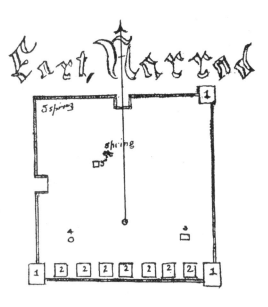

VAN CLEVE'S MAP OF FORT HARROD 1791
This plat is reproduced here exactly as it appears, though slightly smaller, in Bejamin Van Cleve's biographical manuscript memorandum.
Manuscript Complete
September 30, 1929

9-60. *Fort Harrod, Harrodsburg, Ky., 1775-1776. Plan by Benjamin Van Cleve, 1791. (Kentucky Historical Society).*

observation on this building: "The doors in the Ephrata Protestant Convent, about thirteen or fourteen miles from Lancaster [Pa.] are so narrow that only one person can pass through at a time, and if he is fat he cannot get in at all. Our Royal Councillor Cedercreutz would therefore have to stay out. The doors are made of a single board of the Liriodendron tulipifera or tulip tree (June 13, 1750)."[86]

The Ephrata community numbered about 300 at its height and strove to be self-sufficient. As would be the case with similar communities, several of which were founded in later years, the original fervor died away, and the Society was finally dissolved in 1934. Since 1941 the site has been under the Pennsylvania Historical and Museum Commission and is now operated as a museum.

THIS ACCOUNT of American colonial architecture will close not with an original building but with a replica, and perhaps not a very good one at that. The significance of the original for what would happen next in the new United States should not be underestimated, however. Some measure of peace having been attained by the Treaty of 1763, tentative efforts at settlement were beginning to move west of the Alleghenies following the French and Indian War. Harrodsburg became the first settlement

in the then territory of Kentucky, and Fort Harrod was built in 1775-1776. A description written in 1791 was the basis for the reconstruction of the fort in 1923-1928 [9-60 and 9-61].[87]

The original fort was 264 feet square, with blockhouses on either end of the south side and cabins between. On the north side was another blockhouse on the east and a spring on the west. Another spring, a blacksmith shop, and a schoolhouse were also included. The stockade itself was oak logs, set four feet into the ground and rising ten feet high. Built all of timber and with even the roofs slanting inward to lessen the hazard of burning enemy torches, the fort was not unlike the Scandinavian courtyard farms. A similar fort had been built at Boonesborough nearby just previously. Like Port Royal both resembled walled manorial enclosures, but were built with the notched log construction soon to be so characteristic of the new frontier.

THIS IS WHERE THE WHEEL of adventure and migration comes full circle. The story began with trans-Atlantic explorations from an established Western European culture. From hazardous and often unsuccessful attempts to transplant this culture to an

9-61. *Fort Harrod, Harrodsburg. Reconstruction of 1923-1928. (Photo: M. C. Donnelly).*

unknown wilderness, colonists had been able to secure their positions on the Atlantic seaboard and build flourishing towns and cities. These were never of European grandeur, but they were graced with thoughtfully designed and well-constructed buildings of which their inhabitants could be justly proud. American architecture had come of age. As the waves of migration spread westward, across mountains rather than seas, the settlers of the wildernesses of the new United States could look to their home towns and cities for building fashions that could be adopted as soon as their situations permitted. The era of the great revivals was close at hand, and as architects in the coastal cities seized upon the new European fashions of Greek, Roman, and Gothic, these, more than the Palladian, would become the fashions west of the Alleghenies. None of this would have become possible if the confidence of the colonial American patriot, independent in spirit long before July 1776, had not been matched by the skill and confidence of the colonial American architect.

Notes to Chapter 9

1. There is of course an extensive literature on church building in colonial America. Some of the earlier general works are Aymar Embury II, *Early American Churches* (Garden City, N.Y.: Doubleday, Page and Company, 1914); Edward F. Rines, *Old Historic Churches of America* (New York: MacMillan, 1936); Stephen P. Dorsey, *Early English Churches in America* (New York: Oxford University Press, 1936); and Edmund W. Sinnott, *Meetinghouse and Church in Early New England* (New York: McGraw-Hill, 1963). The most comprehensive and best illustrated general survey is Harold W. Rose, *The Colonial Houses of Worship in America* (New York: Hastings House, 1963).

2. Anna Wells Rutledge, "The Second St. Philip's, Charleston, 1710-1835," *JSAH* 18, no. 3 (October 1959): 112-114; and Mills Lane, *Architecture of the Old South* (New York: Abbeville Press, 1993), 25.

3. Marcus Whiffen and Frederick Koeper, *American Architecture, 1607-1976* (Cambridge, Mass.: MIT Press, 1981), 61.

4. Frederick Dalcho, *An Historical Account of the Protestant Episcopal Church in South Carolina* (Charleston: 1820), 120-126.

5. Nikolaus Pevsner and Alexandra Wedgwood, *The Buildings of England. Warwickshire* (Harmondsworth: Penguin Books, Ltd., 1966), 107.

6. Suzanne Foley, "Christ Church, Boston," *OTNE* 51, no. 3 (January-March 1961), 67-85; and Peter T. Mallary, *New England Churches & Meeting Houses [sic], 1680-1830* (New York: Vendome Press, 1985), 61-63.

7. Marcus Whiffen, *Stuart and Georgian Churches* (London: B.T. Batsford, Ltd., 1947), 25-26.

8. Christopher Wren, *Parentalia* (London: 1750, reprinted, Farnborough: Gregg International, 1965), 320.

9. Norman M. Isham, *Trinity Church in Newport, Rhode Island* (Boston: 1936), 36-104; Antoinette Forrester Downing, *Early Homes of Rhode Island* (Richmond, Va.: Garrett and Massie, Inc., 1937), 107-133; Antoinette F. Downing and Vincent J. Scully, Jr., *The Architectural Heritage of Newport, Rhode Island*, 2nd rev. ed. (New York: Clarkson N. Potter, Inc., 1967), 54-57; and Mallary, *New England Churches*, 65-68.

10. For details of Munday's life see Isham, *Trinity Church*, 52-58.

11. Ibid., 37, and Foley, "Christ Church, Boston," 70-71.

12. Robert W. Shoemaker, "Christ Church, St. Peter's, and St. Paul's," *Transactions of the American Philosophical Society* 43, no. 1 (1953): 187-198; and George B. Tatum,

Penn's Great Town (Philadelphia: University of Pennsylvania Press, 1961), 28-30.

13. James Gibbs, *A Book of Architecture* (London: 1728, reprinted, New York: Benjamin Blom, 1968), Plate 21.

14. Terry Friedman, *James Gibbs* (New Haven: Yale University Press, 1984), 54-72.

15. Nikolaus Pevsner, *The Buildings of England. London* (Harmondsworth: Penguin Books, 1962), 451 and 136.

16. Friedman, *James Gibbs*, 68.

17. Carl Bridenbaugh, *Peter Harrison* (Chapel Hill: University of North Carolina Press, 1949), 45-53. This is the standard biography of Harrison and is the source of biographical information in the text.

18. Ibid., 168-170, for the books listed in the inventory of Harrison's estate in 1775 following his death in New Haven, Conn. Other books Harrison may have used in Newport, his long-time home, seem to have found their way to the Redwood Library there. See Helen Park, *A List of Architectural Books Available in America Before the Revolution* (Los Angeles: Hennessey & Ingalls, Inc., 1973).

19. Ibid., 54-63, and Mallary, *New England Churches*, 73-78.

20. The drawing reproduced in Figure 16 is conjectural, by David Powers. It is based on a description of Harrison's intention published in 1784 and quoted in Bridenbaugh, *Peter Harrison*, 59. While the details of the drawing are admittedly speculative, the general scheme was evidently intended to reflect the tower of St. Martin-in-the-Fields.

21. Priscilla Metcalf, "Boston Before Bulfinch: Harrison's King's Chapel," *JSAH* 13, no. 1 (March 1954), 11.

22. Kerry Downes, *Hawksmoor* (London: Thames and Hudson, 1969), 132-138.

23. Metcalf, "Boston Before Bulfinch," 13.

24. Friedman makes the very interesting observation that the timber for St. Paul's Church in Halifax, Nova Scotia, was framed in Boston in 1749 and that contemporary sources describe it as being based on Marylebone Chapel (Friedman, *James Gibbs*, 277-299). He goes on to suggest that because of certain relationships between Gibbs and those concerned with Nova Scotia that Gibbs himself supplied the design. Would it not be more likely that, the framing being done in Boston, the design came from Harrison, who was there working from the same model?

25. The bills for William Burbeck's work are discussed in Henry Wilder Foote, *Annals of King's Chapel*, 2 vols. (Boston: 1882-96).

26. George W. Williams, *St. Michael's, Charleston, 1751-1951* (Columbia: University of South Carolina Press, 1951), 129-151; Dorsey, *Early English Churches*, 102-105; and Lane, *Architecture of the Old South*, 55-57.

27. Harley J. McKee, "St. Michael's Church, Charleston, 1752-1762," *JSAH* 23, no. 1 (March 1964): 39-43.

28. Williams, *St. Michael's, Charleston*, 142. The "massy foundation" has enabled St. Michael's tower to withstand the impact of repeated hurricanes.

29. Ibid., 348.

30. Adolph B. Benson, rev. and ed., *Peter Kalm's Travels in North America* (New York: Dover Publications, 1966), 1:21.

31. Shoemaker, "Christ Church, St. Peter's, and St. Paul's," 189.

32. Morgan Dix, *A History of the Parish of Trinity Church in the City of New York*, 3 vols. (New York: G. P. Putnam's Sons, 1898), 2; Dorsey, *Early English Churches*, 142-147; Hugh Morrison, *Early American Architecture: From the First Colonial Settlement to the National Period* (New York: Dover Publications, 1987 [1952]), 553-555; and Rose, *Colonial Houses of Worship*, 295-297. Small and fragile compared to the present-day surrounding skyscrapers on the tip of Manhattan, St. Paul's Chapel narrowly escaped obliteration when the neighboring World Trade Center towers were attacked and collapsed on September 11, 2001. The old tree in the cemetery churchyard was destroyed but the chapel survived and became a place of solace and recuperation for the scores of firemen, police, and volunteers who slowly removed the debris of the towers in the following months, extracting the remains of hundreds of victims. The old pews became makeshift beds for the searchers. [Ed.]

33. Dorsey, *Early English Churches*, 72-75; Morrison, *Early American Architecture*, 349-350; James Scott Rawlings, *Virginia's Colonial Churches* (Richmond: Garrett & Massie, 1963), 120-127; Rose, *Colonial Houses of Worship*, 501-502; and Louise B. Dawe, *Christ Church: Lancaster County, Virginia 1732 and the Life Around It* (Irvington, Va.: Foundation for Historic Christ Church, 1970).

34. J. Frederick Kelly, *Early Connecticut Meetinghouses*, 2 vols. (New York: Columbia University Press, 1948), 1:45-51; Louise Kingsley, "Old Trinity Church, Brooklyn, Connecticut," *OTNE* 42, no. 3 (January-March 1952): 73-77; Rose, *Colonial Houses of Worship*, 119-120; and Mallary, *New England Churches*, 83-87.

35. Rawlings, *Virginia's Colonial Churches*, 228-232; and Rose, *Colonial Houses of Worship*, 510-512.

36. Benjamin B. Wisner, *The History of the Old South Church in Boston* (Boston: Crakes and Brewster, 1830); Justin Winsor, *The Memorial History of Boston*, 4 vols. (Boston: James R. Osgood and Company, 1880-1881), 2:514-517; and Mallary, *New England Churches*, 69-72.

37. A persistent error in the general histories of American colonial architecture is the statement that the Old South Meeting House was designed by Robert Twelves. This

goes back to Hamilton A. Hill, *History of the Old South Church, Boston, 1669-1884* (Boston and New York: Houghton, Mifflin and Co., 1890), 1:450, "Robert Twelves is said to have been the builder." Place made this an assertion in "From Meeting House to Church," page 114, and the damage was done. Robert Twelves built the first meeting house of the Third Church in 1669, not the later one, Samuel A. Bates, ed., *Records of the Town of Braintree, 1640-1793* (Randolph, Mass.: D. H. Huxford, printer, 1886), 693.

38. Having been taken out of use for church services after a fire in 1872, Old South was for a time to be demolished. The reversal of this intention is one of the earliest of American efforts in historic preservation.

39. Kelly, *Early Connecticut Meetinghouses*, 1:157-169; and Mallary, *New England Churches*, 88-93.

40. Kelly, *Early Connecticut Meetinghouses*, 1:162; and Peter Benes, "Sky Colors and Scattered Clouds: The Decorative and Architectural Painting of New England Meeting Houses [sic], 1738-1834," in *New England Meeting House [sic] and Church: 1630-1850*, ed. P. Benes (Dublin, N.H.: Boston University Press for The Dublin Seminar for New England Folklife: Annual Proceedings for 1979, 1979) 63-66.

41. J. Frederick Kelly, "Raising Connecticut Meeting Houses," *OTNE* 27, no. 1 (July 1936): 3-9.

42. Kelly, *Early Connecticut Meetinghouses*, 1:32-44 and 2:286-295.

43. Park Pressey, "When Grandma Went to Meeting as a Little Girl," *OTNE* 35, no. 4 (April 1945): 60-62; Alice Winchester, "Meeting House at Sandown," *Antiques* 48, no. 6 (December 1945): 336-337; and William E. Hennessy, "The Old Church at Sandown," *New Hampshire Profiles*, no. 3 (August 1954): 28-32.

44. Batty Langley and Thomas Langley, *The Builder's Jewel* (London: 1746, reprinted, New York: Benjamin Blom, Inc., 1970), Plate 4.

45. Benes, "Sky Colors," 51-62.

46. Ibid., 62-64.

47. Lyman Beecher, *Autobiography of Lyman Beecher*, ed. Barbara Cross (Cambridge, Mass.: Belknap Press of Harvard University Press, 1961), 1:152.

48. Kelly, *Early Connecticut Meetinghouses*, 1:166.

49. Benes, "Sky Colors," 66-69; and Bettina A. Norton, "Anglican Embellishments: The Contributions of John Gibbs, Junior, and William Price to the Church of England in Eighteenth-Century Boston," in *New England Meeting House [sic] and Church: 1630-1850*, ed. P. Benes (Dublin, N.H.: Boston University Press for The Dublin Seminar for New England Folklife: Annual Proceedings for 1979, 1979), 80-84.

50. Frederic C. Detwiller, "Thomas Dawes's Church in Brattle Square," *OTNE* 69, nos. 3 and 4 (Winter/Spring 1979): 1-17. For additional information on Dawes and his domestic work see Frederic C. Detwiller, "Thomas Dawes: Boston's Patriot Architect," *OTNE* 68, nos. 1-2 (July-December 1977): 1-18.

51. Detwiller, "Thomas Dawes's Church," 4-5; Norman M. Isham, *Meeting-house of the First Baptist Church in Providence* (Providence: Akerman-Standard Co., 1925); Henry M. King, "The First Baptist Church, Providence, Rhode Island," *OTNE* 34, no. 3 (January 1944): 39-43; and Rose, *Colonial Houses of Worship*, 402-404.

52. Isham, *Meeting-house*, 2

53. Detwiller, "Thomas Dawes's Church," 4.

54. For drawings of the three churches see ibid., 8-9.

55. Edward F. Rines, *Old Historic Churches of America* (New York: MacMillan, 1936), 153.

56. John Hall, *History of the Presbyterian Church in Trenton, N.J., from the first settlement of the town* (New York: A. D. F. Randolph, 1975 [1859]), 37.

57. Marian Card, *Early Church Architecture in New Jersey* (Master's thesis, Oberlin College, 1948), 55-56.

58. The brick at Daretown is laid in plain Flemish bond, but the region is notable for much more elaborate effects. See Paul Van Derveer Love, "Patterned brickwork in Southern New Jersey," *Proceedings of the New Jersey Historical Society* 73 (July 1955): 182-208.

59. Kelly, *Early Connecticut Meetinghouses*, 1:xxviii.

60. Theodore Chambers, *The Early Germans of New Jersey: Their History, Churches, and Genealogies* (Baltimore: Geneaological Pub. Co., 1969), 83.

61. Rose, *Colonial Houses of Worship*, 318.

62. Ibid., 316-317.

63. Ibid., 376.

64. Rines, *Old Historic Churches*, 155-156; and, Rose *Colonial Houses of Worship*, 29.

65. For a short history of the Jewish people in early America see ibid., 415.

66. Bridenbaugh, *Peter Harrison*, 98-104; Downing and Scully, *Architectural Heritage*, 84-87; and Nancy H. Schless, *Peter Harrison, the Touro Synagogue, and the Wren City Church* (Chicago: University of Chicago Press, 1973).

67. For a review of the details and their possible sources see Fiske Kimball, "The Colonial amateurs and their models: Peter Harrison," *Architecture* 53, no. 6 (June 1926): 155-160; and also Bridenbaugh, *Peter Harrison*, 100-104.

68. Esther Schwartz, "Touro Synagogue Restored, 1827-29," *JSAH* 17, no. 2 (Summer 1958): 23-26.

69. Edward M. Riley, *Independence National Historic Park, Philadelphia, Pa.*, rev. ed. (Washington D.C.: 1956), 2-52.

70. Norman M. Isham, "The Colony House at Newport, Rhode Island," *OTNE* 8, no. 2 (December 1917): 3-20; and Downing and Scully, *Architectural Heritage*, 60-63.

71. Marcus Whiffen, "The Early County Courthouses of Virginia," *JSAH* 18, no. 1 (March 1959): 2-10.

72. Whiffen, *Public Buildings*, 152-161.

73. For discussion of colonial commercial interests and rivalries see Carl Bridenbaugh, *Cities in the Wilderness; the First Century of Urban Life in America, 1625-1742* (New York: The Ronald Press Company, 1938), 330-363.

74. Morrison, *Early American Architecture*, 439-442.

75. Frank Chouteau Brown, "John Smibert, Artist, and the First Faneuil Hall," *OTNE* 31, no. 2 (October 1940): 45-51.

76. Carl Bridenbaugh, ed., *Gentleman's Progress* (Chapel Hill: University of North Carolina, 1948), 111.

77. Norman M. Isham, "Report on the Old Brick Market or Old City Hall at Newport, Rhode Island," *OTNE* 6, no. 2 (January 1916): 3-11; and Bridenbaugh, *Peter Harrison*, 107-112.

78. Josiah Quincy, *The History of Harvard University* (New York: Arno Press, 1900), 2:113-114, and Bainbridge Bunting, *Harvard: An Architectural History* (Cambridge, Mass.: Belknap Press of Harvard University Press, 1985), 28-35.

79. Bridenbaugh, *Peter Harrison*, 45-51; and Downing and Scully, *Architectural Heritage*, 80-83.

80. For the development of libraries, both private and public, in the colonies see Bridenbaugh, *Cities*, 291-296.

81. Andrea Palladio, *Architecture in Four Books containing a dissertation on the five orders & ye most necessary observations relating to all kinds of buildings....*, trans. Edward Hoppus (London: B. Cole & J. Wilcox, 1736), Book IV, Frontispiece.

82. Charles E. Peterson, "Carpenters' Hall," *Historic Philadelphia, from the founding until the early nineteenth century; papers dealing with its people and buildings* (Philadelphia: American Philosophical Society, 1953): 96-126; and Charles E. Peterson, "Benjamin Loxley and Carpenters' Hall," *JSAH* 15, no. 4 (December 1956): 23-26. For the history of the Carpenters' Company see Charles E. Peterson, ed., *The Rules of Work of the Carpenters' Company* (Princeton: The Pyne Press, 1971), ix-xviii; and Roger W. Moss, Jr., "The Origins of the Carpenters' Company of Philadelphia," in *Building Early*

America, ed. Charles E. Peterson (Radnor: Chilton Book Company, 1976), 35-53. See also Charles E. Peterson, "Philadelphia Carpentry According to Palladio," in *Building by the Book*, ed. di Valmarana, 3 vols. (Charlottesville, Va.: The University of Virginia Press, 1984) 3:1-52.

83. Marcus Whiffen, *The Eighteenth-Century Houses of Williamsburg* (Williamsburg: Colonial Williamsburg, 1984), 146-160.

84. Ivor Noël Hume, *Archaeology and Wetherburn's Tavern* (Williamsburg: Colonial Williamsburg, 1969).

85. Horace H. F. Jayne, "The Cloisters at Ephrata," *American Magazine of Art* 29, no. 9 (September 1936): 594-598 and 620-622; and G. Edwin Brumbaugh, "Medieval Construction at Ephrata," *Antiques* 46, no. 1 (July 1944): 18-20.

86. Benson, ed., *Peter Kalm's Travels*, 2:685.

87. Rexford Newcomb, *Architecture in Old Kentucky* (Urbana: University of Illinois Press, 1953), 34.

⊰ Bibliography ⊱

"Information and directions formerly given to such persons as went over to settle in America: but particularly to those from England, who first peopled the now flourishing province in Pennsylvania." *Pennsylvania Magazine of History and Biography* 4 (1880): 331-342.

"Letter from Edward Howes, March 26, 1632." In Adam Winthrop. 3:73. *Winthrop Papers.* Boston: Massachusetts Historical Society, 1929-1947.

Acrelius, Israel. *A History of New Sweden,* translated and edited by William M. Reynolds. Philadelphia: The Historical Society of Pennsylvania, 1874.

Addleshaw, G. W. O., and Frederick Etchells. *The Architectural Setting of Anglican Worship: An Inquiry into the Arrangement for Public Worship in the Church of England from the Reformation to the Present Day.* London: Faber and Faber, 1948.

Addyman, P. V., D. Leigh, and M. J. Hughes. "Anglo-Saxon Houses at Chalton, Hampshire." *Medieval Archaeology* 16 (1972): 13-21.

Amadas, Philip, and Arthur Barlow. "First Voyage." 8:309. In *The Principal navigations, voyages, traffiques & discoveries of the English Nation, made by sea or overland to the remote and farthest distant quarters of the earth at any time within the compass of these 1600 years,* compiled by Richard Hakluyt. London: J. M. Dent and Sons, LTD, 1927-28.

Amman, Jost, and Hans Sachs. *The Book of Trades.* New York: Dover Publications, 1973 [1568].

Andrews, Charles McLean. *The Colonial Period of American History.* New Haven: Yale University Press, 1934.

Andrews, Stephenson B., ed. *Bacon's Castle.* Richmond, Va.: Association for the Preservation of Virginia Antiquities, 1984, revised edition, 2001.

Appleton, William Summer. "The Province House, 1928." *OTNE* 62 (Spring 1972): 88-91.

Arber, Edward, ed. *Travels and Works of Captain John Smith: President of Virginia and Admiral of New England, 1580-1631.* Edinburgh: John Grant, 1910.

Archer, John. "Puritan Town Planning in New Haven." *JSAH* 35 (May 1975): 140-149.

Bailey, Rosalie Fellows. *Pre-Revolutionary Dutch Houses and Families in Northern New Jersey and Southern New York.* New York: Dover Publications, 1968.

Baker, Nancy T. "Annapolis, Maryland 1695-1730." *Maryland Historical Magazine* 81 (Fall 1986): 191-202.

Baltimore, Cecilius Lord. "Instructions…directed by the Right Honorable Cecilius Lord Baltimore…." In *Narratives of Early Maryland, 1633-1684,* edited by Clayton Coleman Hall. New York: C. Scribner's Sons, 1910.

Bates, Samuel A., ed. *Records of the Town of Braintree, 1640-1793.* Randolph, Mass.: D. H. Huxford, printer, 1886.

Bealer, Alex W. *The Tools that Built America.* New York: Bonanza Books, 1980.

Beckerdite, Luke. "William Buckland and William Bernard Sears: The Designer and the Carver." *Journal of Early Southern Decorative Arts* 8 (November 1982): 7-40.

Beckerdite, Luke. "William Buckland Reconsidered: Architectural Carving in the Chesapeake." *Journal of Early Southern Decorative Arts* 8 (November 1982): 43-88.

Beecher, Lyman. *Autobiography of Lyman Beecher,* edited by Barbara Cross. Cambridge, Mass.: Belknap Press of Harvard University Press, 1961.

Beirne, Rosamund Randall, and John H. Scarff. *William Buckland (1734-1774): Architect of Virginia and Maryland.* [1958] Baltimore: Board of Regents of Gunston Hall and Hammond-Harwood House Association, 1970.

Benes, Peter, ed. *New England Meeting House [sic] and Church: 1630-1850.* Dublin, N.H.: Boston University Press for The Dublin Seminar for New England Folklife: Annual Proceedings for 1979, 1979.

Benes, Peter. "Sky Colors and Scattered Clouds: The Decorative and Architectural Painting of New England Meeting Houses [sic], 1738-1834." In *New England Meeting House [sic] and Church: 1630-1850,* edited by Peter Benes. Dublin, N.H.: Boston University Press for The Dublin Seminar for New England Folklife: Annual Proceedings for 1979, 1979.

Benson, Adolph B., rev. and ed. *Peter Kalm's Travels in North America.* New York: Dover Publications, 1966.

Betts, Edwin M. *Thomas Jefferson's Farm Book.* Philadelphia: The American Philosophical Society, 1944.

Betts, Edwin M., and Hazlehurst B. Perkins. *Thomas Jefferson's Garden Book.* Philadelphia: The American Philosophical Society, 1944.

Betts, Edwin M., and Hazlehurst B. Perkins. *Thomas Jefferson's Garden at Monticello.* Charlottesville: University of Virginia Press, 1971.

Beverley, Robert. *The History and Present State of Virginia,* edited by Louis B. Wright. Chapel Hill: University of North Carolina Press, 1947.

ARCHITECTURE IN COLONIAL AMERICA

The Bi-centennial Book of Malden. Boston: 1850.

Bishop, James Leander. *A History of American Manufactures from 1608 to 1860.* Philadelphia: Edward Young and Co., 1868.

Bivins, John, and J. Thomas Savage. "The Miles Brewton House, Charleston, South Carolina." *The Magazine of Antiques* 143 (February 1993): 294-307.

Blackburn, Roderic Hall. "Architecture: The Dutch Colony." In *Encyclopedia of the North American Colonies,* edited by Jacob E. Cooke. New York: Charles Scribner's Sons, 1993.

Bradford, William. *Of Plymouth Plantation, 1620-1647,* edited by Samuel E. Morison. New York: Knopf, 1952.

Brand, Barbara. "The Work of William Buckland in Maryland." Master's thesis, George Washington University, 1979.

Brand, Barbara. "William Buckland, Architecture in Annapolis." In *Building by the Book,* edited by Mario. di Valmarana, 2:65-100. 3 vols. Charlottesville, Va.: The University Press of Virginia for the Center for Palladian Studies in America, 1984.

Braun, Lucy E. *Deciduous Forests of Eastern North America.* New York: Hafner Pub. Co., 1964.

Bridenbaugh, Carl, ed. *Gentleman's Progress.* Chapel Hill: University of North Carolina, 1948.

Bridenbaugh, Carl. *Cities in the Wilderness; the First Century of Urban Life in America, 1625-1742.* New York: The Ronald Press Company, 1938.

Bridenbaugh, Carl. *Peter Harrison.* Chapel Hill: University of North Carolina Press, 1949.

Brown, Frank Chouteau. "John Smibert, Artist, and the First Faneuil Hall." *OTNE* 31 (October 1940): 45-51.

Browne, John. *Description and Use of an Ordinary Joynt-Rule.* London: J. Brown and H. Sutton, 1675.

Browne, William H., ed. *Archives of Maryland, Proceedings and Acts of the General Assembly of Maryland, October 1678- November 1683.* Baltimore: Maryland Historical Society, 1889.

Brownell, Charles E. et al. "Architectural Drawings and Design, 1770-1870." In *The Making of Virginia Architecture,* edited by Charles E. Brownell et al. Richmond: Virginia Museum of Fine Arts, 1992.

Brownell, Charles E., et al, eds. *The Making of Virginia Architecture.* Richmond: Virginia Museum of Fine Arts, 1992.

Brumbaugh, G. Edwin. "Medieval Construction at Ephrata." *Antiques* 46 (July 1944): 18-20.

Buchanan, Paul E. "The Eighteenth-Century Frame Houses of Tidewater Virginia." In *Building Early America,* edited by Charles E. Peterson. Radnor: Chilton Book Company, 1976.

The Builder's Dictionary: or, Gentleman and architect's companion; being a complete unabridged reprint of the earlier works published by A. Bettesworth and C. Hitch. Washington D.C.: Association for Preservation Technology, 1981 [1734].

Bunting, Bainbridge. *Early Architecture in New Mexico.* Albuquerque: University of New Mexico Press, 1976.

Bunting, Bainbridge. *Harvard: An Architectural History.* Cambridge, Mass.: Belknap Press of Harvard University Press, 1985.

Burnaby, Andrew. *Burnaby's Travels Through North America.* Edited by Rufus Rockwell Wilson. New York: A. Wessels Co., 1904.

Burrage, Henry S., ed. *Early English and French Voyages, Chiefly from Hakluyt, 1534-1608.* N.p., n.d..

Camp, Helen B. *Archaeological Excavations at Pemaquid, Maine, 1965-1974.* Augusta: Maine State Museum, 1976.

Campbell, Colin. *Vitruvius Britannicus.* 3 vols. London, 1715-1725.

Candee, Richard M. "Merchant and Millwright." *OTNE* 60 (Spring 1970): 131-149.

Card, Marian. *Early Church Architecture in New Jersey.* Master's thesis, Oberlin College, 1948.

Carr, Lois Green. "The Metropolis of Maryland: A Comment on Town Development Along the Tobacco Coast." *Maryland Historical Magazine* 69 (Summer 1974): 124-145.

Carroll, Kenneth L. *Three Hundred Years and More of Third Haven Quakerism.* Easton, Md.: Published for Third Haven Meeting of Friends by the Queen Anne Press, 1984.

Carson, Cary, et al. "Impermanent Architecture in the Southern American Colonies." *Winterthur Portfolio* 16 (Summer/Autumn 1981): 196.

Cartier, Jacques. "Third Voyage of Discovery." 8:267. In *The Principal navigations, voyages, traffiques & discoveries of the English Nation, made by sea or overland to the remote and farthest distant quarters of the earth at any time within the compass of these 1600 years,* compiled by Richard Hakluyt. London: J. M. Dent and Sons, LTD, 1927-28.

Chadwell, Pauline Soroka. "The Colonel Jeremiah Lee Mansion." *Antiques* 48 (December 1945): 353-355.

Chambers, Theodore. *The Early Germans of New Jersey: Their History, Churches, and Genealogies.* Baltimore: Geneaological Pub. Co., 1969.

Chase, Sara B. "A Brief Survey of the Architectural History of the Old State House, Boston, Massachusetts." *OTNE* 68 (Winter/Spring, 1978): 31-49.

Chiappelli, Fredi, Michael J. B. Allen, and Robert Louis Benson, eds. *First Images of America: The Impact of the New World on the Old.* Berkeley: University of California Press, 1976.

Chinard, Gilbert, ed. *Un Français en Virginie.* Paris: Librairie E. Droz, 1932.

Chippendale, Thomas. *The Gentleman and Cabinet Maker's Guide.* London: 1754, reprinted, New York: Dover, 1966.

Claiborne, Herbert A. *Commentary on Virginia Brickwork Before 1800.* Boston: Walpole Society, 1957.

Clifton-Taylor, Alec. *The Pattern of English Building.* London: B. T. Batsford, Ltd., 1962.

Colin, Thomas J. "Solving the Mystery of Gunston Hall." *Historic Preservation* 36 (June 1984): 41-45.

Colvin, Howard. *Biographical Dictionary of English Architects, 1600-1840.* 2nd ed. London: John Murray, 1978.

Comenius, Johann Amos. *The Orbis Pictus of John Amos Comenius,* ed. C. W. Bardeau. Syracuse, N.Y.: C. W. Bardeau, 1887.

Comstock, Helen. "Mount Pleasant, the most elegant seat in Pennsylvania." *Connoisseurs* 156 (August 1964): 226-231.

Condit, Carl. *American Building: Materials and Techniques from the First Colonial Settlements to the Present.* Chicago: University of Chicago Press, 1982.

Condon, Thomas J. *New York Beginnings: The Commercial Origins of New Netherland.* New York: New York University Press, 1968.

Cooke, Jacob E., ed. *Encyclopedia of the North American Colonies.* New York: Charles Scribner's Sons, 1993.

Cornelius, Charles. "Wentworth-Gardner House." *Metropolitan Museum of Art Bulletin* 14 (February 1919): 24-31.

Corner, William. *San Antonio de Bexar: A Guide and History* (San Antonio: 1890). Quoted in *The Alamo Chain of Missions,* by Marion A. Habig. Chicago: Franciscan Herald Press, 1976.

Cotter, John L. *Archaeological Excavations at Jamestown Colonial National Historic Park and Jamestown National Historic Site, Virginia.* Washington D.C.: National Park Service, 1958.

Cousins, Frank, and Phil M. Riley, *The Colonial Architecture of Philadelphia.* Boston: Little, Brown, and Company, 1920.

Cox, Warren J. "Four Men, the *Four Books* and the Five-Part House." 2:117-146. In *Building by the Book,* edited by Mario di Valmarana. 3 vols. Charlottesville, Va.: The University Press of Virginia for the Center for Palladian Studies in America, 1984.

Crossley, Frederick Herbert. *Timber Building in England: From Early Times to the End of the Seventeenth Century.* London: Batsford, 1951.

Crouch, Dora P., Daniel J. Garr, and Axel I. Mundigo. *Spanish City Planning in North America.* Cambridge, Mass.: MIT Press, 1982.

Cumming, William Patterson, R. A. Skelton, and David B. Quinn. *The Discovery of North America.* New York: American Heritage Press, 1972.

Cummings, Abbott L. *The Framed Houses of Massachusetts Bay, 1625-1725.* Cambridge, Mass.: Belknap Press, 1979.

Cummings, Abbott L., ed. *Architecture in Colonial Massachusetts.* Boston: Colonial Society of Massachusetts, 1979.

Cummings, Abbott L., ed. *Architecture in Early New England.* Sturbridge, Mass.: Old Sturbridge Village, 1958.

Cummings, Abbott L. "The Beginnings of Provincial Renaissance Architecture in Boston, 1690-1725." *JSAH* 42 (March 1983): 43-53.

Cummings, Abbott L. "The Foster-Hutchinson House." *OTNE* 54 (January-March 1964): 59-76.

Cummings, Abbott L. "The Parson Barnard House." *OTNE* (October-December 1956), 29-40.

Cushing, John D. "Town Commons of New England, 1640-1840." *OTNE* 51 (January-March 1961): 86-94.

Dahlgren, Stellan, and Hans Norman. *The Rise And Fall of New Sweden: Governor Johan Risingh's Journal 1654-1655 in its Historical Context.* Uppsala: Almqvist & Wiksell International, 1988.

Dalcho, Frederick. *An Historical Account of the Protestant Episcopal Church in South Carolina.* Charleston: 1820.

Dana, Henry W. L. "The Longfellow House, Cambridge, Massachusetts." *OTNE* 37 (April 1948): 82-98.

Danckaerts, Jasper. *Journal of a Voyage to New York.* Ann Arbor, Mich.: University Microfilms, 1966 [1867].

Danckaerts, Jasper. *Journal of Jasper Danckaerts, 1679-1680.* New York: C. Scribner's Sons, 1913 [1867].

Davis, Deering. *Annapolis Houses 1700-1775.* New York: Architectural Book Publishing Company, 1947.

Davis, Richard B., ed. *William Fitzhugh and his Chesapeake World, 1676-1701: The Fitzhugh Letters and Other Documents.* Chapel Hill: University of North Carolina Press, 1963.

Dawe, Louise B. *Christ Church: Lancaster County, Virginia 1732 and the Life Around It.* Irvington, Va.: Foundation for Historic Christ Church, 1970.

de Champlain, Samuel. *Voyages of Samuel de Champlain, 1604-1618,* edited by William Lawson Grant. New York: C. Scribner's Sons, 1907.

de Charlevoix, Pierre François Xavier. *Journal of a Voyage to North America,* quoted in *Town Planning in Frontier America,* by John William Reps. Princeton: Princeton University Press, 1969.

de Costa, Benjamin Franklin. "A Relation of a Voyage to Sagadahoc." In *Early English and French Voyages, Chiefly from Hakluyt, 1534-1608,* edited by Henry S. Burrage. N.p., n.d..

de Forest, Elizabeth. *The Gardens and Grounds at Mount Vernon: How George Washington Planned and Planted Them.* Mount Vernon, Va.: Mount Vernon Ladies' Association of the Union, 1982.

de la Croix, Horst, and John R. Hale. *Renaissance Fortification : Art or Engineering?* London: Thames and Hudson, 1977.

de la Croix, Horst. *Military Considerations in City Planning: Fortifications.* New York: G. Braziller, 1972.

de la Treille, François, Giovanni Battista de' Zanchi, and Robert Corneweyle. *La manière de fortifier villes* (The maner of Fortification of Cities, Townes, Castelles and Other Places). Farnborough: Gregg, 1972.

de Laudonnière, R. G. "The Second Voyage into Florida." In *The Principal navigations, voyages, traffiques & discoveries of the English Nation, made by sea or overland to the remote and farthest distant quarters of the earth at any time within the compass of these 1600 years,* compiled by Richard Hakluyt. London: J. M. Dent and Sons, LTD, 1927-28.

de Rasières, Isaack. "Letter of September 23, 1626." In *Documents Relating to New Netherland, 1624-1626, in the Henry E. Huntington Library,* translated and edited by Arnold Van Laer. San Marino, Calif.: The Henry E. Huntington Library and Art Gallery, 1924.

de Rasières, Isaack. "Letter of September 23, 1626." In *Documents Relating to New Netherland, 1624-1626, in the Henry E. Huntington Library,* translated and edited by Arnold Van Laer. San Marino, Calif.: The Henry E. Huntington Library and Art Gallery, 1924.

de v. Pratt, Harden. "The Restoration of Christ's Cross, New Kent County, Virginia." *Virginia Magazine of History and Biography* 65 (July 1957): 328-331.

de Vries, David Pietersz. *Korte historiael ende journaels aenteyckeninge van verscheyden voyagiens in di vier deelen des wereldtsronde, als Europa, Africa, Asia, ende Amerika gedaen.* 's-Gravenhage: M. Nijhoff, 1911 [1655].

Detwiller, Frederic C. "The Evolution of the Shirley-Eustis House." *OTNE* 70 (1980): 17-30.

Detwiller, Frederic C. "Thomas Dawes: Boston's Patriot Architect." *OTNE* 68 (July-December 1977): 1-18.

Detwiller, Frederic C. "Thomas Dawes's Church in Brattle Square." *OTNE* 69 (Winter/Spring 1979): 1-17.

di Valmarana, Mario, ed. *Building by the Book.* 3 vols. Charlottesville: Published for the Center for Palladian Studies in America by the University Press of Virginia, 1984.

Diderot, Denis, et al. *Receuil des planches pour la nouvelle èdition du Dictionnaire raisonnè…avec leur explication.* Geneva: Pallet, 1776-1777.

Dilliard, Maud Esther. *An Album of New Netherland.* New York: Bramhall House, 1963.

Dix, Morgan. *A History of the Parish of Trinity Church in the City of New York.* 3 vols. New York: G. P. Putnam's Sons, 1898.

Dixon, Carolyn Wyche. "The Miles Brewton House: Ezra Waite's Architectural Design Books and Other Possible Sources." *South Carolina Historical Magazine* 82 (April 1981): 118-42.

Dominguez, Fray Angelico Atanasio. *The Missions of New Mexico, 1776,* translated by Eleanor B. Adams and Fray Angelico Chavez. Albuquerque: University of New Mexico Press, 1956.

Donnelly, Marian C. *The New England Meeting Houses of the Seventeenth Century.* Middletown, Conn.: Wesleyan University Press, 1968.

Dorsey, Stephen P. *Early English Churches in America.* New York: Oxford University Press, 1936.

Downes, Kerry. *Hawksmoor.* London: Thames and Hudson, 1969.

Downey, Fairfax. *Louisbourg: Key to a Continent.* Englewood Cliffs, N.J.: Prentice-Hall, 1965.

Downing, Antoinette Forrester, and Vincent J. Scully, Jr. *The Architectural Heritage of Newport, Rhode Island.* 2nd rev. ed. New York: Clarkson N. Potter, Inc., 1967.

Downing, Antoinette Forrester. *Early Homes of Rhode Island.* Richmond, Va.: Garrett and Massie, Inc., 1937.

Durant, David N. *Ralegh's Lost Colony.* New York: Atheneum, 1981. *Early Records of the Town of Dedham.* 3 vols. Dedham: 1892-1899.

Eberlein, Harold D. *The Architecture of Colonial America.* 2nd ed. Boston: Little, Browne and Co., 1927.

Eburne, Richard. *A Plain Pathway to Plantations (1624).* Ithaca, N.Y.: Cornell University Press, 1962.

Eekhof, Albert. *Jonas Michaëlius, founder of the church in New Netherland, his life and work, together with the facsimile, transcription and English of an extensive unknown autographical Latin letter.* Leyden: A. W. Sijthoff, 1926.

Embury II, Aymar. *Early American Churches.* Garden City, N.Y.: Doubleday, Page and Company, 1914.

Erixon, Sigurd Emanuel. *Svensk byggnadskultur studier och skildringar belysande den svenska byggnadskulturens historia.* Stockholm: Aktiebolaget Bokvert, 1947.

Erixon, Sigurd Emanuel. "The North-European Technique of Timber Construction." *Folkliv,* 1 (1937): 13-60.

Evans, Joan. *Monastic Architecture in France.* Cambridge: Cambridge University Press, 1964.

Faulkner, Gretchen F. "A History of Archaeological Investigation on St. Croix." University of Maine, 1982.

Fernow, Berthold, ed. *Documents Relating to the History of the Dutch and Swedish Settlements on the Delaware River.* Albany: The Argus Company, Printers, 1877.

Foley, Suzanne. "Christ Church, Boston." *OTNE* 51 (January-March 1961), 67-85.

Foote, Henry Wilder. *Annals of King's Chapel.* 2 vols. Boston, 1882-96.

Force, Peter. *Tracts and other papers relating principally to the origin, settlement, and progress of the colonies in North America: from the discovery of the country to the year 1776.* New York: P. Smith, 1947.

Forman, Benno. "Mill Sawing in Seventeenth-Century Massachusetts." *OTNE* 60 (Spring 1970): 110-149.

Forman, Henry Chandler. *Jamestown and St. Mary's: Buried Cities of Romance.* Baltimore: Johns Hopkins Press, 1938.

Forman, Henry Chandler. *The Architecture of the Old South: The Medieval Style, 1585-1850.* Cambridge, Mass.: Harvard University Press, 1948.

Fortier, John. *Fortress of Louisbourg.* Toronto: Oxford University Press, 1979.

Friedman, Terry. *James Gibbs.* New Haven: Yale University Press, 1984.

Froissart, Sir John. *The Chronicles of England, France, Spain, Etc.,* translated by Thomas Johnes. New York: J. M. Dent; E. P. Dutton, 1940 [1906].

Garvan, Anthony N. B. *Architecture and Town Planning in Colonial Connecticut.* New Haven: Yale University Press, 1951.

Gibbs, James. *A Book of Architecture.* London: 1728, reprinted, New York: Benjamin Blom, 1968.

Goelet, Francis. "Journal of Capt. Francis Goelet." *New England Historical Genealogical Register* 24 (1870): 62.

Goodman, William Louis. *The History of Woodworking Tools.* London: G. Bell, 1964.

Gowans, Alan. *Church Architecture in New France.* New Brunswick: Rutgers University Press, 1955.

Gowans, Alan. *Images of American Living: Four Centuries of Architecture and Furniture as Cultural Expression.* Philadelphia: J. B. Lippincott, 1964.

Great Britain Public Records Office. *Calendar of State Papers, Colonial Series.* London: 1860-1969.

Gunter, Edmund. *De sectore et radio (The description and vse of the sector, the crosse-staffe and other instruments for such as are studious of mathematicall practise).* London: Printed by Willia[m] Jones, 1624.

Habig, Marion A. *The Alamo Chain of Missions*. Chicago: Franciscan Herald Press, 1976.

Hadlock, Wendell S. *A Report of the Archeological Work Performed 1961-62 on United States Government Property: the Islesford Historical Museum Grounds, Islesford, Little Cranberry Island, Maine*. N.p., 1962.

Hakluyt the Elder, Richard. "Notes." 7:248. In *The Principal navigations, voyages, traffiques & discoveries of the English Nation, made by sea or overland to the remote and farthest distant quarters of the earth at any time within the compass of these 1600 years*, compiled by Richard Hakluyt. London: J. M. Dent and Sons, LTD, 1927-28.

Hakluyt, Richard and Richard Hakluyt. "Discourse on the Western Planting." 2:211-326. In *The Original Writings & Correspondence of the Two Richard Hakluyts*, edited by E. G. R. Taylor. London: Printed for the Hakluyt Society, 1935.

Hakluyt, Richard, comp. "The letters patents granted by the Queens Majestie to Sir Walter Ralegh." 8:290. In *The Principal navigations, voyages, traffiques & discoveries of the English Nation, made by sea or overland to the remote and farthest distant quarters of the earth at any time within the compass of these 1600 years*. London: J. M. Dent and Sons, LTD, 1927-28.

Hakluyt, Richard, comp. *The Principal navigations, voyages, traffiques & discoveries of the English Nation, made by sea or overland to the remote and farthest distant quarters of the earth at any time within the compass of these 1600 years*. London: J. M. Dent and Sons, LTD, 1927-28.

Hakluyt, Richard. *Divers voyages touching the discoverie of America*. Ann Arbor, Mich.: University Microfilms, 1966.

Halevy, Daniel. *Vauban: Builder of Fortresses*, translated by Cecil J. C. Street. New York: Dial Press, 1925.

Halfpenny, William. *The Modern Builder's Assistant*. London: 1742.

Hall, Clayton Coleman. *Narratives of Early Maryland, 1633-1684*. New York: C. Scribner's Sons, 1910.

Hall, James Anthony. "William Buckland's Anglo-Palladian Interior Ornamentation at Gunston Hall." Architectural History Master's thesis, University of Virginia, 1989.

Hall, John. *History of the Presbyterian Church in Trenton, N.J., from the first settlement of the town*. New York: A. D. F. Randolph, 1975 [1859].

Hallenbeck, Cleve. *Spanish Missions of the Old Southwest*. Garden City, N.Y.: Doubleday, Page and Company, 1926.

Hamor, Ralph. *A True Discourse of the Present State of Virginia*. Richmond: Virginia State Library, 1957.

Hariot, Thomas. *A Brief and True Report of the New Found Land of Virginia*. New York: History Book Club, 1951 [1588].

Harrington, J. C. *Search for the Cittie of Ralegh: Archeological Excavations at Fort Raleigh National Historic Site, North Carolina*. Washington D.C.: National Park Service, U.S. Dept. of the Interior, 1962.

Harrington, J. C. *Seventeenth Century Brickmaking and Tilemaking at Jamestown, Virginia*. Virginia Magazine of History and Biography, 1950.

Harris, John. "The Pattern Book Phenomenon." 2:101-116. In *Building by the Book*, edited by Mario di Valmarana. 3 vols. Charlottesville, Va.: The University Press of Virginia for the Center for Palladian Studies in America, 1984.

Harris, Kenneth D. "Restoration of the Habitation of Port Royal, Lower Granville, Nova Scotia." *Royal Architecture Institute of Canada* 17 (July 1940): 111-116.

Hartley, Edward Neal. *Ironworks on the Saugus; the Lynn and Braintree Ventures of the Company of Undertakers of the Ironworks in New England*. Norman: University of Oklahoma Press, 1957.

Hatch, Jr., Charles E. *America's Oldest Legislative Assembly*. Washington D.C.: n.p., 1956.

Hatch, Jr., Charles E. *Jamestown, Virginia: The Townsite and its Story*. Washington, D.C.: U.S. Dept. of the Interior, National Park Service, 1957.

Hawthorne, Nathaniel. *Twice Told Tales*. 2:3. 2 vols. Boston: Desmond Publishing Co., 1900.

Hening, William Waller, ed. *The Statutes at Large; Being a Collection of all the Laws of Virginia, from the First Session of the Legislature in the Year 1619*. Charlottesville: University Press of Virginia, 1969 [1819].

Hennessy, William E. "The Old Church at Sandown." *New Hampshire Profiles* (August 1954): 28-32.

Higginson, Francis. "New-Englands Plantation" (London, 1630). In *Chronicles of the First Planters of the Colony of Massachusetts Bay, 1623-1636*, by Alexander Young. Boston: C. C. Little and J. Brown, 1846.

Higginson, Francis. *New-Englands Plantation*. Amsterdam: Theatrum Orbis Terrarum; New York: Da Capo Press, 1970 [1630].

Hill, Hamilton A. *History of the Old South Church, Boston, 1669-1884*. Boston and New York: Houghton, Mifflin and Co., 1890.

Hindle, Brooke, ed. *Material Culture of the Wooden Age*. Tarrytown, N.Y.: Sleepy Hollow Press, 1981.

Historic American Building Survey (HABS): New York. 8 vols. New York: Garland Publishing, Inc., 1979.

Historic American Buildings Survey (HABS): Virginia Catalog. Charlottesville: University Press of Virginia, 1976.

Hitchcock, Henry Russell. *Netherlandish Scrolled Gables of the Sixteenth and Early Seventeenth Centuries*. New York: New York University Press for the College Art Association of America, 1978.

Hoffecker, Carol E., et al. *New Sweden in America*. Newark: University of Delaware Press, 1995.

Holme, Thomas. "A Short Advertisement upon the Scituation and extent of the City of Philidelphia and the Ensuing Plat-form Thereof." In *Narratives of Early Pennsylvania, West New Jersey and Delaware, 1630-1707*, edited by Albert Cook Myers. New York: C. Scribner's Sons, 1912.

Huber, Leonard Victor, and Samuel Wilson, Jr. *Baroness Pontalba's Buildings, their Site and the Remarkable Woman who Built them*. New Orleans: New Orleans Chapter of the Louisiana Landmarks Society, 1964.

Hudde, Andries. "A brief, but true Report of the Proceedings of Johan Prints [Printz], Governor of the Swedish forces at the South-River of New-Netherland, also of the garrisons of the aforesaid Swedes, found on that River, the first of November 1645." In *Documents Relating to the History of the Dutch and Swedish Settlements on the Delaware River*, edited by Berthold Fernow. Albany: The Argus Company, Printers, 1877.

Hulton, P. H., and David B. Quinn, eds. *The American Drawings of John White, 1577-1590, with Drawings of European and Oriental Subjects*. London: Trustees of the British Museum; Chapel Hill: University of North Carolina Press, 1964.

Hume, Ivor Noël. *Archaeology and Wetherburn's Tavern*. Williamsburg: Colonial Williamsburg, 1969.

Hume, Ivor Noël. *Digging for Carter's Grove*. Williamsburg: Colonial Williamsburg, 1974.

Hummel, Charles F. *English Tools in America: the Evidence of the Dominys*. South Burlington, Vermont: Early American Industries Association, 1976.

Innocent, Charles Frederick. *The Development of English Building Construction*. Newton Abbot, David and Charles, 1971 [1916].

Isham, Norman M. "Report on the Old Brick Market or Old City Hall at Newport, Rhode Island." *OTNE* 6 (January 1916): 3-11.

Isham, Norman M. "The Colony House at Newport, Rhode Island." *OTNE* 8 (December 1917): 3-20.

Isham, Norman M. *Meeting-house of the First Baptist Church in Providence*. Providence: Akerman-Standard Co., 1925.

Isham, Norman M. *Trinity Church in Newport, Rhode Island*. Boston: 1936.

Isham, Norman M., and Albert F. Brown. *Early Rhode Island Houses: An Historical and Architectural Study*. Providence, R.I.: Preston & Rounds, 1895.

James, John. *The Theory and Practice of Gardening*. London: 1712, reprinted, Farnborough: Gregg, 1969.

Jameson, Franklin J., ed. *Narratives of New Netherland, 1609-1664*. New York: Charles Scribner's Sons, 1909.

Jayne, Horace H. F. "The Cloisters at Ephrata." *American Magazine of Art* 29 (September 1936): 594-622.

Jefferson, Thomas. *Thomas Jefferson's Architectural Drawings*. Edited by Frederick Nichols. Boston: Massachusetts Historical Society, 1978.

Jogues, Father Isaac. "Novum Belgium." In *Narratives of New Netherland, 1609-1664*, edited by Franklin J. Jameson. New York: Charles Scribner's Sons, 1909.

Johnson, Amandus. *The Swedish Settlements on the Delaware, 1638-1664*. Baltimore: Genealogical Publishing Co., 1969 [1911].

Johnson, Edward. *Johnson's Wonder-Working Providence, 1628-1651*. New York: C. Scribner's Sons, 1910.

Johnson, Edward. *Wonder-Working Providence of Sions Saviour in New England*. Andover, Mass.: W. F. Draper, 1867.

Johnson, Paul C., ed. *The California Missions: A Pictorial History*. Menlo Park, Calif.: Lane Magazine and Book Company, 1968.

Johnson, Robert. "New Life of Virginia." 1:14. In *Peter Force, Tracts and other papers relating principally to the origin, settlement, and progress of the colonies in North America: from the discovery of the country to the year 1776*. New York: P. Smith, 1947.

Jones, Hugh. *The Present State of Virginia* (London, 1724), edited by Richard L. Morton. Chapel Hill: University of North Carolina Press, 1956.

Jordan, Terry G. *American Log Buildings: An Old World Heritage*. Chapel Hill: University of North Carolina Press, 1985.

Josselyn, John. *An Account of Two Voyages to New-England, Made During the Years 1638, 1663*. Boston: Veazie, 1865.

Joyner, Georgina Louise. "William Buckland in England and America: His Apprenticeship, English Early Georgian Influences on his Style and New Evidence at Gunston Hall." Master's thesis, University of Notre Dame, 1985.

Judge, Joseph. "Where Columbus Found the New World: Island of Landfall." *National Geographic* 170 (November 1986): 566-599.

Juet, Robert. "Third Voyage of Master Henry Hudson." In *Narratives of New Netherland, 1609-1664*, edited by Franklin J. Jameson. New York: Charles Scribner's Sons, 1909.

Keeler, Robert W. *The Homelot on the Seventeenth-Century Chesapeake Tidewater Frontier*. Ann Arbor, Mich.: University Microfilms International, 1980.

Kelly, J. Frederick. "Restoration of the Henry Whitfield House, Guilford, Connecticut." *OTNE* 29 (January 1939): 75-89.

Kelly, J. Frederick. "Raising Connecticut Meeting Houses." *OTNE* 27 (July 1936): 3-9.

Kelly, J. Frederick. *Early Connecticut Meetinghouses*. 2 vols. New York: Columbia University Press, 1948.

Kelly, J. Frederick. *Early Domestic Architecture of Connecticut*. New Haven: Yale University Press, 1924.

Kelly, J. Reaney. "Cedar Park, Its People and Its History." *Maryland Historical Magazine* 58 (March 1963): 30-53.

Kelso, William M. *Kingsmill Plantations, 1619-1800: Archeology of Country Life in Colonial Virginia*. Orlando: Academic Press, 1984.

Kennedy, Rick. "Thomas Brattle, mathematician-architect in the transition of the New England mind, 1690-1700." *Winterthur Portfolio* 24 (Winter 1989): 231-45.

Kent, William. *Designs of Inigo Jones and Others*. London: 1727.

Kettel, Russell H. "Repair and Restoration of Eleazar Arnold's Splendid Mansion." *OTNE* 43 (October 1952): 29-35.

Kimball, Fiske. "The Colonial amateurs and their models: Peter Harrison." *Architecture* 53 (June 1926): 155-160.

Kimball, Fiske. *Domestic Architecture of the American Colonies and of the Early Republic*. New York: Dover Publications, 1966 [1922].

Kimball, Fiske. *Thomas Jefferson, Architect*. Cambridge: Riverside Press, 1916.

King, Henry M. "The First Baptist Church, Providence, Rhode Island." *OTNE* 34 (January 1944): 39-43.

Kingsbury, Susan Myra, ed. "An Answer to a Declaration of the Present State of Virginia, May 1623." 4:143. In *The Records of the Virginia Company of London*. Washington D.C.: Government Printing Office, 1906-1935.

Kingsbury, Susan Myra, ed. "Notes for an Answer." 4:259. In *The Records of the Virginia Company of London*. Washington D.C.: Government Printing Office, 1906-1935.

Kingsbury, Susan Myra, ed. "Parts of Drafts of a Statement touching the Miserable Condition of Virginia, May or June 1623." 1:176. In *The Records of the Virginia Company of London*. Washington D.C.: Government Printing Office, 1906-1935.

Kingsbury, Susan Myra, ed. *The Records of the Virginia Company of London*. Washington D.C.: Government Printing Office, 1906-1935.

Kingsley, Louise. "Old Trinity Church, Brooklyn, Connecticut." *OTNE* 42 (January-March 1952): 73-77.

Kornwolf, James D. *"So Good a Design," The Colonial Campus of the College of William and Mary: Its History, Background, and Legacy*. Williamsburg: Joseph and Margaret Muscarelle Museum of Art, College of William and Mary, 1989.

Kouwenhoven, John A. *The Columbia Historical Portrait of New York*. New York: Doubleday & Co., 1953.

Kubler, George. *The Religious Architecture of New Mexico*. 4th ed. Albuquerque: University of New Mexico Press, 1972.

Lagerlöf, Erland. *Medeltida träkyrkor II*. Stochholm: Riksantikvarieämbetet, 1985.

Lane, Mills. *Architecture of the Old South*. New York: Abbeville Press, 1993.

Lane, Mills. *Architecture of the Old South: South Carolina*. Savannah, Ga.: Beehive Press, 1984.

Lane, Richard B. "The Fortress at Louisbourg." *Archaeology* 19 (October 1966): 258-267.

Lane, William C. "The Building of Massachusetts Hall, 1717-1720." *Publications of the Colonial Society of Massachusetts* 24 (1920-1922): 81-110.

Langley, Batty, and Thomas Langley. *The Builder's Jewel*. London: 1746, reprinted, New York: Benjamin Blom, Inc., 1970.

Langley, Batty. *The Builder's and Workman's Treasury of Designs*. London: 1740.

Le Moyne de Morgues, Jacques. "Narrative." In *The New World: The First Pictures of America*, edited by Stefan Lorant. New York: Duell, Sloan, and Pearce, 1965.

Leighton, Ann. *American Gardens in the Eighteenth Century*. Boston: Houghton Mifflin Company, 1976.

Lescarbot, Marc. "Nova Francia: A Description of Acadia, 1606." 2:807. In *A Collection of Voyages and Travels*, compiled by Thomas Osborne. London: T. Osborne, 1745.

Lindsay, G. Carroll. "Plantagenet's Wigwam." *JSAH* 15 (November 1958): 31-35.

Little, Nina Fletcher. *American Decorative Wall Painting 1700-1850*. Sturbridge, Mass.: Old Sturbridge Village, 1952.

Lorant, Stefan, ed. *The New World: The First Pictures of America*, New York: Duell, Sloan, and Pearce, 1965.

Loth, Calder. "Notes on the Evolution of Virginia Brickwork from the Seventeenth Century to the Late Nineteenth Century." *Bulletin of the Association for Preservation Technology* 6 (1974): 82-120.

Loth, Calder. "Palladio in Southside Virginia: Berandon and Battersea." 1:25-46. In *Building by the Book*, edited by Mario di Valmarana. 3 vols. Charlottesville, Va.: The University of Virginia Press, 1984.

Lounsbury, Carl. "An elegant and Commodious Building: William Buckland and the Design of the Prince William County Courthouse." *JSAH* 96 (September 1987): 228-40.

Lounsbury, Carl. "The Structure of Justice: The Courthouses of Colonial Virginia." In *Perspectives in Vernacular Architecture*, vol. 3. Columbia, Mo.: University of Missouri Press, 1989.

Lounsbury, Carl. "Beaux-Arts Ideals and Colonial Reality: The Reconstruction of Williamsburg's Capitol, 1928-1934." *JSAH* 44 (December 1990): 373-389.

Love, Paul Van Derveer. "Patterned brickwork in Southern New Jersey." *Proceedings of the New Jersey Historical Society* 73 (July 1955): 182-208.

Lowery, Woodbury. *The Spanish Settlements within the Present Limits of the United States, Florida, 1562-1574*. New York: G. P. Putnam's Sons, 1905.

Lunn, John. "Louisbourg—the Forgotten Fortress." *Antiques* 97 (June 1970): 872-879.

Lynn, Catherine. *Wallpaper in America*. New York: W. W. Norton and Company, 1980.

Lyon Gardiner Tyler, ed. *Narratives of Early Virginia, 1606-1625*. New York: C. Scribner's Sons, 1907.

Mallary, Peter T. *New England Churches & Meeting Houses [sic], 1680-1830*. New York: Vendome Press, 1985.

Manucy, Albert C. *The Building of Castillo de San Marcos*. Washington D.C.: United States Government Publishing Office, 1942.

Marzio, Peter C. "Carpentry in the Southern Colonies during the Eighteenth Century with Emphasis on Maryland and Virginia." *Winterthur Portfolio* 7 (1972): 229-250.

Mason, George C. "The Colonial Churches of James City County, Virginia." *William and Mary Quarterly* 19 (October 1939): 515.

Mason, George C. "Colonial Architecture-II." *American Architect and Building News* 10 (August 20, 1881): 83-85.

Mason, George C. *Colonial Churches of Tidewater Virginia*. Richmond: Whittet and Shepperson, 1945).

Mathews, Maurice. "A Contemporary View of Carolina in 1680." *South Carolina Historical Review* 55 (1954): 154.

Maverick, Samuel. "A Briefe description of New England and the Several Towns Therein." *Proceedings of the Massachusetts Historical Society* 1, Series 2 (1884-1885), 325.

McCready, Eric S. "The Architecture of Richard Taliaferro." Master's thesis, University of Oregon, 1968.

McIlwaine, H. R., ed. *Journals of the House of Burgesses of Virginia, 1619-1776*. Richmond, Va.: Colonial Press, E. Waddey Co., 1905-1915.

McKearin, George S., and Helen A. McKearin. *American Glass*. New York: Crown Publishers, 1941.

McKee, Harley J. "St. Michael's Church, Charleston, 1752-1762." *JSAH* 23 (March 1964): 39-43.

McLennan, Katherine. *Fortress of Louisbourg National Historic Park*. Ottawa: n.p., 1963.

Mercer, Henry C. *Ancient Carpenters' Tools: Together with Lumbermans', Joiners' and Cabinet Makers' Tools in Use in the Eighteenth Century*. Doylestown, Penn.: Horizon Press, 1975.

Messer, Nellie Stearus. "The Ropes Memorial at Salem, Massachusetts." *OTNE* 17 (April 1924): 146-163.

Metcalf, Priscilla. "Boston Before Bulfinch: Harrison's King's Chapel." *JSAH* 13 (March 1954), 11.

Metcalf, Priscilla. "Which John James was in Boston in 1736." *OTNE* 43 (October/December 1952): 54-56.

Miller, The Rev. John. *A Description of the Province and City of New York with Plans of the City and Several Parts as they Existed in the Year 1695*. London: Thomas Rodd, 1843.

Montgomery, Charles Franklin "Thomas Banister on the New Sash Windows, Boston, 1701." *JSAH* 24 (May 1965): 169-170.

Montgomery, Charles Franklin, ed. *Joseph Moxon's Mechanick Exercises; or, The Doctrine of Handy-works Applied to the Arts of Smithing, Joinery, Carpentry, Turning, Bricklaying*. London: Praeger, 1970 [1703].

Moogk, Peter N. "Architecture: The French Colonies." In *Encyclopedia of the North American Colonies*, edited by Jacob E. Cooke. New York: Charles Scribner's Sons, 1993.

Morison, Samuel Eliot. "A Conjectural Restoration of the 'Old College' at Harvard." *OTNE* 23 (April 1933): 131-138.

Morison, Samuel Eliot. *Admiral of the Ocean Sea: A Life of Christopher Columbus*. Boston: Brown and Co., 1942.

Morison, Samuel Eliot. *Harvard College in the Seventeenth Century*. 2 vols. Cambridge, Mass.: Harvard University Press, 1936.

Morison, Samuel Eliot. *The European Discovery of America*. New York: Oxford University Press, 1971-74.

Morris, Robert. *Select Architecture; being regular designs of plans and elevations well suited to both town and country*. New York: Da Capo Press, 1973 [1757].

Morrison, Hugh. *Early American Architecture: From the First Colonial Settlement to the National Period*. New York: Dover Publications, 1952, 1987.

Morse, Jedidiah. *The American Geography*. London: 1794.

Morton, Thomas. *The New English Canaan* (London: 1634). In *Publications of the Prince Society* 14 (1883): 43.

Moss, Jr., Roger W. "The Origins of the Carpenters' Company of Philadelphia." In *Building Early America*, edited by Charles E. Peterson. Radnor: Chilton Book Company, 1976.

Mulholland, James A. *A History of Metals in Colonial America*. Tuscaloosa, Ala.: University of Alabama Press, 1981.

Munsell, Joel. *The Annals of Albany*. 10 vols. Albany: J. Munsell, 1850-1859.

Myers, Albert Cook, ed. *Narratives of Early Pennsylvania, West New Jersey and Delaware, 1630-1707*. New York: C. Scribner's Sons, 1912.

Nairn, I. A., and Nikolaus Pevsner. *Buildings of England: Sussex, by Ian Nairn and Nikolaus Pevsner*. Harmondsworth, Middlesex: Penguin Books, 1965.

Neve, Richard. *The City and countrey purchaser, and builder's dictionary, or, the compleat builder's guide*. London: Printed for J. Sprint, G. Conyers, and T. Ballard, 1703.

Newcomb, Rexford. *Architecture in Old Kentucky*. Urbana: University of Illinois Press, 1953.

Newcomb, Rexford. *Old Mission Churches and Historic Houses of California*. Philadelphia: J. B. Lippincott Company, 1925.

Newcomb, Rexford. *Spanish-Colonial Architecture in the United States*. New York: J. J. Augustine, 1937.

Nichols, Frederick D. "Drayton Hall, plantation house of the Drayton family." *Antiques* 97 (April 1970): 576-583.

Nichols, Frederick D., and James Bear. *Monticello*. Monticello, Va.: Thomas Jefferson Memorial Foundation, 1967.

Nichols, Frederick D., and Ralph Griswold. *Thomas Jefferson, Landscape Architect*. Charlottesville: University Press of Virginia, 1978.

Norton, Bettina A. "Anglican Embellishments: The Contributions of John Gibbs, Junior, and William Price to the Church of England in Eighteenth-Century Boston." In *New England Meeting House [sic] and Church: 1630-1850*, edited by P. Benes. Dublin, N.H.: Boston University Press for The Dublin Seminar for New England Folklife: Annual Proceedings for 1979, 1979.

Nuttall, Zelia. "Royal Ordinances Concerning the Laying Out of New Towns." *The Hispanic American Historical Review* [Spanish] 4 (1921): 743-753, [English] 5 (1922): 249-254.

O'Callaghan, E. B. *History of New Netherland or New York under the Dutch*. New York: D. Appleton, 1966 [1846].

O'Callaghan, E. B., ed. *The Documentary History of the State of New York: Arranged Under Direction of the Hon. Christopher Morgan, Secretary of State*. Albany: Weed, Parsons & Co., Public Printers, 1849-1851.

Ochse, Orpha. *The History of the Organ in the United States*. Bloomington: University of Indiana Press, 1975.

O'Dea, Shane. "The Tilt: Vertical Log Construction in Newfoundland." *Perspectives in Vernacular Architecture* 1 (1982): 55-64.

O'Mara, James. "Town Founding in Seventeenth-Century North America: Jamestown in Virginia." *JSAH* 8 (1982): 1-11.

O'Neal, William B. *Jefferson's Fine Arts Library for the University of Virginia, with Additional Notes on Architectural Volumes Known to Have Been Owned by Jefferson*. Charlottesville, University of Virginia Press, 1956.

O'Neal, William B. *Jefferson's Fine Arts Library: His Selections for the University of Virginia, Together with his own Architectural Books*. Charlottesville: University Press of Virginia, 1976.

O'Neal, William B. "Pattern Books in American Architecture, 1730-1930." 1:47-74. In *Building by the Book*, edited by Mario di Valmarana. 3 vols. Charlottesville, Va.: The University Press of Virginia for the Center for Palladian Studies in America, 1984.

Orcutt, Philip Dana. *The Moffatt Ladd House*. Portsmouth: N. H. Society of Colonial Dames of America, 1935.

Osborne, Thomas, comp. *A Collection of Voyages and Travels*. London: T. Osborne, 1745.

Oviatt, Edwin. *The Beginnings of Yale*. New Haven: Yale University Press, 1926.

Oviedo y Valdès, Gonzalo. *Natural History of the West Indies*. Chapel Hill: University of North Carolina Press, 1959.

Owen, Scott Campbell. "George Washington's Mount Vernon as British Palladian Architecture." Architectural History Master's thesis, University of Virginia, 1991.

Palladio, Andrea. *Architecture in Four Books containing a dissertation on the five orders & ye most necessary observations relating to all kinds of buildings....*, translated by Edward Hoppus. London: B. Cole & J. Wilcox, 1736.

Palladio, Andrea. *The Four Books of Architecture*, translated by Giacomo Leoni. 2 vols. London: 1715.

Park, Helen. *A List of Architectural Books Available in America Before the Revolution*. Los Angeles: Hennessey and Ingalls, 1973.

Parkhurst, Henry. "Report of the true state and commodities of Newfoundland." In *The Principal navigations, voyages, traffiques & discoveries of the English Nation, made by sea or overland to the remote and farthest distant quarters of the earth at any time within the compass of these 1600 years*, compiled by Richard Hakluyt. London: J. M. Dent and Sons, LTD, 1927-28.

Parkinson, John. *Paridisus in Sole*. London: 1629.

Parry, J. H. *Age of Reconnaissance*. Berkeley: University of California Press, 1981.

Paschall, Thomas. "Letter to J. J. of Chippenham, January 31, 1684." In *Narratives of Early Pennsylvania, West New Jersey and Delaware, 1630-1707*, edited by Albert Cook Myers. New York: C. Scribner's Sons, 1912.

Patton, Glenn. "The College of William and Mary, Williamsburg, and the Enlightenment." *JSAH* 29 (March 1970): 24-32.

Pearson, Danella. "Shirley-Eustis House Landscape History." *OTNE* 70 (1980): 1-16.

Peckham, Sir George. "A true reporte of the late discoveries...." 8:113-117. In *The Principal navigations, voyages, traffiques & discoveries of the English Nation, made by sea or overland to the remote and farthest distant quarters of the earth at any time within the compass of these 1600 years*, compiled by Richard Hakluyt. London: J. M. Dent and Sons, LTD, 1927-28.

Pemberton, Thomas. "A Topographical and Historical Description of Boston." *Collections of the Massachusetts Historical Society* 3 (1974): 250-251.

Penn, William. "A Further Account of the Province of Pennsylvania." In *Narratives of Early Pennsylvania, West New Jersey and Delaware, 1630-1707*, edited by Albert Cook Myers. New York: C. Scribner's Sons, 1912.

Penn, William. "A Letter from William Penn proprietary and govenour of Pennsylvania in America, to the committee of the Free Society of Traders of that province, residing in London." In Albert Cook Myers, *Narratives of Early Pennsylvania, West New Jersey and Delaware, 1630-1707*. New York: C. Scribner's Sons, 1912.

Penn, William. "Instructions given by me, William Penn...." In *William Penn and the Founding of Pennsylvania*, edited by Jean R. Soderland. Philadelphia: University of Pennsylvania Press, 1983.

Percy, George. "Observations gathered out of a Discourse of the Plantation of the Southerne Colonie in Virginia by the English, 1606." 1:lxx. In *Travels and Works of Captain John Smith: President of Virginia and Admiral of New England, 1580-1631*, edited by Edward Arber. Edinburgh; John Grant, 1910.

Peterson, Charles E. "Benjamin Loxley and Carpenters' Hall." *JSAH* 15 (December 1956): 23-26.

Peterson, Charles E. "Carpenters' Hall." *Historic Philadelphia, from the founding until the early nineteenth century; papers dealing with its people and buildings*. Philadelphia: American Philosophical Society, 1953.

Peterson, Charles E. "Early Ste. Genevieve and its Architecture." *Missouri Historical Review* 35 (January 1941): 207-232.

Peterson, Charles E. "French Houses of the Illinois Country." *Missouriana* 1 (August/September 1938): 9-12.

Peterson, Charles E. "French Landmarks along the Mississippi." *Antiques* 53 (April, 1948): 286-288.

Peterson, Charles E. "Notes on Old Cahokia." *The French American Review* 1 (July-September 1948): 184-225.

Peterson, Charles E. "Philadelphia Carpentry According to Palladio." 3:1-52. In *Building by the Book*, edited by Mario di Valmarana. 3 vols. Charlottesville, Va.: The University of Virginia Press, 1984.

Peterson, Charles E. *Building Early America*. Radnor: Chilton Book Company, 1976.

Peterson, Charles E. *Colonial St. Louis: Building a Creole Capital*. Saint Louis: Missouri Historical Society, 1949.

Peterson, Charles E., ed. *The Rules of Work of the Carpenters' Company*. Princeton: The Pyne Press, 1971.

Pevsner, Nikolaus, and Alexandra Wedgwood. *The Buildings of England. Warwickshire*. Harmondsworth: Penguin Books, Ltd., 1966.

Pevsner, Nikolaus. *The Buildings of England. London*. Harmondsworth: Penguin Books, 1962.

Phillips, Sir Thomas. *Londonderry and the London Companies, 1609-1629: Being a Survey and Other Documents Submitted to King Charles I*. Belfast: H.M.S.O., 1928.

Pickens, Buford. *Mr. Jefferson as Revolutionary Architect*. Philadelphia: Society of Architectural Historians, 1975.

Pierson, William Harvey. *American Buildings and their Architects, I: The Colonial and Neoclassical Styles*. New York: Oxford University Press, 1986.

Plantagenet, Beauchamp. *A Description of the province of New Albion... with a brief of the charge of victual, and necessaries, to transport and buy stock fro each planter, or labourer, there to get his master fifty pounds per annum, or more, in twelve trades, and at ten pounds per annum, or more, in twelve trades, and at tem pounds charges onely a man*. London: Printed by James Moxon, 1650.

Plowden, Sir Edmund, attr. "A Description of the Province of New Albion." 2:31. In *Tracts and other papers relating principally to the origin, settlement, and progress of the colonies in North America: from the discovery of the country to the year 1776*, edited by Peter Force. New York: P. Smith, 1947 [1836].

Plowden, Sir Edmund. "American Notes." *JSAH* 15 (October 1956): 2.

Poore, Benjamin Perley, comp. *The Federal and State Constitutions, Colonial Charters, and Other Organic Laws of the United States.* Washington D.C.: Government Printing Office, 1878.

Pressey, Park. "When Grandma Went to Meeting as a Little Girl." *OTNE* 35 (April 1945): 60-62.

Printz, Governor Johan. "Report to the Right Honorable West India Company." In Albert Cook Myers, *Narratives of Early Pennsylvania, West New Jersey and Delaware, 1630-1707.* New York: C. Scribner's Sons, 1912.

Quincy, Josiah. *The History of Harvard University.* New York: Arno Press, 1900.

Quinn, David B., Alison M. Quinn, and Susan Hillier, eds. *English Plans for North America: The Roanoke Voyages, the New England Ventures.* New York: Arno Press, 1979.

Quinn, David B., Alison M. Quinn, and Susan Hillier, eds. *New American World: A Documentary History of North America to 1612.* New York: Arno Press, 1979.

Radoff, Morris L. *Buildings of the State of Maryland at Annapolis.* Annapolis: Hall of Records Commission, 1954.

Rahtz, Philip. "Buildings and Rural Settlement." In *The Archaeology of Anglo-Saxon England,* edited by David M. Wilson. London: Methuen, 1976.

Randall, T. Henry. "Colonial Annapolis." *Architectural Record* 1 (January 1891): 309-43.

Rasmussen, William M. S. "Architectural Drawings and Design in the Virginia Colony." In *The Making of Virginia Architecture,* edited by Charles E. Brownell et al. Richmond: Virginia Museum of Fine Arts, 1992.

Rasmussen, William M. S. "Palladio in Tidewater Virginia: Mount Airy and Blandfield." In *Building by the Book,* edited by Mario di Valmarana. 3 vols. Charlottesville, Va.: The University Press of Virginia for the Center for Palladian Studies in America, 1984.

Rasmussen, William M. S. "Sabine Hall, a Classical Villa in Virginia." *JSAH* 39, no.4 (December 1980):286-296.

Ravenel, Beatrice. *Architects of Charleston.* Charleston: Carolina Art Association, 1945.

Rawlings, James Scott. *Virginia's Colonial Churches.* Richmond: Garrett & Massie, 1963.

Records of the Church in Brattle Square. Boston: 1902.

The Records of the Town of Cambridge. Cambridge, Mass.: 1901.

Re-dedication of the Old State House, Boston, July 11, 1882. 3rd ed. Boston: 1885.

Reiff, Daniel. *Small Georgian Houses in England and Virginia: Origins and Development Through the 1750s.* Newark: University of Delaware Press, 1986.

Reps, John William. *The Making of Urban America: A History of City Planning in the United States.* Princeton: Princeton University Press, 1965.

Reps, John William. *Tidewater Towns: City Planning in Colonial Virginia and Maryland.* Williamsburg, Va.: Colonial Williamsburg Foundation; University Press of Virginia, 1972.

Reps, John William. *Town Planning in Frontier America.* Princeton: Princeton University Press, 1965.

Reynolds, Helen Wilkinson. *Dutch Houses in the Hudson Valley before 1776.* New York: Payson and Clarke, 1929.

Ridout, Orlando. "An Architectural History of Third Haven Meetinghouse." In *Three Hundred Years and More of Third Haven Quakerism,* Kenneth L. Carroll, ed. Easton, Md.: Published for Third Haven Meeting of Friends by the Queen Anne Press, 1984.

Ridout, Orlando. "The James Brice House, Annapolis, Maryland." Master's thesis, University of Maryland, 1978.

Riley, Edward M. *Independence National Historic Park, Philadelphia, Pa.* Revised edition. Washington D.C.: 1956.

Rines, Edward F. *Old Historic Churches of America.* New York: MacMillan, 1936.

Rising, Johan. "Report of Govenor Johan Rising." In *Narratives of Early Pennsylvania, West New Jersey and Delaware, 1630-1707,* edited by Albert Cook Myers. New York: C. Scribner's Sons, 1912.

Roach, Hannah B. "The Planting of Philadelphia, a Seventeenth-Century Real Estate Development." *Pennsylvania Magazine of History and Biography* 92 (1968): 3-47 and 143-194.

Robb, Colin Johnston. "Loughgall, Ireland." *Architectural Record* 98 (August 1945): 146.

Robinson, Willard B. *American Forts: Architectural Form and Function.* Urbana: University of Illinois Press, 1977.

Roos, Frank John. *Bibliography of Early American Architecture: Writings on Architecture Constructed before 1860 in Eastern and Central United States.* Urbana: University of Illinois Press, 1968.

Rose, Harold Wickliffe. *The Colonial Houses of Worship in America.* New York: Hastings House, 1963.

Rose-Troup, Frances James. *John White, the Patriarch of Dorchester (Dorset) and the Founder of Massachusetts, 1575-1648, with an Account of the Early Settlements in Massachusetts, 1620-1630.* New York: G. P. Putnam's Sons, 1930.

Roubo, Audrè. *L'art du menuisier.* 3 vols. Paris: Leonce Laget, 1976.

Rutledge, Anna Wells. "The Second St. Philip's, Charleston, 1710-1835." *JSAH* 18 (October 1959): 112-114.

Salaman, R. A. *Dictionary of Woodworking Tools.* New York: Charles Scribner's Sons, 1980.

Salmon, William. *Palladio Londinensis.* London: 1734.

Salzmann, F. *English Industries of the Middle Ages.* Boston and New York: Houghton Mifflin Company, 1913.

Sanford, Trent. *The Architecture of the Southwest.* New York: W. W. Norton and Company, 1950.

Scarlett, Charles, Jr. "Governor Horatio Sharpe's Whitehall." *Maryland Historical Magazine* 46 (March 1951): 8-26.

Schimmelman, Janice G. *Architectural Treatises and Building Handbooks Available in American Libraries and Bookstores through 1800.* Worcester, Mass.: American Antiquarian Society, 1986.

Schless, Nancy Halverson. *Peter Harrison, the Touro Synagogue, and the Wren City Church.* Chicago: University of Chicago Press, 1973.

Schless, Nancy Halverson. "Dutch Influence on the Governor's Palace, Williamsburg." *JSAH* 38 (December 1969): 254-270.

Schless, Nancy Halverson. "The Province House; English and Netherlandish Forms in Gables and Chimneys." *OTNE* 62 (Spring 1972): 114-123.

Scholes, France V. "Documents for the History of the New Mexico Missions in the Seventeenth Century." *New Mexico Historical Review* 4 (January 1929): 49.

Scholes, France V. "The Supply Service of the New Mexico Missions in the Seventeenth Century." *New Mexico Historical Review* 5 (January 1930): 103-104.

Schuetz-Miller, Mardith K. "Architecture: The Spanish Borderlands," In *Encyclopedia of the North American Colonies,* edited by Jacob E. Cooke. New York: Charles Scribner's Sons, 1993.

Schwartz, Esther. "Touro Synagogue Restored, 1827-29." *JSAH* 17 (Summer 1958): 23-26.

Seymour, George Dudley. "Henry Caner, 1680-1731, master carpenter, builder of the first Yale College building, 1718, and of the rector's house, 1722." *OTNE* 15 (1925): 99-124.

Shepherd, Jr., Raymond J. "Cliveden." *Historic Preservation* (July-September 1972): 4-11.

Shoemaker, Robert W. "Christ Church, St. Peter's, and St. Paul's." *Transactions of the American Philosophical Society* 43 (1953): 187-198.

Shurtleff, Harold R. *The Log Cabin Myth: A Study of the Early Dwellings of the English Colonists in North America.* Gloucester, Mass.: P. Smith, 1967 [1937].

Shurtleff, Nathaniel B. *A Topographical and Historical Description of Boston.* Boston: 1871.

Shurtleff, Nathaniel B., ed. *Records of the Governor and Company of the Massachusetts Bay in New England.* 5 vols. Boston: 1853-1854.

Singer, Charles Joseph, et al. *A History of Technology.* Oxford: Clarendon Press, 1954-1978.

Sinnott, Edmund W. *Meetinghouse and Church in Early New England.* New York: McGraw-Hill, 1963.

Sloan, Eric. *A Museum of Early American Tools.* New York: Wilfred Funk, Inc., 1964.

Small, Edwin W. "The Derby House." *OTNE* 47 (April-June 1957): 101-107.

Smith, J. Frazer. *White Pillars.* New York: William Helburn, Inc., 1941.

Smith, John. "A Map of Virginia." In *Narratives of Early Virginia, 1606-1625,* edited by Lyon Gardiner Tyler. New York: C. Scribner's Sons, 1907.

Smith, John. "A True Relation." In *Travels and Works of Captain John Smith: President of Virginia and Admiral of New England, 1580-1631,* edited by Edward Arber. Edinburgh; John Grant, 1910.

Smith, John. "Advertisements." In *Travels and Works of Captain John Smith: President of Virginia and Admiral of New England, 1580-1631,* edited by Edward Arber. Edinburgh; John Grant, 1910.

Smith, John. "Description of Virginia." In *Narratives of Early Virginia, 1606-1625,* edited by Lyon Gardiner Tyler. New York: C. Scribner's Sons, 1907.

Snow, Caleb H. *A History of Boston.* 2nd ed. Boston: Abel Bowen, 1828.

Soderland, Jean R., ed. *William Penn and the Founding of Pennsylvania.* Philadelphia: University of Pennsylvania Press, 1983.

Stanislawski, Dan. *Early Spanish Town Planning in the New World.* New York: American Geographical Society, 1947.

Stechow, Wolfgang. *Dutch Landscape Painting of the Seventeenth Century.* London: Phaidon, 1966.

Stephenson, Mary A. *Carter's Grove Plantation: A History.* Williamsburg: 1964.

Stevenson, Frederic R., and Carl Feiss. "Charleston and Savannah." *JSAH* 10 (December 1951): 3-9.

Stokes, Isaac Newton Phelps. *The Iconography of Manhattan Island, 1498-1909.* New York: Arno Press, 1967 [1915].

Stone, Garry Wheeler. "Society, Housing, and Architecture in Early Maryland: John Lewger's St. John's." Ph.D. diss., University of Pennsylvania, 1952, n.p.

Stone, Garry Wheeler. "St. John's Archaeological Questions and Answers." *Maryland Historical Magazine* 69 (Summer 1974): 146-168.

Stoney, Samuel Gaillard. *Plantations of the Carolina Low Country.* Charleston: The Carolina Art Association, 1966.

Strachey, William. "A true repertory of the wracke, and redemption of Sir Thomas Gates…his coming to Virginia, and the estate of that Colonie then, and after, vnder the gouernment of the Lord [de La] Warre, Iuly 15, 1610." In *A Voyage to Virginia in 1609; Two Narratives: Strachey's "True reportory" and Jourdain's "Discovery of the Bermuda,"* edited by Louis B. Wright. Charlottesville: University Press of Virginia, 1964.

Sturtevant, William C. "First Visual Images." In *First Images of America: The Impact of the New World on the Old,* edited by Fredi Chiappelli, Michael J. B. Allen, and Robert Louis Benson. Berkeley: University of California Press, 1976.

Summerson, John. *Architecture in Britain 1530 to 1830.* Baltimore: Penguin Books, 1954.

Swan, Abraham. *A Collection of Designs in Architecture.* London: 1757, reprinted, Farnborough: Gregg, 1972.

Swan, Abraham. *The British Architect.* London: 1745, reprinted, New York: Da Capo Press, 1967.

Sweeney, John A. H. *Grandeur on the Appoquinimink: The House of William Corbit at Odessa, Delaware.* Newark: University of Delaware Press, 1959.

Sweeney, Kevin M. *Mansion People: Kinship, Class, and Architecture in Western Massachusetts.* N.p., 1984.

Tatum, George B. *Penn's Great Town.* Philadelphia: University of Pennsylvania Press, 1961.

Taylor, Benjamin C. *Annals of the Classis of Bergen.* New York: Board of Publication of the Reformed Protestant Dutch Church, 1857.

Taylor, E. G. R., ed. *The Original Writings & Correspondence of the Two Richard Hakluyts*. London: Printed for the Hakluyt Society, 1935.

Thane, Elswyth. *Mount Vernon Is Ours: The Story of its Preservation*. New York: Duell, Sloan and Pearce, 1966.

Thomas, Gabriel. "An Historical and Geographical Account of Pennsylvania and of West New-Jersey." In *Narratives of Early Pennsylvania, West New Jersey and Delaware, 1630-1707*, edited by Albert Cook Myers. New York: C. Scribner's Sons, 1912.

Tinkcom, Margaret B. "Cliveden: The Building of a Philadelphia Countryseat, 1763-1767." *Pennsylvania Magazine of History and Biography* 88 (January 1964): 2-36.

Town Records, Ipswich, Mass.

Town Records, Middleboro, Mass.

Town Records, Sudbury, Mass.

Town Records, Weymouth, Mass.

Trostel, Michael F. "The Annapolis Plan in America." In *Building by the Book*, edited by Mario di Valmarana, 2:1-34. 3 vols. Charlottesville: The University Press of Virginia for the Center for Palladian Studies in America, 1984.

Tuck, James A. "A 16th-Century Basque Whaling Station in Labrador." *Scientific American* 245 (November 1981): 183.

Tuck, James A., and Robert Grenier. *Red Bay, Labrador: World Whaling Capitol A.D. 1550-1600*. St. John's, Newfoundland: Atlantic Archaeology, 1989.

Tutt, Hannah. *The Lee Mansion*. Marblehead: Marblehead Historical Society, 1911.

Two Hundredth Anniversary of the Clinton Congregational Church. Clinton, Conn.: 1867.

Tyler, Lyon Gardiner, ed. *Narratives of Early Virginia, 1606-1625*. New York: C. Scribner's Sons, 1907.

Ullän, Marian. *Medeltida träkyrkor*. Stockholm: Riksantikvarieämbetet, 1983.

Upton, Dell. "Architectural Change in Colonial Rhode Island: The Mott House as a Case Study." *OTNE* 69 (Winter/Spring 1979): 19-28.

Upton, Dell. "Architecture: The British Colonies." In *Encyclopedia of the North American Colonies*, edited by Jacob E. Cooke. New York: Charles Scribner's Sons, 1993.

Upton, Dell. "Ordinary Buildings: A Bibliography on American Vernacular Architecture." *American Studies International* 19 (Winter 1981): 57-75.

Upton, Dell. "The Power of Things: Recent Studies on American Vernacular Architecture." *American Quarterly* 35 (1983): 262-79.

Upton, Dell. "Traditional Timber Framing." In *Material Culture of the Wooden Age*, edited by Brooke Hindle. Tarrytown, N.Y.: Sleepy Hollow Press, 1981.

Upton, Dell. "Vernacular Domestic Architecture in Eighteenth-Century Virginia." *Winterthur Portfolio* 17 (Summer/Autumn 1982): 95-119.

Upton, Dell. *Holy Things and Profane: Anglican Parish Churches in Colonial Virginia*. New York and Cambridge: Architectural History Foundation and MIT Press, 1986.

Van der Donck, Adriaen, attr. "The Representation of New Netherland Concerning its Location, Productiveness and Poor Condition." in *Narratives of New Netherland, 1609-1664*, edited by Franklin J. Jameson. New York: Charles Scribner's Sons, 1909.

Van Derpool, James Grote. "The Restoration of St. Luke's, Smithfield, Virginia." *JSAH* 17 (March 1958): 12-18.

Van Laer, Arnold, trans. and ed. "Instructions for Willem Verhulst." In *Documents Relating to New Netherland, 1624-1626, in the Henry E. Huntington Library*. San Marino, Calif.: The Henry E. Huntington Library and Art Gallery, 1924.

Van Laer, Arnold, trans. and ed. "Special Instructions for Cryn Fredericksz Regarding the laying out of the fort." In *Documents Relating to New Netherland, 1624-1626, in the Henry E. Huntington Library*. San Marino, Calif.: The Henry E. Huntington Library and Art Gallery, 1924.

Van Laer, Arnold, trans. and ed. *Documents Relating to New Netherland, 1624-1626, in the Henry E. Huntington Library*. San Marino, Calif.: The Henry E. Huntington Library and Art Gallery, 1924.

Van Laer, Arnold, trans. and ed. *Van Riensselaer Bowier Manuscripts*. Albany: University of the State of New York, 1908.

Van Tienhoven, Cornelis. "Information Relative to Taking Up Land in New Netherland." In *The Documentary History of the State of New York: Arranged Under Direction of the Hon. Christopher Morgan, Secretary of State*, edited by E. B. O'Callaghan. Albany: Weed, Parsons & Co., Public Printers, 1849-1851.

Van Wassenaer, Nicolaes. *Historisch verhael alder ghedenck-weerdichste geschiedenisse(n) die hier en daer in Europa, als in Duijtsch-lant, Vranckrijck, Enghelant...en Neder-lant, van den beginne des jaers 1621, tot den herfst toe, voorgevallen syn*. t'Amstelredam: Bij Ian Evertss, 1622-1635.

Verey, David. *The Buildings of England: Gloucestershire, I: The Cotswolds*. Harmondsworth: Penguin Books, 1970.

Vermeulen, Frans Audrè Jozef. *Handboek tot de geschiedenis der Nederlandsche bouwkunst*. 's Gravenhage: M. Nijhoff, 1931.

Waddell, Gene. "The First Monticello." *JSAH* 46 (March 1987): 5-29.

Waterman, Thomas. *The Mansions of Virginia*. New York: Bonanza Books, 1945.

Waterman, Thomas, and John Barrows. *Domestic Colonial Architecture of Tidewater Virginia*. New York: Charles Scribner's Sons, 1932.

Waterman, Thomas. *The Dwellings of Colonial America*. Chapel Hill: University of North Carolina Press, 1950.

Watkins, Walter Kendall. "The Early Use and Manufacture of Paper-Hangings in Boston." *OTNE* 12 (January 1922), 112.

Watkins, Walter Kendall. "The Hancock House and its Builder." *OTNE* 17 (July 1926): 3-19.

Watkins, Walter Kendall. "Three contracts for seventeenth-century building construction in Massachusetts." *OTNE* 12 (July 1921): 31-32.

Welsh, Peter C. *Woodworking Tools, 1600-1900*. Washington D.C.: Smithsonian Institution, 1966.

Wenger, Mark R. "Jefferson's designs for remodeling the Governor's Palace." *Winterthur Portfolio* 32 (Winter 1997): 223-242.

Wenger, Mark R. "The Central Passage in Virginia: Evolution of an Eighteenth-Century Living Space." *Perspectives in Vernacular Architecture* 2 (1986): 137-149.

Wenger, Mark R. "Westover: William Byrd's Mansion Reconsidered." Master's thesis, University of Virginia, 1981.

Wertenbaker, Thomas J. *The Founding of American Civilization: The Middle Colonies*. New York: C. Scribner's Sons, 1938.

Wertenbaker, Thomas J. *The Puritan Oligarchy*. New York: C. Scribner's Sons, 1947.

Weslager, C. A. *The Log Cabin in America: From Pioneer Days to the Present*. New Brunswick, N.J.: Rutgers University Press, 1969.

West, Stanley E. *West Stow, the Anglo-Saxon Village*. Ipswich: Suffolk County Planning Dept., 1985.

West, Trudy. *The Timber-frame House in England*. New York: Architectural Book Pub. Co., 1971.

Whiffen, Marcus, and Frederick Koeper. *American Architecture, 1607-1976*. Cambridge, Mass.: MIT Press, 1981.

Whiffen, Marcus. "Some Virginia House Plans Reconsidered." *JSAH* 16 (May 1957): 17-19.

Whiffen, Marcus. "The Early County Courthouses of Virginia." *JSAH* 18 (March 1959): 2-10.

Whiffen, Marcus. *Stuart and Georgian Churches*. London: B.T. Batsford, Ltd., 1947.

Whiffen, Marcus. *The Eighteenth-Century Houses of Williamsburg*. Williamsburg: Colonial Williamsburg, 1984.

Whiffen, Marcus. *The Public Buildings of Williamsburg*. Williamsburg: Colonial Williamsburg, 1959.

White, Hunter. *Old St. Paul's in Narragansett*. Wakefield, R.I.: 1957.

Whitehill, Walter M. *Boston, a Topographical History*. Cambridge: Belknap Press of Harvard University Press, 1959.

Wieder, Frederik C. *De Stichting von New York in Juli 1625. Reconstructies en nieuwe gegevens ontleend aan de van Rappard documenten*. 's-Gravenhage: M. Nijhof, 1925.

Williams, Edward. *Explication of the saw-mill*. London: 1650.

Williams, Edward. *Virginia: more especially the south part thereof, richly and truly valued viz. the fertile Carolana, and no lesse excellent isle of Roanoak, of latitude from 31. to 37. degr. Relating the meanes of raysing infinite profits to the adventurers and planters*. London: J. Stephenson, 1650.

Williams, George W. *St. Michael's, Charleston, 1751-1951*. Columbia: University of South Carolina Press, 1951.

Willsford, Thomas. *Architectonice: The Art of Building, or An Introd. to All Young Surveyors in Common Structures*. London: Brook, 1659.

Wilson, David M., ed. *The Archaeology of Anglo-Saxon England*. London: Methuen, 1976.

Wilson, Jr., Samuel. "An Architectural History of the Royal Hospital and the Ursuline Convent of New Orleans." *The Louisiana Historical Quarterly* 29 (July 1946): 572-602.

Wilson, Jr., Samuel. "Louisiana drawings by Alexandre de Batz." *JSAH* 22 (May 1963): 76-78.

Wilson, Jr., Samuel. "Religious Architecture in French Colonial Louisiana." *Winterthur Portfolio* 8 (1973): 91-97.

Wilson, Richard Guy, ed. *Buildings of Virginia: Tidewater and Piedmont*. New York : Oxford University Press, 2002.

Winchester, Alice. "Meeting House at Sandown." *Antiques* 48 (December 1945): 336-337.

Winfield, Charles H. *History of the County of Hudson, New Jersey*. New York: Kennard and Hay, 1874.

Winsor, Justin. *The Memorial History of Boston*. 4 vols. Boston: James R. Osgood and Company, 1880-1881.

Winthrop, Adam. *Winthrop Papers*. Boston: Massachusetts Historical Society, 1929-1947.

Winthrop, John. *Winthrop's Journal, "History of New England," 1630-1649*. Edited by James Hasmer. New York: C. Scribner's Sons, 1908.

Wisner, Benjamin B. *The History of the Old South Church in Boston*. Boston: Crakes and Brewster, 1830.

Wittkower, Rudolf. *Palladio and Palladianism*. New York: George Braziller, 1974.

Wood, Charles B. "A Survey and Bibliography of Writings on English and American Architectural Books Published before 1895." *Winterthur Portfolio* 2 (1965): 127-137.

Wood, Joseph. "Village and Community in Early Colonial New England." *Journal of Historical Geography* 8 (October 1982): 333-346.

Wood, Joseph. *The New England Village*. Baltimore: Johns Hopkins University Press, 1997.

Wood, William. *New-England's Prospect*. Edited by Alden T. Vaughan. Amherst: University of Massachusetts Press, 1977.

Wren, Christopher. *Parentalia*. London: 1750, reprinted, Farnborough: Gregg International, 1965.

Wright, Louis B., ed. *A Voyage to Virginia in 1609; Two Narratives: Strachey's "True reportory" and Jourdain's "Discovery of the Bermuda."* Charlottesville, University Press of Virginia, 1964.

Young, Alexander. "Memoirs of Capt. Roger Clap." In *Chronicles of the First Planters of the Colony of Massachusetts Bay, 1623-1636*. Boston: C. C. Little and J. Brown, 1846.

Young, Alexander. *Chronicles of the First Planters of the Colony of Massachusetts Bay, 1623-1636*. Boston: C. C. Little and J. Brown, 1846.

Young, Gordon. "Colonial Building Techniques." *Vernacular Architecture* 17 (1986): 6.

Zanchi, Giovanni Battista de'. *Del modo di fortificar le Città*. Venetia: 1560.

⊰ Index ⊱